HANDBOOK
ON THE BRITISH ARMY 1943

HANDBOOK ON THE BRITISH ARMY 1943

Edited by
Chris Ellis and Peter Chamberlain

London: Arms & Armour Press
New York: Hippocrene Books, Inc.

This edition published in Great Britain, 1976
by Arms and Arms Press
2-6 Hampstead High Street
London NW3 1PR
ISBN 0 85368 181 3

Published in the United States, 1976
by Hippocrene Books, Inc.,
171 Madison Avenue,
New York,
N.Y. 10016
ISBN 0-88254-409-8
LC 76-13830

Original edition, published 1943, TM 30-410

Printed and bound in Great Britain by Redwood Burn Limited, Trowbridge & Esher

INTRODUCTION

While it is well-known that the U.S. Army produced manuals on the German Army in World War 2 (eg., *Handbook on German Military Forces*), several editions of which have been reprinted in recent years, a much rarer work which is of great value to students of military history is TM 30-410, *Handbook on the British Army*, which was produced early in 1943 to give an overall picture of the British Army, its equipment, uniforms, organisation, and tactics, to the American soldier. The book fills a considerable gap in available reference material, the British Army of World War 2 having been somewhat overlooked in the spate of military equipment and uniform publications which have appeared in recent years. This edition is basically a reprint of the original TM 30-410 but it has been considerably edited to correct errors which were made in the original and to eliminate the flimsy fold-out charts of the original and incorporate them in the text pages. Cross-references have been amended to take account of changes made. Omitted completely are some inadequate supplements on the RAF and Civil Defence, and chapters of social rather than military interest which dealt with forms of address, comparisons of every day language, and so on. Also omitted is a chapter on British maps which merely covers the British Ordnance Survey system, and a glossary of both military and every day abbreviations, most of which can be found in any dictionary. We have replaced several illustrations and added some completely new ones. The original Fig 1 is the only omission from what is published in this edited version, and that was merely a map of the British Isles. This version of the book should make it a valuable and compact guide to the British Army as it was in the middle of World War 2. There were, of course, a number of detail changes in organisation of units and command structures during the course of World War 2, but the 1943 period represents a good average of the World War 2 organisation of the British Army in general. There are a few extra points of interest. British Airborne Forces did not really come into their own until 1944, and they are covered in this book while still in their formative stages; the Bailey Bridge, as is now well-known, became *the* most standardised Allied bridging equipment, but did not fully come into its own until 1944, thus accounting for its less than prominent (though adequate) coverage in this book. The 2-pounder gun on a Carrier chassis, of which much is made on page 152, did not, in fact, see much service, and what is referred to as a 'trailer' on page 31 and elsewhere is what the British Army referred to as an 'ammunition limber'. Some late-war weapons (eg., 17-pounder, PIAT) are not covered at all here, while others (eg., the 4.2 inch mortar) are mentioned only in passing. Overall, however, this is a most useful work of reference for all military enthusiasts, and is greatly commended.

Chris Ellis/Peter Chamberlain

CONTENTS

ILLUSTRATIONS

INSIGNIA PLATES

Chapter 1

INTRODUCTION

1. Purpose.—The object of this handbook is to furnish a simple guide for the U. S. soldier cooperating with the British.

2. Arrangement and scope.—Within the limitations imposed by security and size, the handbook shows, in order, the relation between the British Army and Government; the organization and equipment of the various arms and services; and some of the principles practiced by the forces operating in the field. Information on ranks, uniforms, insignia, abbreviations, and pertinent miscellaneous topics has been included to permit ready reference and a reasonable understanding of the British military system.

3. Difficulties of terminology.—*a.* Familiar words used in unfamiliar senses by the British may at times be confusing. Differences in both terminology and meaning are indicated throughout the text, but some terms recur so frequently that they must be discussed briefly here.

b. The use of the terms "unit" and "formation" differs from that in the U. S. Army. In general, in British terminology a "unit" is an organization of a single arm or service operating both tactically and administratively under a single commander, whereas a "formation" is a combination of units of different arms and services to the strength of a brigade or more. The largest unit is ordinarily called a battalion, but cavalry (horse and mechanized), artillery, and reconnaissance regiments are also units, since they operate both tactically and administratively under a single commander. Brigades, divisions, corps, armies, and groups of armies are formations.

c. The term "regiment" as used by the British may have several meanings.

(1) "Regiment" is used to designate a combatant arm such as the Royal Regiment of Artillery. (See pars. 20*a* and 28*a*.)

(2) Mechanized cavalry includes such units as the armoured car regiments and the various tank regiments of the Royal Armoured Corps (see pars. 37*a* and 167*b*). An artillery "regiment" indicates an artillery unit composed of a standard number of officers, men, and

1

weapons, but the number varies according to the type (field, medium, anti-aircraft, anti-tank, etc.—see par. 28a).

(3) "Regiment" may be used to designate a parent organization for a number of infantry battalions. For example, The Royal Sussex Regiment (see par. 167g) might include any number of infantry battalions which have neither trained nor fought together but which have a historic name in common (see par. 23).

(4) On occasion, in order to obtain brevity, a battalion of the Royal Tank Regiment (R Tanks) may be referred to, for example, as 6 R Tanks (i. e., the 6th Battalion of the Royal Tank Regiment—see pars. 37a and 168a).

d. In tactical organizations the British term "brigade" indicates an organization roughly equivalent to a U. S. reinforced regiment (see par. 25 and fig. 107), and British "battery" indicates an artillery unit which is comparable in size to a U. S. field artillery battalion rather than a U. S. battery (see par. 28c).

Chapter 2

GENERAL

5. British Empire.—The British Empire, or the British Common-wealth of Nations as it is now frequently termed, is an association of some 60 separate territories, scattered across every continent, owing a common allegiance to the British Crown. British territories include dominions, colonies, the Indian Empire, protectorates, and mandates.

a. Dominions.—Dominions (Canada, Australia, New Zealand, and South Africa) are autonomous communities within the British Empire, equal in status and in no way subordinate one to another in any aspect of their domestic or external affairs. No formal written document binds the dominions to the United Kingdom (par. 6) and their virtual independence as sovereign states was recognized by the Parliament of the United Kingdom in the Statute of Westminister (1931). In fact, only the link of a common sovereign and a common tradition—stronger than any written document or treaty—holds this free association of peoples together.

b. Colonies.—Colonies are territories in a state of dependency toward the United Kingdom. This dependence varies according to the degree of social development of the colony. The more advanced, such as Ceylon, enjoy their own local legislatures.

c. Indian Empire.—The Indian Empire, a subcontinent in itself, stands in a separate category. Its constitution is in process of transition toward a federal system of government comprising both British India and the Native States, the latter of which are administered by their own rulers. India's eventual entry into the comity of dominions is an expressed aim of British policy.

d. Protectorates.—Protectorates, such as Zanzibar, for the most part retain their own native or tribal rulers, but relations with foreign states are conducted by the British Government, which is also responsible for their protection.

e. Mandates.—Mandates, such as Palestine, are territories, formerly belonging to enemy countries in the First World War, submitted to British trusteeship under the Covenant of the League of Nations.

6. United Kingdom.—*a.* The United Kingdom consists of Great Britain (England and Wales, and Scotland), Northern Ireland, the Channel Islands, and the Isle of Man.

b. The United Kingdom is a constitutional or limited monarchy, that is, a Parliamentary democracy in which the King "reigns, but does not rule." The King is the legal head of the state, and embodies the unity of the nation. He can exercise the royal prerogative in a wide variety of ways, and all acts of Parliament require his assent. Yet in practice he performs no official act without the advice of one of his Ministers. Parliament itself is opened with a speech by the King, but it is a speech prepared by his Ministers, who are drawn from the majority party in Parliament in peacetime or from several parties as in the present wartime coalition.

7. Houses of Parliament.—The Houses of Parliament, consisting of the House of Lords and the House of Commons, comprise the supreme lawmaking body of the realm.

a. House of Commons.—Members of the House of Commons (MP's) are elected by universal adult franchise. The life of an ordinary Parliament may be 5 years, but the present wartime Parliament has extended its duration by majority vote in order to avoid interruption of the war effort. Any voter may offer himself as a candidate for election in any constituency in the country, no matter where his ordinary residence may be, provided he receives the required number of nominations and pays a deposit of $600, which is subject to forfeit if he fails to obtain one-eighth of the total votes polled. Most members of the House of Commons are elected on a party program. In the present House of Commons the Conservative Party has the largest representation; then come the Labour Party and the Liberal Party. Other parties with small representation are the Independent Labour and the Communist.

b. House of Lords.—The House of Lords consists of peers who have a hereditary or official right to attend, together with persons raised to the peerage in recognition of their public services. The Archbishops of Canterbury and York and 21 other bishops also sit in the House of Lords. The main function of the House of Lords today is to act as a check on legislation: it cannot initiate legislation, but it can delay, or recommend amendments to, any bill except one that authorizes taxation or expenditure. If, however, the House of Commons passes a bill for the third time in spite of its rejection by the House of Lords, the latter must acquiesce, and the bill becomes law when the King's assent is given. In principle the King may veto legislation, but the right has not been used for so many years that it may be said to be obsolete. (On the peerage, see also par. 163.)

8. Cabinet.—*a.* The simplest description of the Cabinet is that it is a bridge between the legislative and executive organs of government. The Ministers who compose it are, or become, members of one of the two Houses. The Cabinet must derive support from a majority in the House of Commons, and its members, except when there is a coalition or national government, are drawn from the predominant party in that House.

b. The functions of Cabinet Ministers correspond closely to those of the secretaries of the executive departments of the United States Government. In normal times each Minister except the Prime Minister is in charge of some department of government, but in the present Cabinet there are several members who have been freed of departmental duties in order to devote greater time to the direction of the war.

c. The Cabinet depends for its tenure on the support of the majority of the House of Commons. If that support is withdrawn, either on a vote of confidence or on the rejection of major legislation, the Prime Minister and the Cabinet are bound by custom, though only by custom, to resign. In practice, however, it would be impossible for any Cabinet which lacked the confidence of the Commons to continue long in office, since proposed legislation could be rejected by the House of Commons, which also controls the purse strings of government. Historically and in name the Cabinet is the working committee of government; in fact its members are appointed by the King on the Prime Minister's recommendation.

d. All sessions of the Cabinet are secret. Theoretically, no differences of opinion can exist within it, and externally none do exist. It stands or falls as a unit.

e. At the present time there exists an inner War Cabinet consisting of seven members, including the Prime Minister.

9. Privy Council.—The Privy Council, out of which the Cabinet historically grew, is a body of advisers to the King which sanctions acts of government that are not within the province of Parliament. Its size is not limited. Under special wartime legislation certain emergency powers are conferred upon the Privy Council.

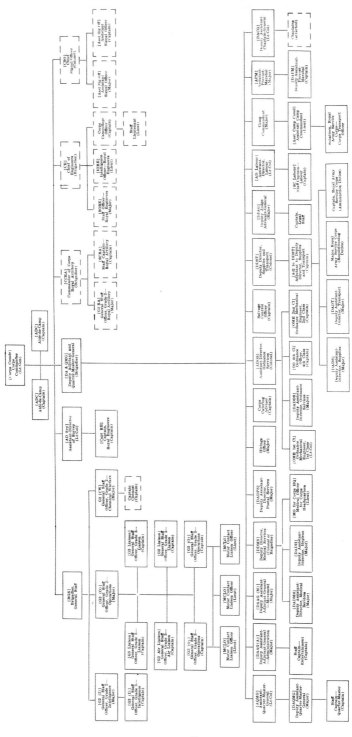

FIGURE 3.—Organization of the corps staff.

NOTE : 1. The letters shown in brackets are the British abbreviations for the official titles. The ranks of the officers normally holding these titles are shown in parentheses.
2. The positions shown in broken lines are not an integral part of the staff organization but are normally attached to the corps staff for advisory or technical services.

6

Chapter 3

ORGANIZATION

Section I

SUPREME COMMAND

11. General.—The armed forces of the nation—the Royal Navy, the Army, and the Royal Air Force—function under separate Ministries: namely, the Admiralty, the War Office, and the Air Ministry. These Ministries are coordinated by the War Cabinet.

12. Army Council.—The Army is directly under the command of the Army Council. The senior military member is the Chief of the Imperial General Staff. All orders are issued in the name of the Army Council, not by the Secretary of State for War, who is, however, individually responsible to the War Cabinet for the business of the Army.

13. War Office.—Under the direction of the Army Council is the War Office, the organization of which (fig. 2) is fundamentally similar to that of the War Department of the United States.*

14. General Staff.—*a.* The Department of the Chief of the Imperial General Staff is divided into the following directorates:

---

* The U. S. "war department" itself was called "War Office" from its foundation in 1777 until 1789.

7

(1) Directorate of Military Operations.
(2) Directorate of Military Intelligence.
(3) Directorate of Signals.
(4) Directorate of Staff Duties.
(5) Directorate of Military Training.
(6) Directorate of Weapons and Vehicles.
(7) Directorate of Armoured Fighting Vehicles.
(8) Directorate of Royal Artillery.
(9) Directorate of Air.
(10) Directorate of the Home Guard and Territorial Army.
(11) Directorate of American Liaison and Munitions.

The Directorate of Anti-Aircraft and Coast Defence has been abolished, and its functions have been taken over mainly by the Directorate of Royal Artillery. The Directorate of Air handles for the War Office the problems of air-borne forces and air-ground cooperation. The Directorate of Staff Duties is responsible through the War Establishments Committee for the preparation of the War Establishments of all British Army units and formations. The War Establishments in the British service are the equivalent of the Tables of Organization in the U. S. Army. The War Establishment of a formation or of a unit changes from time to time according to the exigencies of the service.

b. The Department of the Chief of the Imperial General Staff is basically concerned with military policy (which includes war-planning, training, historical research, and military intelligence) and with coordinating the activities of the other staff departments.

c. The Department of the Adjutant-General to the Forces is concerned with personnel, which includes recruiting, organization, administration, military discipline, and medical services. In general, its functions are a combination of those of G–1, The Adjutant General, The Surgeon General, and The Judge Advocate General in the U. S. Army.

d. The Department of the Quarter-Master-General is concerned with quartering the Army, with road, railway, and sea transport, with construction and maintenance of buildings and fortifications, with supply of food, forage, and fuel, and with remount and veterinary service. In general, its functions include those of G–4 and some of those of The Quartermaster General and the Chief of Engineers in the U. S. Army.

e. The Department of the Director-General of Army Requirements is concerned with formulating Army material requirements and transmitting them to and coordinating them with the Ministry of Supply.

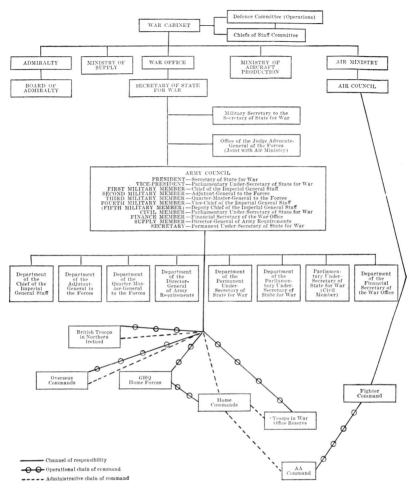

FIGURE 2.—Organization of the War Office (showing its relation to other Ministries).

15. Permanent Under-Secretary of State for War.—The Department of the Permanent Under-Secretary of State for War is charged with the conduct of War Office business, including all finance and accounting, and with administration of the Royal Army Chaplains' Department and the Royal Army Pay Corps. This conservative civilian department, because of its powers of veto in financial matters, has great influence in the War Office even in time of war.

SECTION II

HIGHER ORGANIZATIONS

16. General.—*a.* At the declaration of war on September 3, 1939, the British Army consisted of the Regular Army, the Territorial Army (corresponding to the National Guard in the United States), and several reserve forces. Soon thereafter all elements were consolidated into a single "British Army" and, except for certain legal differences, the distinctions between these several elements have now vanished.

b. In general, the British Army consists of the Home Forces, the Anti-Aircraft Command, the British Forces in the Middle East, the British Forces in India, and a considerable number of scattered commands throughout the world. These elements are all commanded directly from the War Office.

17. Home Forces.—*a.* The Home Forces, with its own Commander-in-Chief [1] and its own GHQ, comprises all field forces located in the United Kingdom. It is responsible for the defence of the British Isles, and it consists of all corps, divisions, and separate units assigned to defend Great Britain against invasion.

b. The Home Guard, which is within the Home Forces, was organized hastily in May 1940 as the Local Defence Volunteers. It consists of volunteer unpaid, part-time troops formed into units for the local defence of communities, airfields, and communications, and for general observation purposes. Its members, who are regularly enrolled in the military forces and would come to full-time duty in case of invasion, are equipped with rifles and with some automatic weapons, anti-tank rifles, grenades, submachine guns, etc. The Home Guard has little transportation and can be depended upon only for local defence purposes.

18. Corps and army.—The organization of the corps and the field army is similar to that in the U. S. Army, each consisting of a headquarters, certain organic troops, and a variable number of divisions and corps, respectively, as determined by the War Office. (For the organization of the corps staff, see fig. 3.)

---

[1] The following troops are not under the command of the Commander-in-Chief, Home Forces:

1. Anti-aircraft formations, which are under the operational control of the Fighter Command of the Royal Air Force (RAF).

2. Transportation troops held in reserve under War Office control.

3. Training units and establishments except those allotted an operational role, and then only in an emergency.

4. Forces in Northern Ireland, which are commanded by the General Officer Commanding (GOC), British Troops in Northern Ireland, under the War Office.

SECTION III

ADMINISTRATION

19. General.—*a.* For administrative purposes the United Kingdom is divided into six military commands and two military districts (fig. 4). Commands are subdivided into areas. Northern Ireland and London are the two districts; the commands are as follows:

(1) Southern.	(4) Eastern.
(2) Western.	(5) South-eastern.
(3) Northern.	(6) Scottish.

b. The chain of command for operational (tactical) matters is from GHQ, Home Forces, through commands to tactical corps. Areas are operationally under corps. In the event of operations taking place in the United Kingdom, commands become headquarters of armies.

c. In administrative matters the chain of command is from the War Office to commands, then direct to both corps and areas. The area, as has been stated above, comes under the corps only operationally.

d. A district functions in the same manner as a command.

e. The commands are in charge of army commanders, whose staffs are similar to corps staffs on an enlarged scale.

20. Arms of the Service.—All branches, taken collectively, are called the "Arms of the Service." The combatant branches are called "The Arms"; the administrative branches, "The Services." The principal branches in order of precedence are as follows:

a. The Arms:

Cavalry (Cav).[2]

Royal Armoured Corps (RAC).[2]

Royal Regiment of Artillery (RA).[3]

Corps of Royal Engineers (RE).

Royal Corps of Signals (R Sigs).

Infantry (Inf).

Reconnaissance Corps (Recce Corps).[4]

---

[2] All except two of the cavalry regiments have been mechanized, and now constitute a part of the Royal Armoured Corps. (See pars. 37 and 167b.) The term "Royal" is given to a regiment or corps as a special mark of favor for distinguished service. As a further distinction, the King will honor the regiment or corps by becoming its colonel-in-chief.

[3] The Royal Regiment of Artillery retains the name "regiment" for traditional reasons. (See par. 28a.)

[4] The units of the Reconnaissance Corps are distributed throughout the various formations of the Army, a regiment (battalion), for example, being furnished to each infantry division. (See par. 26e and fig. 11.)

FIGURE 4.—Military commands and districts.

12

b. The Services:

Royal Army Chaplains' Department (RAChD).
Royal Army Service Corps (RASC).
Royal Army Medical Corps (RAMC).
Royal Army Ordnance Corps (RAOC).
Royal Electrical and Mechanical Engineers (REME).
Royal Army Pay Corps (RAPC).
Royal Army Veterinary Corps (RAVC).
Army Educational Corps (AEC).
The Army Dental Corps (AD Corps).
Pioneer Corps (P Corps).[5]
Intelligence Corps (IC).[6]
Army Catering Corps (ACC).
Army Physical Training Corps (APTC).
Corps of Military Police (CMP).
Military Provost Staff Corps (MPSC).
Queen Alexandra's Imperial Military Nursing Service (QAIMNS).
Auxiliary Territorial Service (ATS).
Officers' Training Corps (OTC).

SECTION IV

TACTICAL STAFFS

21. Division and brigade staffs.—For the purpose of illustrating staff duties, two representative staffs are presented in detail.

a. Infantry division staff (fig. 5).—(1) *Duties and office organization.*—(a) *GSO 1—General Staff Officer, Grade 1.*—GSO 1 (Chief of Staff) is responsible for—

    1. Policy as directed by the General Officer Commanding (GOC), including policy for training.

    2. Coordination and general supervision of all work of divisional Hq.

---

[5] Formerly known as the Auxiliary Military Pioneer Corps (AMPC).
[6] The units of the Intelligence Corps are distributed throughout the various formations of the Army, a section, for example, being furnished to each divisional Hq. (See ch. 7, especially pars. 141 and 142.)

(*b*) *GSO 2—General Staff Officer, Grade 2.*—GSO 2 is responsible for—

1. Orders and instructions as ordered by GSO 1.
2. Organization and working of "G" (Operations and Intelligence) office.
3. Detail of duty officers at Hq.
4. Control and interviewing of liaison officers at divisional Hq.
5. Arrangements with the Officer Commanding, Divisional Signals (OC Div Sigs), and the Camp Commandant (officer responsible for local administration of Hq as a whole) for moves of divisional Hq.
6. Moves by road; he is assisted by DAQMG (Deputy Assistant-Quarter-Master-General) for movement (march) tables (see par. 131 and fig. 116).

(*c*) *GSO 3 (O)—General Staff Officer, Grade 3 (Operations).*—GSO 3 is the understudy to GSO 2 and is responsible for—

1. Operations as directed by GSO 1 or GSO 2.
2. Moves by road (as allotted by GSO 2).
3. Distribution of maps.
4. Supervision of "G" draftsmen, who make tabulations, charts, and sketch maps.
5. Location statement (each evening).
6. Circulation of situation reports.
7. Supervision of the acknowledgment register (a receipt diary for messages).
8. Codes and ciphers.
9. "G" war diary.
10. Detailed orders for move of "O" Group (Operations Group).

(*d*) *GSO 3 (I)—General Staff Officer, Grade 3 (Intelligence).*—GSO 3 (I) is responsible for—

1. Coordination of all intelligence work in the divisional area.
2. Situation map.
3. Divisional commander's battle map.
4. Divisional intelligence summaries.
5. Deductions from information received.
6. Confirmation of uncertain information.
7. Reporting to GOC on requests for bomber support by brigades.[7]
8. Liaison with the Air Intelligence Liaison Officer (AILO) on operational matters.

---

[7] This arrangement is known as Army Air Support Control (AASC).

9. Ordering and interpretation of air photographs.

10. Distribution of intelligence of air photographs.

11. Maintenance of diary showing identifications, enemy order of battle, and any other necessary items (less enemy artillery information, which is the duty of the Intelligence Officer, Royal Artillery (IORA)).

12. Arrangements for preliminary examination of prisoners and deserters (carried out by IO (Intelligence Officer)).

13. Liaison with IORA.

14. Report of enemy identifications to higher authority.

15. Circulation of intelligence.

(e) *GSO 3 (CW)—General Staff Officer, Grade 3 (Chemical Warfare).*—GSO 3 (CW) is responsible for—

1. Advice on chemical warfare, including, when necessary, a CW appreciation of the situation.

2. Anti-gas training.

3. Study of the divisional area in order to assess the probable dangers from enemy use of gas.

4. Chemical warfare intelligence in conjunction with the intelligence staff.

5. Examination of specimens of technical interest in conjunction with anti-gas mobile laboratory.

6. Meteorological arrangements for chemical warfare.

7. Chemical warfare map.

(f) *IO—Intelligence Officer.*—His duties are similar to those of GSO 3 (I) and he is responsible to him. These two officers are interchangeable and one is always at divisional Hq. In principle, the Intelligence Officer and his staff are primarily concerned with the detailed examination of messages, documents, prisoners, etc., and with the keeping of records. GSO 3 (I) is primarily concerned with insuring that steps are taken to obtain information and that proper use is made of information obtained.

(g) *MCLO's—3 Motor Contact Liaison Officers.*—These officers are charged with liaison with infantry brigades (brigades are equivalent to U. S. regiments), flank formations, units on each flank, and corps Hq. They keep in constant touch with signal offices (message centers), calling for messages, etc., on outward journeys and reporting any information such as locations, etc., on return journeys.

(h) *Cipher Officer.*—This officer, who is responsible to OC Div Sigs for all matters other than technical cipher duties, conducts the cipher office. He and his staff will be prepared to assist the "G" Staff when not fully occupied on cipher duties.

(i) AA & QMG—Assistant-Adjutant and Quarter-Master-General.—This officer is charged with administrative staff work and with coordination of the work of the services. He is in close touch with the "G" Staff.

(j) DAAG—Deputy Assistant-Adjutant-General.—DAAG is responsible for—

1. Reinforcements.
2. Medical services (with the Assistant-Director of Medical Services (ADMS)).
3. Spiritual welfare (with the Senior Chaplain).
4. Graves.
5. Pay.
6. Personnel services, including discipline (with the Deputy Assistant-Provost-Marshal (DAPM)), leave, and prisoners of war.
7. "A" "Q" war diary.
8. Discipline (courts-martial).
9. Morale.
10. Traffic control with DAPM.

(k) DAQMG—Deputy Assistant-Quarter-Master-General.—DAQMG is responsible for—

1. Supplies, petrol (gasoline), oil, and lubricants (POL), and ammunition (with the Commander, Royal Army Service Corps (CRASC)).
2. Ordnance services (with the Assistant-Director of Ordnance Services (ADOS)).
3. Detailed quartering of troops in consultation with the "G" Staff.
4. Moves by road (with GSO 2).
5. Moves other than by road.

(l) ADC—Aide-de-Camp.—ADC has the following duties:

1. The personal comfort of the division commander.
2. When the division commander wishes, he acts as his staff officer.
3. On return from visits to troops, he makes certain that the Signalmaster (officer in charge of the signal office) knows the latest locations of the troops he has visited.
4. Assistant to the Camp Commandant in his duties (e. g., he may act as Camp Commandant for advanced Hq when it is formed).

(*m*) *Catering Adviser.*—The Catering Adviser is responsible for—

1. Advising unit commanders on all matters concerning food preservation, cooking, preparation of diets, and dietetic hygiene.
2. Arranging the relief or transfer of Army Catering Corps (ACC) personnel throughout various units of the division (cooks of all units being ACC personnel but under the command of the unit to which they are attached).
3. Training ACC personnel in their specialist duties within the division.

(*n*) *Chief Clerks, "A" and "G"* (*RSM—Regimental Sergeant-Major* [8] (warrant officer, class I) *and CSM—Company Sergeant-Major* (warrant officer, class II)).—These clerks are responsible for—

1. Organization and supervision of clerical duties in their offices.
2. Checking, correct assembly, numbering, and dispatch of orders, messages, etc.
3. Detailing clerk to keep a record of "in" and "out" messages.
4. Insuring that reliefs are carried out so that clerks get meals and rest.
5. The acknowledgment register (see (*c*)7, above).

(2) *General organization.*—See figure 5, paragraph 24, and figure 7. On the inclusion of a tank brigade in the (infantry) division, see paragraph 25*b*. For the armoured division staff, see paragraph 38*b*.

b. Infantry brigade staff (fig. 6).—(1) *Duties and office organization.*—(*a*) *BM—Brigade Major* (*Executive and S–3*).—The Brigade Major is responsible for—

1. All the staff work at brigade Hq (he can allocate this work, subject to his commander's approval, as he thinks fit).
2. Initiation of plans, subject to the commander's orders.
3. Preparing and issuing operational orders and instructions.
4. Transmission of information to divisional Hq and to neighboring troops.
5. Training.
6. Reports.
7. Reports on officers.
8. Honors and awards.

(*b*) *Bde IO—Brigade Intelligence Officer* (*S–2*).—For full details of the responsibilities of Bde IO (or BIO), see paragraph 137.

---

[8] "Serjeant" is the official British Army form, but the spelling "sergeant," which is official in the Royal Air Force, is adopted throughout for the sake of uniformity.

(c) *MCLO's—3 Motor Contact Liaison Officers.*—These officers are responsible for liaison with battalion, flank units, and divisional Hq. Their duties in connection with signal offices (message centers) are the same as on the infantry division staff. (See *a*(1)(*g*), above.)

(d) *Bde Sigs—Brigade Signal Officer (Communication Officer).*— This officer is responsible for—

1. Command, administration, and technical efficiency of the brigade signal section.
2. His turn of duty at brigade Hq as an officer of the brigade staff.
3. Advice on signal matters, especially with reference to the intercommunication paragraphs of operation orders.
4. Liaison with BM and Bde IO to obtain adequate information on which to base his signal plans.
5. Reporting to BM any failure in signal communications or delays in the transmission of messages.
6. Advice to battalion commanders on their own signal communications and cooperation with battalion signal officers, including all possible assistance to them.
7. Siting at brigade Hq, and general tactical control of divisional wireless (radio) sets, Royal Air Force wireless tender (for tactical reconnaissance), and wireless set (Army) for AASC.[9]
8. Administration of attached details of other signal units and RAF personnel at brigade Hq.
9. First-line repairs to signaling equipment of battalions.

(e) *SC—Staff Captain (S–1 and S–4).*—This officer is responsible for—

1. Personnel.
2. Casualties.
3. Spiritual welfare.
4. Discipline.
5. Sanitation.
6. Prisoners of war.
7. Police.
8. Routine duties.
9. Ceremonial.
10. Distribution and detail of billets.
11. Supplies (including food), petrol, ammunition, water, equipment, clothing, etc.

---

[9] See *a*(1)(*d*)7, above, and note.

12. Preparation of administrative paragraph of operation orders.

13. Traffic control.

14. Reconnaissance of sites for brigade Hq—and allotment.

15. Control of transport arriving at brigade Hq.

(*f*) *Captain, RASC—Royal Army Service Corps (S–4).*—This officer has the following duties (with the Staff Captain):

1. Represents CRASC at brigade Hq.

2. Advises on RASC questions.

3. Maintains personal liaison with units to insure smooth working of RASC services.

4. Assists the Staff Captain in all matters relating to RASC supplies (including food).

5. Forecasts requirements of petrol and oil and gives early warning of any abnormal demand.

(*g*) *Bde TO—Brigade Transport Officer.*—This officer is responsible for—

1. Command of "B" echelon (rear echelon of first-line transport), including "B" echelon transport units when brigaded (that is, when sub-units of arms such as artillery and engineers are under the command of the brigade). (On "B" echelon, see par. 57*a* and figs. 107 and 115.)

2. Defence of "B" echelon area.

3. Mechanical transport.

4. Use of petrol.

5. Reconnaissance of site for "B" echelon.

(*h*) *Chief Clerk (S/Sgt—Staff Sergeant).*—The chief clerk is charged with—

1. Organization and supervision of clerical duties.

2. Checking, correct assembly, numbering, and dispatch of orders, messages, etc.

3. Insuring that incoming orders, messages, etc., are at once passed to the officer concerned, and that they are subsequently seen, as necessary, by other officers and filed (this duty may be allotted to Bde IO).

4. Insuring that all waste paper, carbons, etc., are burned.

5. Insuring that reliefs are carried out so that clerks get meals and rest.

(*i*) *OME—Ordnance Mechanical Engineer (warrant officer, class I), RAOC (Royal Army Ordnance Corps)) (S–4).*—This warrant officer has the following duties (under the Staff Captain):

1. Represents ADOS (Assistant-Director of Ordnance Services).

    2. Advises on RAOC questions.

    3. Assists the Staff Captain in all matters relating to ordnance stores.

    (*j*) *Brigade CQMS* (*Company Quarter-Master Sergeant*).—CQMS is charged with—

    1. Assisting the Staff Captain.

    2. Drawing and accounting for equipment and stores.

    3. Accounting for and repair of brigade Hq property.

    4. Interior economy and discipline of OR's—other ranks (enlisted men).

    5. Messing of OR's (including Sigs); arranging special meals, haversack rations, etc.; informing personnel when meals are ready and keeping meals for, or sending tea, etc., to, those unable to attend; making special point of insuring that all concerned, including visiting personnel, get meals.

    6. Ordering rations, etc.

    7. Pay rolls.

    (*k*) *Brigade Transport Sergeant.*—This sergeant is charged with—

    1. Assisting the Brigade Transport Officer.

    2. Drawing and accounting of motor-transport (MT) vehicles and spare parts.

    3. Maintenance of MT.

    4. Petrol.

    (2) *General organization.*—See figure 6, paragraph 25, and figure 8.

    22. Infantry and other battalions.—The channel of operational and administrative command passes from the commanding officer (usually a lieutenant-colonel) of the unit by way of the Adjutant to the remainder of the unit. Officers of subordinate units may advise the commanding officer on specific subjects, but normally they have no power outside their own units. A major is second-in-command. The Adjutant (a captain) is the executive of the commanding officer. All correspondence, requests for interviews, and the like are directed to him, and he deals with all subjects, passing on to the commanding officer all those which are of sufficient importance to demand the commanding officer's attention.

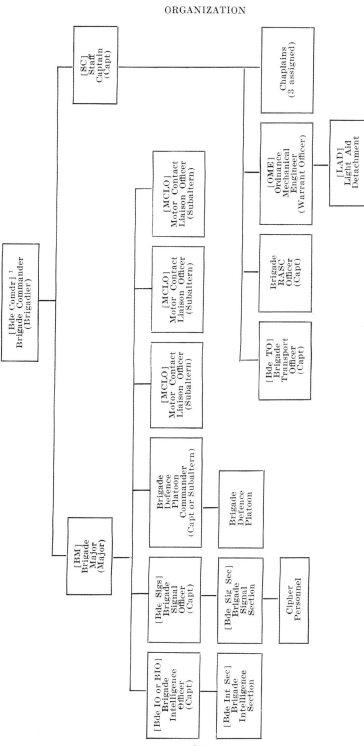

FIGURE 6.—Organization of the infantry brigade staff.

[1] The letters shown in brackets are the British abbreviations for the official titles. The ranks of the men normally holding these titles are shown in parentheses.

21

SECTION V

INFANTRY

23. General.—The infantry of the British Army is organized into 5 Foot Guards Regiments (The Brigade of Guards) and 64 regiments of the line, but since the outbreak of war the number of battalions has been considerably increased (see par. 167*f* and *g*). An infantry regiment is a parent organization only and has no tactical functions. In time of peace most regiments consisted of two Regular Army battalions and from two to five Territorial battalions. The regular battalions have almost never served together, but they have regimental training depots in common. In time of war newly organized battalions are assigned by War Establishments to a regiment, generally according to geographical origin. Thus a regiment may have an indefinite number of battalions; during the First World War this number was sometimes as high as 60. The infantry battalion is the basic combat unit. Infantry battalions are assigned to brigades for operational purposes without regard to regimental unity. There are five general types of battalions: namely, rifle battalion, machine-gun battalion, motor battalion, motorized battalion (an infantry battalion carried in Royal Army Service Corps transport), and divisional reconnaissance regiment (battalion) (see par. 26*e*).

24. Division.—*a.* One type of (infantry) division (fig. 7) consists of 2 infantry brigades and 1 tank brigade, the infantry brigades being composed of 3 rifle battalions each and the tank brigade of 3 tank battalions. The supporting arms consist of 3 field (artillery) regiments, 1 medium (artillery) regiment,[10] 1 anti-tank regiment, 1 light anti-aircraft regiment; 1 divisional reconnaissance regiment (battalion); and signal, Royal Army Service Corps (QM), engineer, medical, ordnance, provost, and other units. The war strength of the division is approximately 17,500 officers and enlisted men.

b. Certain divisions, as above, set up for special purposes have organizations that vary from the standard infantry division of three infantry brigades.

c. In army troops and occasionally in corps troops there are a number of troop-carrying companies of the Royal Army Service

---

[10] In Great Britain medium artillery is designated as corps troops, but in operations abroad it is a part of the division. (See par. 30.)

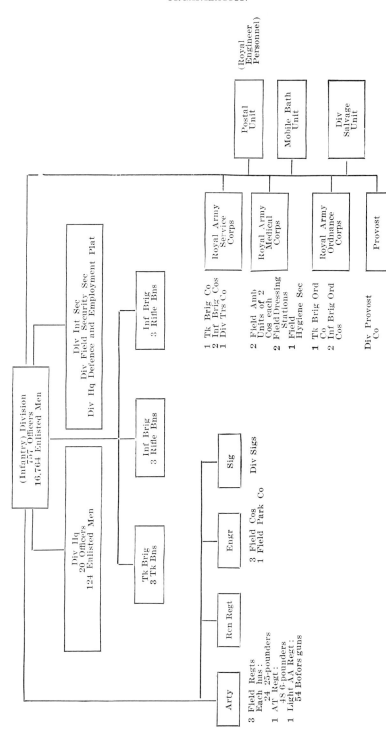

FIGURE 7.—Organization of one type of (infantry) division.

Corps. Each company is capable of carrying one infantry brigade. These RASC companies are not divisional troops in any way.

25. Brigades.—*a. Infantry brigade.*—The accompanying organizational table (fig. 8) shows the present organization of the infantry brigade, which corresponds roughly to the infantry regiment in the U. S. Army. The infantry brigade is the basic unit of the combat team. The brigade has attached to it for combat a defence platoon of 38 men, 1 anti-tank battery, 1 light anti-aircraft battery, a mobile ordnance and motor repair unit—light aid detachment (LAD)—and a signal unit.

b. Tank brigade.—The inclusion of an (army) tank brigade in the organization of the (infantry) division does not mean that the army tank brigade will not operate unattached. See paragraph 39 and figure 20.

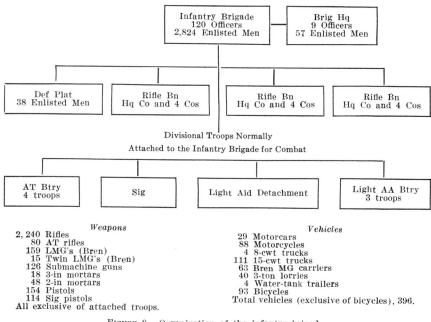

FIGURE 8.—Organization of the infantry brigade.

26. Battalions.—*a. Rifle battalion* (fig. 9).—The rifle battalion organization is based on the Bren caliber .303 light machine gun. This battalion has motorized transport and a war strength of 33 officers and 753 enlisted men.[11] The battalion consists of a head-

---

[11] Throughout the discussion of the organization of formations and units, the term "enlisted men" will include warrant officers.

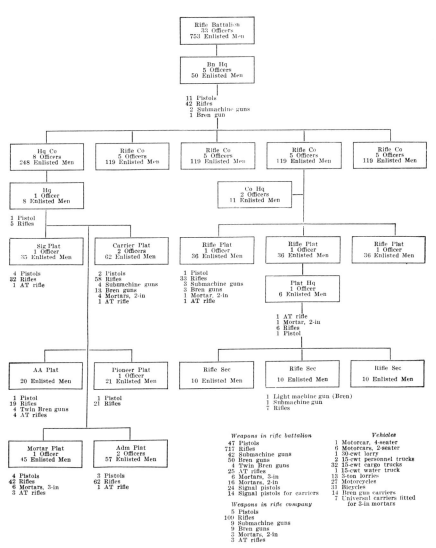

FIGURE 9.—Organization of the rifle battalion.

(Face p. 24)

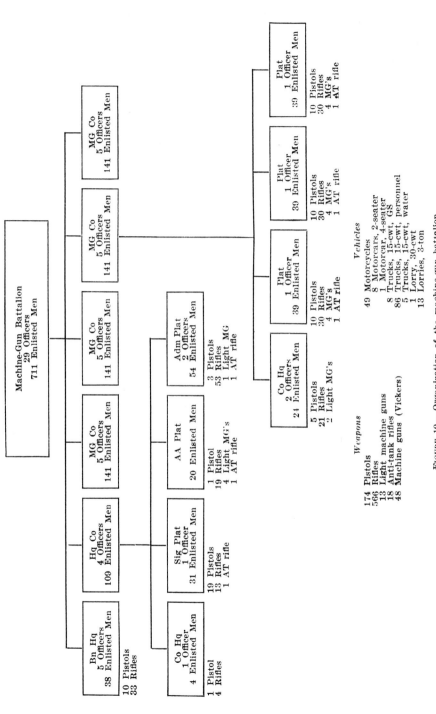

Machine-Gun Battalion
29 Officers
711 Enlisted Men

Bn Hq
5 Officers
38 Enlisted Men

10 Pistols
33 Rifles

Hq Co
4 Officers
109 Enlisted Men

MG Co
5 Officers
141 Enlisted Men

MG Co
5 Officers
141 Enlisted Men

MG Co
5 Officers
141 Enlisted Men

MG Co
5 Officers
141 Enlisted Men

Co Hq
1 Officer
4 Enlisted Men

1 Pistol
4 Rifles

Sig Plat
1 Officer
31 Enlisted Men

19 Pistols
13 Rifles
1 AT rifle

AA Plat
20 Enlisted Men

1 Pistol
19 Rifles
4 Light MG's
1 AT rifle

Adm Plat
2 Officers
54 Enlisted Men

3 Pistols
53 Rifles
1 Light MG
1 AT rifle

Co Hq
2 Officers
24 Enlisted Men

5 Pistols
21 Rifles
2 Light MG's

Plat
1 Officer
39 Enlisted Men

10 Pistols
30 Rifles
4 MG's
1 AT rifle

Plat
1 Officer
39 Enlisted Men

10 Pistols
30 Rifles
4 MG's
1 AT rifle

Plat
1 Officer
39 Enlisted Men

10 Pistols
30 Rifles
4 MG's
1 AT rifle

Plat
1 Officer
39 Enlisted Men

10 Pistols
30 Rifles
4 MG's
1 AT rifle

Weapons

174 **Pistols**
566 **Rifles**
13 **Light machine guns**
18 **Anti-tank rifles**
48 **Machine guns (Vickers)**

Vehicles

49 **Motorcycles**
8 **Motorcars, 2-seater**
1 **Motorcar, 4-seater**
8 **Trucks, 15-cwt, GS**
86 **Trucks, 15-cwt, personnel**
5 **Trucks, 15-cwt, water**
1 **Lorry, 30-cwt**
13 **Lorries, 3-ton**

FIGURE 10.—Organization of the machine-gun battalion.

quarters, a headquarters company, and 4 rifle companies. The headquarters company is composed of a headquarters, a signal platoon, a mortar platoon with six 3-inch mortars, each in a carrier, an anti-aircraft platoon with 4 twin anti-aircraft light machine guns and 4 caliber .55 anti-tank rifles, a carrier platoon with 13 Bren machine-gun carriers, a pioneer platoon, and an administrative platoon. A rifle company consists of 5 officers and 119 enlisted men. It has a 2-inch mortar, 3 Bren light machine guns, 3 submachine guns, and 1 caliber .55 anti-tank rifle. (For discussion of the carrier platoon, see par. 128.)

b. Machine-gun battalion (fig. 10).—The machine-gun battalion, which is at present assigned to corps troops, is based on the caliber .303 Vickers machine gun. It consists of a headquarters, a head-quarters company, and 4 machine-gun companies of 12 guns each. Each company is composed of a headquarters and 3 platoons. The battalion is completely motorized and all personnel are carried in motor transport. It has a strength of 29 officers and 711 enlisted men.

c. Motor battalion.—The motor battalion, assigned to each ar-moured brigade (fig. 19), consists of a headquarters company and 4 motor companies. Each company consists of 3 motor platoons and 1 scout platoon (11 Bren carriers). Each motor platoon consists of 3 sections, each self-contained, operationally and administratively, in 1 vehicle. This battalion, with a strength of 26 officers and 774 enlisted men, has much greater fire power than any other in the British Army.

d. Motorized battalion.—The motorized battalion, formerly assigned to the support group of the armoured division, now forms the infantry component of the infantry brigade in the armoured division (see par. 38a(4)). Its organization is exactly the same as that of a rifle battalion (fig. 9), but it is carried in motor transport.

e. Divisional reconnaissance regiment (battalion) (fig. 11).—This regiment is assigned to each infantry division. It consists of a head-quarters, a headquarters squadron, and 3 squadrons, each of which is composed of a headquarters, 3 scout troops, and an assault troop. Headquarters squadron consists of an anti-aircraft troop, a signal troop, a mortar troop, an anti-tank troop, and an administrative troop. The regiment is wholly motorized, includes 52 armoured reconnaissance cars and 70 carriers, and has a strength of 40 officers and 753 enlisted men. It is actually equivalent to an infantry battalion in composition but has recently adopted cavalry nomen-clature. However, it is composed of specially trained infantrymen, and is under infantry control at the War Office.

SECTION VI

PARACHUTE TROOPS

27. Organization and equipment.—*a. General.*—Paratroops, or parachute troops (figs. 12, 13, and 14), are procured from all branches of the Army and retain the uniforms, insignia, and organizational name of their parent organization. The British Parachute Wing is organized into battalions.[12] These battalions consist of a battalion

FIGURE 12.—Parachute troops.

headquarters, a headquarters company, and 3 or 4 rifle companies, each organized into 3 platoons. The platoon is divided into sections, each section consisting of a sergeant, a corporal, and 8 other men. This section of 10 men is considered as a "dropping" unit, that is, the largest group that can normally be dropped from 1 airplane. The armament includes 3-inch mortars in the mortar platoon of head-quarters company, and light machine guns, submachine guns, rifles,

_____

[12] These battalions have been formed into brigades, which are components of the air-borne division (see par. 185).

and pistols in the rifle companies. The parachute school at which the men are trained is a separate organization from the Parachute Wing.

FIGURE 13.—Parachute troops.

b. Equipment.—When jumping, the parachutist wears or carries the following equipment:

(1) Helmet.

(2) Gabardine jerkin.

(3) Battle-dress uniform.

(4) Knee pads (optional).

(5) Athletic supporter.

(6) Elastic ankle supporter.

FIGURE 14.—Parachute troops.

(7) Jumping boots.

(8) Gas mask (if warranted).

(9) Two empty utility pouches carried high on the sides near the chest (after landing, the parachutist uses these for carrying ammunition which he secures from containers that have been dropped).

(10) Sten machine carbine [13] (for those parachutists armed with the submachine gun)—the gun is carried on one leg and ammunition on the other. When about 100 feet from the ground, the parachutist, in order to lessen his weight and speed a quick release on landing, pulls a

---

[13] The Sten machine carbine (par. 91b) is similar to the U. S. Thompson submachine gun (see the center guardsman in fig. 48).

quick-release attachment and the gun and ammunition drop about 20 feet to the end of a small rope which is attached to the parachutist.

(11) Two grenades—one in each pocket of trousers.

(12) Map, wire cutters, etc., in pockets.

(13) One or two haversacks worn on the thigh—one contains knife, fork, spoon, canteen, and rations for 1 or 2 days; the other contains additional rations and a poncho.

c. Special equipment.—Signal personnel carry radio sets when they jump. Depending on the mission, other special equipment—medical supplies, bicycles, tools, etc.—is dropped.

Section VII

ROYAL REGIMENT OF ARTILLERY

28. General.—*a.* All artillery of the British Army belongs to the Royal Regiment of Artillery (RA), which in organization and magnitude is similar to a corps, but which retains the name "regiment" for traditional reasons.[14] Including Royal Horse Artillery (RHA) and all other types of artillery, it is classified by type as follows:

(1) *Field (Fd).*—Divisional artillery—25-pounder (3.45-inch; 88-mm) gun-howitzer.

(2) *Royal Horse Artillery (RHA).*—Motorized and in armoured divisions (25-pounder).

(3) *Medium (Med).*—4.5-inch gun; 5.5-inch gun-howitzer; 6-inch howitzer (obsolescent).

(4) *Heavy (Hy).*—6-inch gun; 7.2-inch howitzer; 9.2-inch howitzer.

(5) *Super-heavy.*—9.2-inch gun and all greater calibers.

(6) *Special equipment.*

(a) *Anti-tank (A Tk).*—2-pounder (40-mm); 6-pounder (57-mm); 17-pounder (3-inch; 76.2-mm).

(b) *Anti-aircraft (AA).*—20-mm Sten; 40-mm Bofors; 3.7-inch and 4.45-inch heavy AA guns.

---

[14] Cf. The King's Royal Rifle *Corps* and The Rifle *Brigade,* each of which is in reality an infantry *regiment* of the line. See paragraph 167*g.*

(c) *Mountain* (*Mtn*).—2.95-inch (75-mm) gun (pack); 3.7-inch howitzer (pack).

b. All artillery, except for certain specialized units such as coast defence and mountain, is motorized.

c. British artillery unit designations are, in the main, different from those of the U. S. Army. For easy reference, they are tabulated below:

British	*United States*
Regiment	Regiment
Battery	Battalion
Troop	Battery
Section	Platoon
Sub-section	Section

d. Artillery is organized into—

(1) Tactical units.

(2) Technical fire units.

The tactical unit contains more than one fire unit. Normally, this fire unit is the battery, which is fully equipped to. and does, operate independently.

29. Field regiment.—*a.* The field regiment (fig. 15) is the basic tactical unit of British artillery.

b. It is equipped with the 25-pounder (3.45-inch) gun-howitzer. All reports of this weapon are laudatory, and it is replacing both the obsolescent 18-pounder (3.3-inch) and the 4.5-inch howitzer.

c. The field regiment has the following anti-aircraft and anti-tank resources:

	Regt Hq	Btry Hq	Each troop
Anti-aircraft light machine guns	4	4	2
Anti-tank rifles	1	2	1

Anti-aircraft light machine guns have Motley mountings to enable them to be fired from vehicles on the move. Normally, however, the vehicle is halted before the attacker is engaged. Anti-tank rifles are carried in the same vehicles as the anti-aircraft light machine guns.

d. Ammunition.—The ammunition normally transported in the regiment is 160 rounds per gun (90 percent HE; 10 percent smoke), and, in addition, 12 rounds per gun of solid armour-piercing shot, which is carried on the gun tractors. Separate charges are carried for each round of ammunition except armour-piercing, and they include a number of supercharge rounds. The normal distribution of ammunition is as follows:

(1) *In each troop:*

Six tractors, 24 rounds each = 144 rounds.

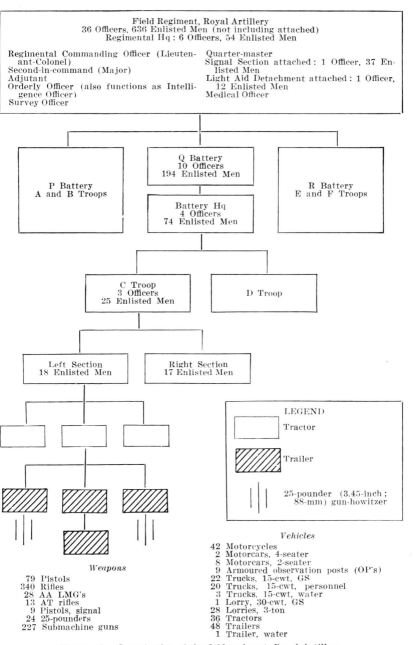

Field Regiment, Royal Artillery
36 Officers, 636 Enlisted Men (not including attached)
Regimental Hq : 6 Officers, 54 Enlisted Men

Regimental Commanding Officer (Lieutenant-Colonel)
Second-in-command (Major)
Adjutant
Orderly Officer (also functions as Intelligence Officer)
Survey Officer

Quarter-master
Signal Section attached : 1 Officer, 37 Enlisted Men
Light Aid Detachment attached : 1 Officer, 12 Enlisted Men
Medical Officer

P Battery
A and B Troops

Q Battery
10 Officers
194 Enlisted Men

Battery Hq
4 Officers
74 Enlisted Men

R Battery
E and F Troops

C Troop
3 Officers
25 Enlisted Men

D Troop

Left Section
18 Enlisted Men

Right Section
17 Enlisted Men

LEGEND

Tractor

Trailer

25-pounder (3.45-inch ; 88-mm) gun-howitzer

Vehicles

42 Motorcycles
2 Motorcars, 4-seater
8 Motorcars, 2-seater
9 Armoured observation posts (OP's)
22 Trucks, 15-cwt, GS
20 Trucks, 15-cwt, personnel
3 Trucks, 15-cwt, water
1 Lorry, 30-cwt, GS
28 Lorries, 3-ton
36 Tractors
48 Trailers
1 Trailer, water

Weapons

79 Pistols
340 Rifles
28 AA LMG's
13 AT rifles
9 Pistols, signal
24 25-pounders
227 Submachine guns

FIGURE 15.—Organization of the field regiment, Royal Artillery.

NOTE.—A British medium regiment, equipped with 6-inch howitzers and 4.5-inch guns or 5.5-inch gun-howitzers, is identical in organization except that there are only two batteries and each section includes only two tractors, each pulling one gun. All ammunition is therefore carried in the ammunition group.

Eight trailers, 32 rounds each=256 rounds.
Total, 400 rounds=100 rounds per gun.

(2) *In each battery ammunition group:*[15]
Two 30-cwt trucks, 56 rounds each=112 rounds.
Two 3-ton trucks, 184 rounds each=368 rounds.
Total, 480 rounds=60 rounds per gun.

e. Fuzes.—Types of fuzes employed are as follows:
(1) Fuze 117_____ Direct action.
(2) Fuze 119_____ Direct action, delayed.
(3) Fuze 210_____ Clockwork for high bursts.
(4) Fuze 221_____ Time.

30. Medium regiment.—*a. Employment.*—In Great Britain medium artillery is a part of corps artillery, but with British troops abroad it is included in the divisional organization. Medium artillery is normally employed on counter-battery work and on other missions where use can be made of its long range.

b. Organization.—The organization of a medium regiment is similar to that of a field regiment except that the former contains only two batteries. (The organization of the field regiment is shown in fig. 15.)

c. Armament.—(1) The medium regiment in the infantry division is armed with the 5.5-inch gun-howitzer or the old 6-inch howitzer. The maximum range of the 6-inch howitzer is 11,400 yards, and that of the 5.5-inch gun-howitzer 16,000 yards.

(2) The medium regiments of corps artillery are armed with 6-inch howitzers or the 4.5-inch gun. The maximum range of the latter is 20,500 yards.

d. Maneuver and deployment.—The medium regiment is organized for maneuver and deploys in the same way as the field regiment. There is one armoured observation post (OP) in each battery.

e. Ammunition.—The medium regiment carries 100 rounds of ammunition per gun, all HE, no smoke being fired by medium artillery. The distribution is as follows:

(1) *On each gun tractor (prime mover).*—Fifty rounds.
(2) *In each battery ammunition group:*
Eight 3-ton lorries, 40 rounds each=320 rounds.
Two 3-ton lorries, 40 rounds each=80 rounds.
Total, 400 rounds=50 rounds per gun.

---

[15] The ammunition group is not shown on the chart in figure 15, since, except on a tactical march, it is a part of Hq.

f. Communications.—Communications are similar to the light artillery nets except that both troops are equipped so that they can act independently. The allotment of wireless sets is three to regimental headquarters, three to each battery headquarters, and two to each troop. There is, in addition, one set for each battery providing wireless-telegraph (W/T) and radio-telephone (R/T) air-ground communication.

g. Survey party.—A survey party is included in regimental headquarters.

h. Anti-aircraft and anti-tank resources.—The medium regiment has the following anti-aircraft and anti-tank resources:

	Regt Hq	Btry Hq	Each troop
Anti-aircraft light machine guns	2	2	1
Anti-tank rifles	1	2	1

31. Anti-aircraft and anti-tank.—*a.* Each infantry division contains an organic light anti-aircraft regiment and an organic anti-tank regiment. In combat, one light anti-aircraft battery (U. S. battalion) and one anti-tank battery (battalion) may be attached to the infantry brigade.

b. The divisional light anti-aircraft regiment is armed with fifty-four 40-mm Bofors AA guns and the divisional anti-tank regiment is armed with forty-eight 6-pounder guns (of the 48 a proportion will eventually be 17-pounder).

32. Adjustment of fire.—*a. Methods in order of preference.*—(1) *Forward observer.*—British opinion believes the best method of getting field artillery fire on a target is by a forward observer connected directly by telephone to the battery. A forward observer with radio is used prior to the establishment of wire communications or when wires are out temporarily or permanently.

(2) *Air observation post (OP).*—(*a*) The artillery air OP is gaining popularity. It is an unarmed airplane equipped with radio-telephone, capable of landing on and taking off from a small space, and piloted by an artillery officer who also acts as observer. The airplane constitutes an elevated OP, fire being conducted from it in the same manner as fire from a ground OP. A second occupant of the airplane serves as lookout to warn the pilot of the approach of enemy aircraft. The airplane ascends to 600 or 1,000 feet and does not fly out over the target area.

(*b*) *Organization of air OP personnel:*
1 artillery officer (pilot).
1 flight mechanic.

1 flight rigger.

1 motorcycle driver.

(c) *Matériel:*

1 airplane.

1 motorcycle.

1 truck (1½-ton).

(d) The ground staff for repairs consists entirely of RAF personnel.

(e) One squadron of four flights of four air OP's each is attached to each corps. One of these flights is allotted to each division and comes under the control of the divisional artillery commander. This provides one air OP to operate with each field regiment of artillery in the division. One air OP is held in reserve for replacement or for leapfrogging.

(3) *Map data corrected by "meteor."*—When maps are available and observed fire is impractical or undesirable, firing is done by map data corrected by "meteor" obtained either from high-burst ranging shots, that is, registration (conducted by specialists with special equipment of the flash-ranging battery of the corps survey regiment), or from a broadcast meteor message like the U. S. "metro message" (see *e*, below.) The meteor obtained by high-burst ranging is the more accurate of the two.

b. Sight and instrument graduations.—The British use degrees, minutes, and tenths of minutes instead of mils. All their sights and instruments are so graduated.

c. Clock code.—The horizontal clock code method of aerial adjustment of fire is now used. Its advantage lies in the fact that the observer need not know the position of the firing battery; he needs only the target and a map.

d. Gridded oblique photographs.—In conjunction with aerial observation of fire, the use of gridded oblique photographs has proved very successful in identifying and locating targets, despite the handicap of the oblique view which the observer has. A system is being developed whereby these gridded oblique photographs may be used as a basis of unobserved prepared fires when maps are lacking. This will be of great value where the taking of vertical aerial photographs involves too great a risk because of enemy anti-aircraft or fighter defence.

e. Meteorological message.—A "metro message" is called a "meteor telegram" by the British. A typical one, with explanations, is given below:

From—			Ground in text	
Originator's number 14		Date 22	In reply to number	
Bar _ _ _ _ _ _ _ _ _ _ _ _ _ _ _ _ _ _	3060	0539	16223	1037
19225 _ _ _ _ _ _ _ _ _ _ _ _ _ _ _ _ _	1535	21230	2033	23231
2530 _ _ _ _ _ _ _ _ _ _ _ _ _ _ _ _ _	25228	3030	26225	3530
28220 _ _ _ _ _ _ _ _ _ _ _ _ _ _ _				
Time of origin 1400 _ _ _ _ _ _	T. O. R.[1]			

[1] Time of receipt.

(1) "Bar 3060" is the height of the barometer in inches, to two places of decimals, at mean sea level (MSL)—here 30.60 inches.

(2) The first two figures in each 4-figure group are the time of flight in seconds.

(3) The last two figures in each 4-figure group give the air temperature in degrees Fahrenheit.

(4) Each 5-figure group relates to the preceding group of four figures.

(5) The first two figures in each 5-figure group give the velocity of the equivalent constant wind in feet per second. To convert feet per second into miles per hour, multiply by 2 and divide by 3. Thus 30 feet per second equals 30 multiplied by 2 and divided by 3, or 20 miles per hour.

(6) The last three figures in each 5-figure group give in degrees the true bearing from which the wind is blowing.

(7) The groups always consist of the number of figures shown, 0's being prefixed if necessary. Thus, 07004 would signify a 7-foot-per-second wind from a bearing of 4°.

33. Communications.—*a.* Dispatch riders, as well as wireless, line, and visual systems, are provided for intercommunication between regimental headquarters and batteries. The wireless layout depends on the number of sets available and on the number of frequencies allotted. The minimum number of sets required to make communication efficient is three for regimental headquarters, three for battery headquarters, and two for each troop. All wireless sets have remote control. One wire is laid from each trop OP to its Gun Position Officer (GPO). The gun positions are linked together by a "link line" (lateral line), through three-way switches at the gun position. The battery command post is connected by a single wire to each troop gun position. The only switchboards are at the battery command post and regimental headquarters.

b. The artillery is responsible for its own communication from the battery down. The regimental signal section, Royal Corps of Signals, which is attached to regimental headquarters from the 2nd Company, Divisional Signals, handles communication from regiment to battery, between batteries, and from the artillery to the infantry. (See fig. 16 for a schematic diagram of field regimental signal communications.)

c. New radio sets have been issued, providing two-way radio-telephone (R/T), as well as radio-telegraph (W/T), communication. These are operated by RA personnel, and will be the standard air-ground communications. Communication from ground to air may also be made by ground strips (identification panels).

34. Maneuver.—*a. Organization.*—For tactical purposes, groups are formed as follows:

(1) *Regimental commander's group.*—The commander with such personnel as he requires when he goes to obtain orders.

(2) *Reconnaissance groups.*—Both regiment and battery personnel required for reconnaissance of regiment, battery, and OP areas.

(3) *Headquarters groups.*—Both regiment and battery personnel necessary to man headquarters and command posts (CP's), and complete technical work and communications required before the guns can open fire. Battery headquarters groups are divided into—

(*a*) "O" party—for the OP area.

(*b*) "G" party—for the gun-position area.

(4) *Gun group.*—The guns and vehicles, and the personnel to work them.

(5) *Ammunition group.*—Reserve ammunition and one gasoline distribution truck to each battery. These may be centralized and moved under orders of regimental headquarters.

(6) *Headquarters group.*—MT (motor transport) stores and technical personnel of regimental headquarters and the attached LAD (light aid detachment—motor maintenance section) normally move with the ammunition group under the regimental quartermaster sergeant.

(7) *"B" echelon.*—As in any other unit, moving under orders of regimental headquarters.

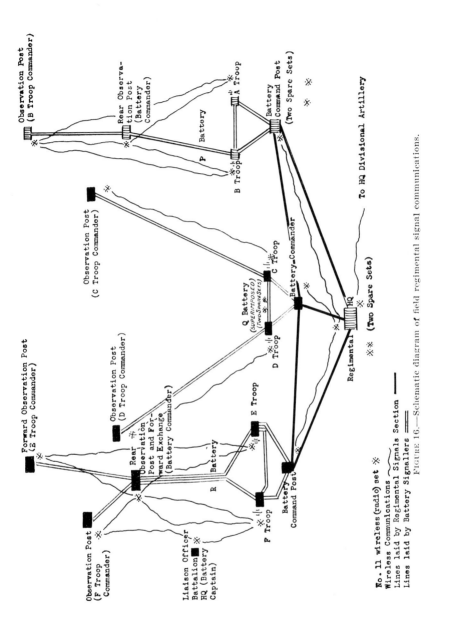

Observation Post
(B Troop Commander)

Rear Observation Post (Battery Commander)

A Troop

P Battery

B Troop

Battery Command Post
(Two Spare Sets)

※ ※

To HQ Divisional Artillery

Observation Post
(C Troop Commander)

C Troop

Battery Commander

Q Battery
(SUPERIMPOSED)
(Two Spare Sets)

D Troop

HQ (Two Spare Sets)

Regimental HQ

※ ※

Observation Post
(D Troop Commander)

Forward Observation Post
(E Troop Commander)

Rear Observation Post and Forward Exchange
(Battery Commander)

R Battery

E Troop

F Troop

Battery Command Post

Observation Post
(F Troop Commander)

Liaison Officer
Battalion ■
HQ (Battery Captain) ※

No. 11 wireless (radio) set ※
Wireless Communications ※
Lines laid by Regimental Signals Section ——
Lines laid by Battery Signallers ══

FIGURE 16.—Schematic diagram of field regimental signal communications.

(Face p. 36)

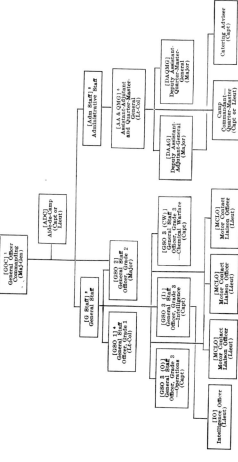

FIGURE 5.—Organization of the infantry division staff.

[GOC] [1]
General Officer
Commanding
(Maj-Gen)

[ADC] [1]
Aide-de-Camp
(Capt or
Lieut)

[G Staff] [2]
General Staff

[GSO 1] [4]
General Staff
Officer, Grade 1
(Lt-Col)

[GSO 3 (O)]
General Staff
Officer, Grade 3
—Operations
(Capt)

[IO]
Intelligence Officer
(Lieut)

[MCLO]
Motor Contact
Liaison Officer
(Lieut)

[GSO 3 (I)]
General Staff
Officer, Grade 3
—Intelligence
(Capt)

[MCLO]
Motor Contact
Liaison Officer
(Lieut)

[GSO 2]
General Staff
Officer, Grade 2
(Major)

[GSO 3 (CW)]
General Staff
Officer, Grade 3
—Chemical Warfare
(Capt)

[MCLO]
Motor Contact
Liaison Officer
(Lieut)

[Adm Staff] [3]
Administrative Staff

[AA & QMG] [5]
Assistant-Adjutant
and Quarter-Master-
General
(Lt-Col)

[DAAG]
Deputy Assistant-
Adjutant-General
(Major)

[DAQMG]
Deputy Assistant-
Quarter-Master-
General
(Major)

Camp
Commandant—
Quarter-Master
(Capt or Lieut)

Catering Adviser
(Capt)

[1] The letters shown in brackets are the British abbreviations for the official titles. The ranks of the officers normally holding these titles are shown in parentheses.

[2] The following headquarters staffs of the arms are attached to divisional Hq and are in close touch with the "G" Staff:
Commander, Royal Artillery (CRA).
Brigade Major, Royal Artillery (BMRA).
Staff Captain, Royal Artillery (SCRA).
Intelligence Officer (et Capt), Royal Artillery (IORA).
Commander, Royal Engineers (CRE).
Adjutant, Royal Engineers.
Officer Commanding, Divisional Signals (OC Div Sigs).

[3] The following headquarters staffs of the services are attached to divisional Hq and are in close touch with the "A" and "Q" Staffs (see note 5, below):
Commander, Royal Army Service Corps (CRASC).
Five officers, Royal Army Service Corps.
Assistant-Director, Medical Services (ADMS).
Deputy Assistant-Director, Medical Services (DADMS).
Deputy Assistant-Provost-Marshal (DAPM).
Assistant-Director, Ordnance Services (ADOS).
Two Deputy Assistant-Directors, Ordnance Services (DADOS [O]) and (DADOS [E]).
Senior Ordnance Mechanical Engineer (SOME).

[4] GSO 1 is responsible for coordination of all staff work at divisional Hq.

[5] AA & QMG (AQ) controls and coordinates the "A" Staff (DAAG) and the "Q" Staff (DAQMG).

b. Deployment.—(1) *Regimental headquarters.*—Before leaving for the place where orders are to be issued, the regimental commander lays down RV's (rendezvous) for all groups. After receiving his orders he normally sends back his second-in-command to supervise the reconnaissance and occupation of the gun-position area, while he, with or without personal reconnaissance, supervises the establishment of OP's. Regimental headquarters is then chosen and communications are opened with the three batteries.

(2) *Batteries.*—A battery can deploy as part of the regiment or independently. In either case speed is usually important. As soon as the battery commander receives his orders, he sends the Command Post Officer (CPO) to the gun-position area, where the latter reconnoiters the command post and troop positions. "G" party is then called up and all preparations are made so that guns can open fire immediately upon arrival. Meanwhile the battery commander has called the forward "O" party and is supervising the establishment of OP's, and communications are being opened between the OP's and the gun positions. As soon as the gun positions are determined, the battery captain arranges a track plan (circulation plan) and, with the Wagon Line Officer (WLO), chooses the wagon-line area (truck park). He then arranges for the anti-aircraft and anti-tank defence of the gun position and wagon lines. At the same time guides go back to the gun group rendezvous, guns are brought into action, and all vehicles not wanted at the gun positions are taken away to the wagon lines.

(3) *Troops.*—Troops can be deployed independently in the same manner under the orders of the troop commander and the troop GPO.

c. Control.—(1) Tactical control is normally the regimental commander's primary responsibility. He usually stays with the commander whom he is supporting, leaving technical control to his second-in-command. Similarly the battery has an officer with the supported unit. If the battery is working "under command" of the unit, it will be normal for the battery commander to be at the unit headquarters; but if the battery is "in support," he may remain with the battery and send the battery captain to the unit.

(2) Technical control is carried out through the command post officer at the battery command posts, and the GPO's (executives) at the troop positions.

d. Liaison.—(1) Liaison is maintained by Forward Observation, or Observing, Officers (FOO's) who keep in touch with forward units, and by an artillery officer at the headquarters of the supported unit.

(2) It is contemplated placing an armoured OP in each troop.

SECTION VIII

ANTI-AIRCRAFT COMMAND

35. General.—*a.* The Anti-Aircraft Command, which controls all anti-aircraft guns, heavy and light, and searchlights in the United Kingdom, is one of the commands which are charged with the joint cooperative mission of the defence of England, Scotland, Wales, and Northern Ireland against attack from the air. The various commands having that mission are collectively referred to under the name "Air Defence of Great Britain" (ADGB). The agencies and the high military commands included within the meaning of this term are shown diagrammatically in figure 17. The organization of the Anti-Aircraft Command itself is illustrated in figure 18.

b. The Anti-Aircraft Command has been organized with the primary consideration of facilitating full cooperation between it and other elements of the Air Defence of Great Britain and particularly between it and the Fighter Command of the Royal Air Force. Although for administrative purposes the Anti-Aircraft Command remains under the War Office and consequently must function through several army commands, the geographical boundaries of the three anti-aircraft corps correspond, nevertheless, with the boundaries of the areas of the six groups of the Fighter Command rather than with the boundaries of the army commands. Each anti-aircraft corps, therefore, covers the same area as two of the groups of the Fighter Command.

c. The Anti-Aircraft Command is under the operational control of the Fighter Command. See paragraph 179*a*(2). Except for that control, however, the Anti-Aircraft Command is a separate tactical unit of the Army charged with the anti-aircraft gun and searchlight defence of Great Britain and is directly responsible to the Army Council. It is commanded by a general.

36. Organization.—*a.* The Anti-Aircraft Command consists of 3 corps and 12 divisions. The corps and divisions are geographical commands, and the units assigned to each vary with their missions.

b. An anti-aircraft division is not a standard tactical unit like an infantry division but is rather a unit charged with the AA defence of a certain area. A division, which is commanded by a major-general, generally consists of a headquarters and three or more brigades, with certain service elements.

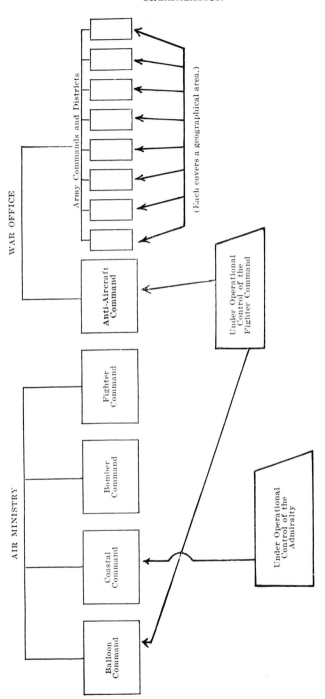

FIGURE 17.—Organization of the Air Defence of Great Britain.

39

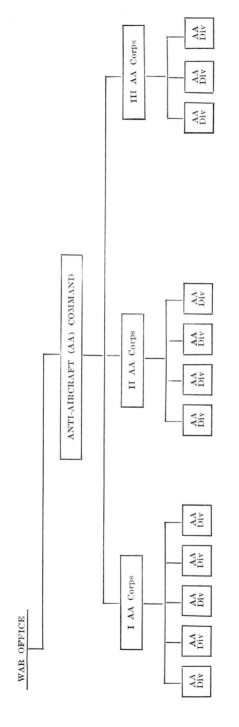

WAR OFFICE

ANTI-AIRCRAFT (AA) COMMAND

I AA Corps

II AA Corps

III AA Corps

AA Div

Brigades—including heavy artillery, or light artillery, or searchlights, or unrotating projectiles (rockets), or a combination of any of the four—are assigned to divisions as required. AA corps, divisions, and brigades have geographical boundaries.

FIGURE 18.—Organization of the Anti-Aircraft Command.

40

c. A brigade, which is commanded by a brigadier, is composed of a headquarters and three or more regiments. The brigade, which has a very flexible organization, may be composed of regiments equipped with heavy or light guns, with searchlights, with rocket guns, or with a combination of any of the four.

d. A regiment, however, normally has but one type of equipment. A regiment consists of 3 or 4 batteries, and can be organized on a mobile or static basis. Regiments organized on a static basis possess transport only for administrative needs. Each regiment has a small headquarters of about 4 or 5 line officers, 1 or 2 medical officers, and about 30 enlisted men, and is commanded by a lieutenant-colonel.

e. Batteries of mixed personnel, men and women, are now actually employed. The women are specially trained members of the Auxiliary Territorial Service (ATS), who are not operationally employed in fighting units outside the Anti-Aircraft Command. They man and operate directors, height-finders, observation telescopes, telephones, and other instruments. Up to the present time they have been operationally employed only in heavy batteries. (On the ATS, see par. 77*b*.)

Section IX

ROYAL ARMOURED CORPS

37. General.—*a.* The Royal Armoured Corps (RAC) represents an amalgamation of the Royal Tank Corps and the mechanized cavalry regiments of the line. The Royal Tank Regiment (formerly called RTR, and now known as R Tanks) consists of various numbered tank battalions: for example, 4 R Tanks (that is, the 4th battalion of the Royal Tank Regiment).[16] The tank regiments of the mechanized cavalry of the RAC have the same main type of organization as the tank battalions of the R Tanks, the only difference being the use of the words "regiment" and "battalion" to designate the respective organizations. The mechanized cavalry also includes the armoured car regiments.

b. There are two general types of armoured units: the armoured division and the army tank brigade.

(1) The armoured division is equipped with cruiser tanks, which have the best all-around combination of speed, armament, and armour for long-range operations and tank combat.

---

[16] See paragraphs 167*b* and 168*a*.

41

(2) The army tank brigade is equipped with heavily armoured infantry ("I") tanks for assault on defended positions in close cooperation with the infantry. In infantry tanks, speed is sacrificed to heavier armour which will afford greater protection against enemy anti-tank guns.

c. The main armament usually consists of one 2-pounder (40-mm) gun [17] mounted co-axially with one machine gun. Close-support (CS) tanks have a 3-inch howitzer instead of the 2-pounder.

38. Armoured division.—*a. Organization.*—(1) The organization of the armoured division has undergone, and is undergoing, continuous changes. Also, the organization of the armoured division in the Middle East differs from that of the Home Forces armoured division (fig. 19), though it is expected that the former will eventually approximate the latter. At the present time, the Home Forces armoured division normally consists of an advanced and a rear headquarters, 1 armoured brigade, 1 armoured car regiment, 1 infantry brigade, divisional artillery, divisional signals, engineer, medical, and provost units, and supply organizations. This division has a total strength of 201 tanks of the cruiser type, 8 of which are at advanced headquarters.[18]

(2) The armoured brigade (with 193 tanks) consists of brigade headquarters (with 10 tanks), 3 armoured regiments (with 61 tanks each), and 1 infantry motor battalion.

(*a*) The armoured regiment consists of a headquarters (with 4 tanks and 10 two-man armoured scout cars) and 3 squadrons. Each squadron consists of a headquarters (with 4 tanks, 2 of which are close-support) and 5 troops (with 3 tanks each).

(*b*) The motor battalion (par. 26*c*) is equipped with 14 scout cars and 44 machine-gun carriers.

(3) The armoured car regiment (with about 60 armoured cars) varies in organization. One type, for operation in the desert, consists of a headquarters (with 4 armoured cars), a headquarters section (with 12 scout cars), and 3 squadrons. Each squadron consists of a headquarters (with 3 armoured cars) and 5 troops (with 3 armoured cars each). Another type, for close-country fighting, consists of 4 squadrons of 5 troops each. Each troop has 3 armoured cars forming a non-dismountable portion, and 2 scout cars, 2 motorcycles, and 2 motorcycle combinations forming the dismountable portion.

---

[17] See paragraph 99*a*.
[18] See paragraph 110 for types of U. S. light and medium tanks used by the British.

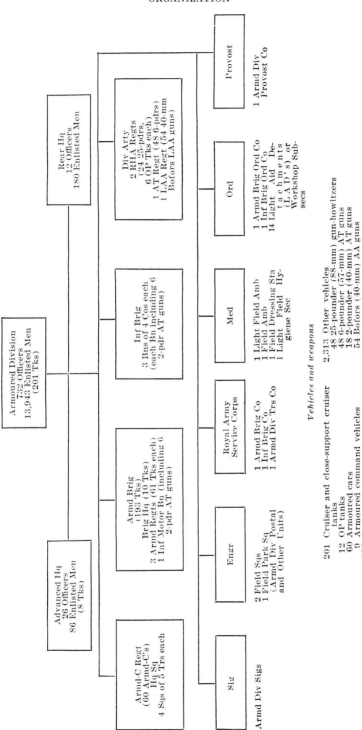

Vehicles and weapons

201 Cruiser and close-support cruiser tanks
 12 OP tanks
 60 Armoured cars
  9 Armoured command vehicles
137 Scout cars

2,313 Other vehicles
  48 25-pounder (88-mm) gun-howitzers
  48 6-pounder (57-mm) AT guns
  18 2-pounder (40-mm) AT guns
  54 Bofors (40-mm) AA guns

FIGURE 19.—Organization of the Home Forces armoured division.

(4) The support group no longer exists, and its place has been taken by an infantry brigade consisting of three (motorized) battalions (par. 26*d*). Each battalion includes six 2-pounder anti-tank guns. The remainder of the supporting element consists of two Royal Horse Artillery regiments, with twenty-four 25-pounders and six observation-post (OP) tanks each; an anti-tank regiment, with forty-eight 6-pounders; and a light anti-aircraft regiment, with fifty-four 40-mm Bofors light anti-aircraft guns.

b. Duties of various staff officers at armoured divisional headquarters.— The various staff officers are charged with the following duties:[19]

(1) *GSO 1.*—Coordinating all branches of the staff and acting as adviser to the commander.

(2) *GSO 2.*—Issuing orders, except over the wireless (this is done by the divisional commander or GSO 1), keeping up the battle map, keeping other armoured command vehicles (ACV's) in touch with the situation and receiving information from them over the house telephone, and directing road movements in conjunction with DAQMG (Deputy Assistant-Quarter-Master-General) and DAPM (Deputy Assistant-Provost-Marshal).

(3) *OC Armd Div Sigs (Officer Commanding, Armoured Divisional Signals).*—Signal communications in the division manned by R Sigs personnel.

(4) *GSO 3 (I) and IO (Intelligence Officer).*—Collecting all intelligence information and producing an estimate of the enemy for the commander; responsible for the production of intelligence ("I") summaries.

(5) *GSO 3 (CW) (Chemical Warfare).*—Chemical warfare adviser to the commander.

(6) *AA & QMG (Assistant-Adjutant and Quarter-Master-General).*— Chief "Q" (Quarter-master) officer in the division. Responsible for all "Q" problems such as replenishment of supplies, etc. Adviser to the commander and GSO 1 on "Q" matters.

(7) *DAQMG (Deputy Assistant-Quarter-Master-General).*—Assists the AA & QMG and is responsible, with GSO 2 and DAPM ("B" echelon in some divisions is controlled by DAAG (Deputy Assistant-Adjutant-General) from rear divisional Hq) for road movements and, with the Staff Captain from each brigade, for sheltering and protecting troops and vehicles for the night, and for "B" echelon (rear echelon of first-line transport).

---

[19] See paragraph 21*a* and figure 5 for the duties of these officers on the infantry division staff.

(8) *CRE (Commander, Royal Engineers).*—Acts as engineer adviser to the commander and commands the engineers in the division.

(9) *DAAG (Deputy Assistant-Adjutant-General).*—Responsible for all personnel matters. In some divisions he controls "B" echelon.

(10) *SC (Staff Captain).*—Assists AQMG and DAQMG and represents them at the rear divisional Hq.

(11) *DAPM (Deputy Assistant-Provost-Marshal).*—Commands the division provost section and assists in arranging for traffic control.

(12) *CRASC (Commander, Royal Army Service Corps).*—Commands the divisional RASC and is responsible for the replenishment of supplies, ammunition, and gasoline.

(13) *SOME (Senior Ordnance Mechanical Engineer).*—Adviser to the commander on ordnance questions.

(14) *DADOS (Deputy Assistant-Director of Ordnance Services).*—Responsible for the supply of ordnance equipment. Either SOME or DADOS will command the ordnance in the division, depending upon which is the senior.

(15) *SMO (Senior Medical Officer).*—Adviser to the commander on all medical matters.

c. Rear divisional headquarters.—(1) The following staff officers and attached officers are normally at rear divisional Hq: DAAG, SC, DAPM, CRASC, SOME, DADOS, and SMO.

(2) These officers normally travel in utility cars or trucks. There are no ACV's at rear divisional Hq.

39. Army tank brigade.—*a.* An army tank brigade (fig. 20) differs from an armoured brigade in that it is built around infantry tanks rather than cruiser tanks. It is composed of 3 battalions rather than 3 regiments, with a total strength of 178 tanks (135 or more infantry tanks, 16 or more cruiser tanks, and 18 close-support cruiser tanks).

b. An army tank battalion consists of a headquarters and a headquarters squadron (with 4 cruiser tanks, 9 scout cars, and 2 carriers) and 3 squadrons. It has a total strength of 58 tanks (45 or more infantry tanks, 4 or more cruiser tanks, and 6 close-support cruiser tanks).

c. A squadron consists of a headquarters (with one infantry or cruiser tank and two close-support cruiser tanks) and five troops (with three infantry tanks each).

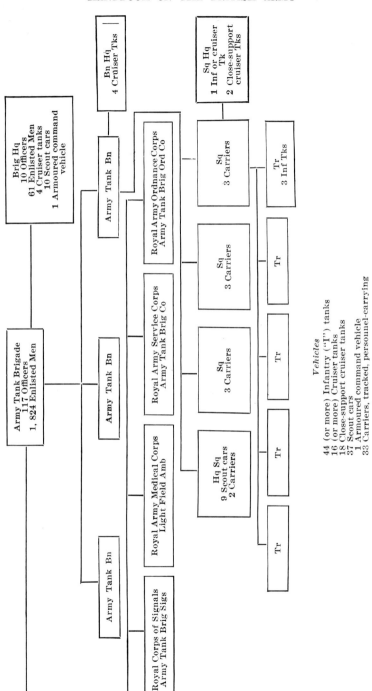

FIGURE 20.—Organization of the army tank brigade.

46

SECTION X

CORPS OF ROYAL ENGINEERS

40. General.—*a. Employment.*—The personnel of the Corps of Royal Engineers (RE) is technically trained and equipped to apply engineering skill and science to the needs of the Army. Officers when first commissioned normally receive nearly 3 years of engineering training; a large number of the enlisted men are "tradesmen" (corresponding generally to specialists in U. S. services). Engineers ("sappers") are also trained to fight, and are, when needed, used as infantry. Such employment is, however, exceptional, since casualties in skilled personnel are difficult to replace. The engineers are equipped with automatic and other weapons on a scale to provide for local protection against personnel, tanks, and aircraft rather than for use in attack.

b. Organization.—The basic engineer unit is the company. Each company is numbered and is administratively independent. Companies are normally grouped under command of a CRE (Commander, Royal Engineers—corresponding to the divisional engineer in the U. S. division). Companies are divided generally into three main types:

(1) *Field and fortress.*—Field units form the engineer element of fighting formations; fortress companies exist only in overseas garrisons such as Gibraltar and Malta.

(2) *Line of communications (L of C).*—Such units provide troops for engineer services in the base and L of C area.

(3) *Transportation.*—Transportation units provide troops for the construction, maintenance, and operation of railways, docks, and inland waterways.

c. Distribution.—The Royal Engineers are normally distributed throughout the Army as follows:

(1) *Infantry division.*
  Hq Divisional RE.
  One Field Park Co.
  Three Field Cos.
(2) *Armoured division.*
  Hq Armoured Divisional RE.
  One Field Park Squadron.
  Two Field Squadrons.

(3) *Corps.*
Three Army Field Cos.
One Corps Field Park Co.
One Corps Field Survey Co.

(4) *Army GHQ and L of C.*—No fixed allotments; may include—
Army Troops Cos.
Engineer Base Workshops.
Engineer Store Base Depots.
Workshop and Park Cos.
Mechanical Equipment Cos.
Electrical and Mechanical Cos.
Forestry Cos.
Quarrying Cos.
Road Construction Cos.
Tunnelling Cos.
General Construction Cos.
Artisan Works Cos.
Aerodrome Maintenance Cos.
Welding Cos.
Welding Sections.
Well-boring Sections.
Army Field Survey Cos.
Transportation Units.

d. Special units.—In addition to typical engineer units, the Royal Engineers contain postal units, mobile bath units, salvage units, bomb disposal units, and chemical warfare groups. Chemical warfare groups receive the same general training as divisional field companies except for training in building bridges, the principle being that they can be converted into field companies, if necessary, with a small amount of instruction. The engineer bridge equipment is carried in a bridge company, which is a Royal Army Service Corps (RASC) unit and not a Royal Engineer unit. The bridge company is a corps unit and is charged with holding and maintaining bridge equipment, but not with constructing the bridge or with maintaining it when built. The company delivers bridging equipment to the engineer organizations when needed.

41. Infantry division.—In the infantry division, the engineers are organized into a headquarters, divisional engineers; 1 field park company; and 3 field companies. All companies are completely self-sustaining. They are not dependent upon the headquarters, divisional engineers, for supplies or administration, although they are under the disciplinary and executive command of the CRE. The field park company corresponds generally to the Headquarters and Service Company in the U. S. Army. The field company, although larger, corresponds to the lettered companies of the U. S. combat engineers. The field companies are organized as company headquarters and 3 sections (platoons). The basic work unit is the section of the field company with a strength of 1 officer and 64 enlisted men; the normal working strength is 48 men in 4 subsections (squads). There are nine basic work units in the divisional engineers. (For organization charts, see figs. 21 and 22.)

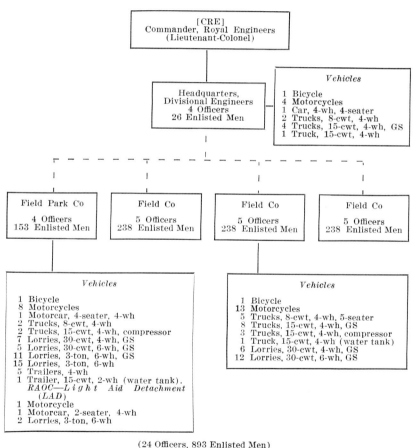

(24 Officers, 893 Enlisted Men)

Chain of Command - - - - -
Chain of Command and Administration ————

FIGURE 21.—Organization of (infantry) divisional engineers.

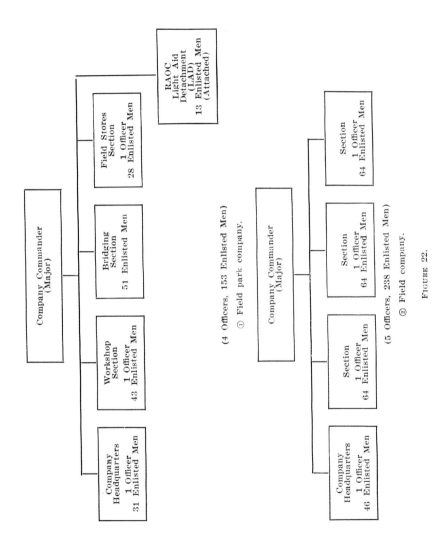

(4 Officers, 153 Enlisted Men)

① Field park company.

(5 Officers, 238 Enlisted Men)

② Field company.

FIGURE 22.

42. Armoured division.—In the armoured division, the engineers are organized into a headquarters, armoured divisional engineers; 1 field park squadron; and 2 field squadrons. The British armoured divisional engineers have a much looser organization than the engineers in a U. S. armored unit. The squadrons are completely self-sustaining and so do not depend upon the headquarters for any administration or supply, although they are directly under the command of the CRE. The field park squadron corresponds generally to the Headquarters and Service Company of the U. S. armored battalion. The field squadrons, although larger than the lettered companies of the U. S. armored battalion, are similar to them. The field squadrons are divided into squadron headquarters and 3 troops, each troop being organized as a headquarters and 4 sections. The section of the troop is the basic work unit, with a strength of 12 enlisted men. There is a total of 24 basic work units in the divisional engineers. (For organization charts, see figs. 23 and 24.)

43. Supply.—Engineer equipment and stores are supplied as follows:

a. Organizational equipment carried by companies is supplied by the Royal Army Ordnance Corps (RAOC).

b. Explosives are ordnance stores, but replenishment in the field is carried out by the supply company, Royal Army Service Corps (RASC).

c. Engineer stores, such as expendable material (cement, timber, barbed wire, etc.) and equipment not included in organizational scales, are supplied by the engineer store service, which includes an engineer store base depot, and workshop and park companies.

d. Bridging equipment is carried in the field by bridge companies (RASC), one of which is normally allotted to each corps. A reserve is also held at the base and at advanced base depots if necessary. The sub-allotment and forward dispatch of bridging equipment is decided by the General Staff at GHQ, army, corps, and, in due course, divisional headquarters, with advice of the Engineer-in-Chief, Chief Engineer, and CRE, respectively.

44. Explosives and demolition.—*a. General.*—The present British standard explosive carried by first-line units is guncotton in slab form. Ammonal and guncotton in the proportion of 9 to 4 are carried by second- and third-line RASC supply units. Further reserves of bulk explosives are held at the base. These reserves may include TNT slabs and plastic HE, which are service explosives, or any suitable commercial explosive such as the nitroglycerin group. Plastic HE, when available in sufficient quantities, will replace all others, since it is equally suitable for use in cutting, mined, or borehole charges. Until such time as plastic HE is available in quantity, explosive 808 is being issued instead.

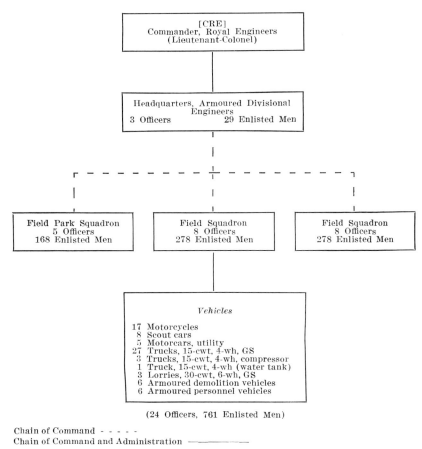

Chain of Command - - - - -
Chain of Command and Administration ————————

FIGURE 23.—Organization of armoured divisional engineers.

b. Characteristics of explosives.—Explosive 808 is a plastic, desensitized polar blasting gelatine which is equally suitable for cutting, mined, or borehole charges, but owing to its slightly rubbery nature it cannot be rammed tightly in boreholes, and, when used as a cutting charge, requires secure fixing. This explosive contains 60 percent nitroglycerin, but it will not be detonated by a rifle bullet. Its strength is 93 percent greater than that of TNT. Since its explosive properties deteriorate rapidly at temperatures of 100° F., it is not suitable for use in climates where such high temperatures are the rule.

It is issued in 4-ounce cylindrical cartridges 1⅜ inches in diameter and 3 inches long and is wrapped in thin paper. The explosive can be used under water, and, when fresh, can be detonated by any detonator or detonating fuze, although primers will give more satisfactory results.

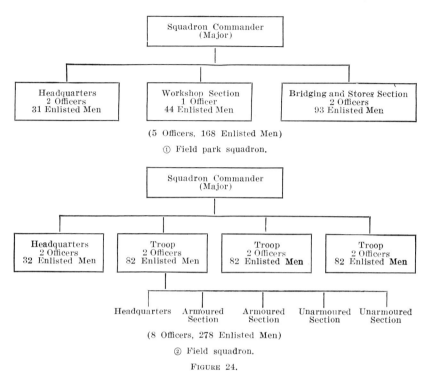

(5 Officers, 168 Enlisted Men)

① Field park squadron.

(8 Officers, 278 Enlisted Men)

② Field squadron.

FIGURE 24.

c. Mines.—(1) *Anti-tank.*—Types of British mines with details of their packing and carriage in the field are shown in figure 25.

(2) *Mk. IV mine.*—(*a*) Details of the standard British anti-tank mine Mk. IV are shown in figure 26. This mine is set to be detonated by pressure of 320 pounds. It will break the track of tanks, but normally does not breach the belly of the tank or injure the crew.

(*b*) The fuze for the Mk. IV mine is shown in figure 26 ①. A steel rod projects from the head of the fuze, through which passes a stiff pin with a strong loop attached and a piece of bent brass wire. To arm the mine, remove the safety (split, or cotter) pin, but do not touch the brass wire. (If the brass wire is not in position as shown in figure 26 ②, the safety pin should not be removed, and the fuze should not be used.) The cover of the mine should next be removed and the fuze inserted in the socket in the top of the body. (The fuze should be an easy fit, and on no account should force be used.) The cover of the mine should then be gently replaced so that the pins engage the straps. To disarm Mk. IV mines, carefully remove the cover and extract the fuze. After the fuze has been removed, a safety pin or small nail should be inserted in the hole in the striker.

(c) The divisional supply company carry 1,232 Mk. II or 880 Mk. IV anti-tank mines. The corps ammunition park carries a sufficient supply to replenish the stocks of the supply companies of all the divisions in the corps.

(3) *Anti-personnel mines.*—Several patterns are in use: in the Middle East they are generally constructed locally.

| Mark | How packed | Diameter (approximate) | Height (approximate) | Weight | | Pistol, or fuze | | Remarks |
				Complete (approximate)	Filling (approximate)	Description	How packed	
		Inches	*Inches*	*Pounds* *Ounces*	*Pounds* *Ounces*			
II [1] ____	Steel box of 8 mines.	$7\frac{1}{2}$	$3\frac{1}{4}$	8 4	4 0	Fuze AT, Mks. I and II	In box with mines.	Obsolescent.
IV [1] ___	Wooden crate of 5 mines.	8	5	12 0	8 4	Fuze AT, No. 3, Mk. I.	Separate wooden box of 4 cylinders, each cylinder of 5 fuzes.	

[1] Mk. II and Mk. IV mines are being issued at present. Mk. I and Mk. III mines are now obsolete. A new model, Mk. V, which has a spider top similar to the U. S. mine and eliminates certain disadvantages of previous marks, is being tested.

FIGURE 25.—Anti-tank mines.

45. Bridging and bridge equipment.—*a. Load classification system.*—The British employ a system of load classification by which they give bridges and vehicles corresponding classification numbers. The classification number painted on any vehicle indicates that it can be safely taken over any bridge having a corresponding or higher classification number. These numbers are approximately equal to the tonnage of the vehicle in long tons (2,240 pounds). For example, a class 24 bridge can carry a 26-ton tank. (See par. 161a.)

b. Bridge types.—The following are the principal types of British mobile bridging equipment:

(1) *Reconnaissance boat.*—The reconnaissance boat (fig. 27) is a pneumatic boat 6 feet $8\frac{1}{2}$ inches by 2 feet $8\frac{1}{2}$ inches built in two

compartments, with a wooden floor-stiffener. It weighs 39 pounds and will carry a two-man load.

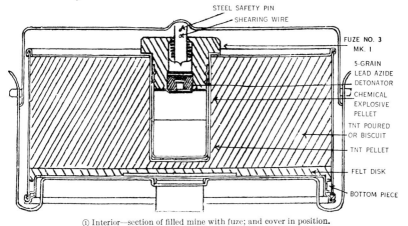

① Interior—section of filled mine with fuze; and cover in position.

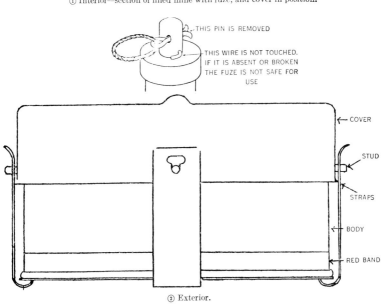

② Exterior.

FIGURE 26.—Anti-tank mine, Mk. IV.

(2) *Assault boat.*—The assault boat (fig. 28) is a wooden folding boat 12 feet 1½ inches by 4 feet 1 inch. It has five paddles, weighs 174 pounds, and carries nine fully armed men.

(3) *Kapok footbridge.*—This equipment is lighter than the U. S. footbridge, but is otherwise similar.

(4) *Folding boat equipment, Mk. III.*—This folding boat equipment (fig. 29) consists of folding boats, superstructure suitable for both

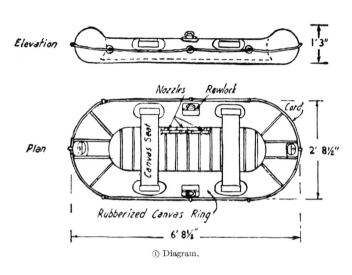

① Diagram.

② Boat being inflated by foot pump.

FIGURE 27.—Reconnaissance boat.

bridge use and rafting, trestles, anchors and anchor stores, auxiliary rafting gear, and folding dinghies for assault boats. The equipment may be made up into rafts for class 5 or class 9 loads, or used as single boats to carry 16 armed men in addition to the commander and crew of 4. The equipment has been designed primarily as a bridge, however, and such will be its normal use. The bridge is constructed by rafts, and the use of connectors permitting only limited articulation gives the bridge sufficient load capacity to carry class 9 loads (about 10 tons). The boats are 21 feet 10 inches by 6 feet 8 inches and weigh 870 pounds.

FIGURE 28.—Assault boat.

(5) *The small box-girder (SBG) bridge, Mk. III.*—This bridge is similar to the U. S. H10 bridge. Two sets are carried in each infantry division, and one special set in each armoured division.

(6) *Mk. V ponton equipment.*—(a) This equipment consists of pontons, Mk. V, trestles, Mk. VII, superstructure, and accessories, including the long landing bay and the sliding bay. The bridge is designed to carry class 24 loads (26 long tons.) The pontons are decked and weigh about 1,450 pounds. In forming a ponton pier two pontons are joined together by means of side and deck ponton couplings. The bridge is constructed by rafts, each raft being coupled together by means of raft connectors. A raft is normally supported on three ponton piers, each consisting of two pontons coupled stern to stern. Across the piers are laid steel I-beams which in turn support a decking of wooden planks, called chesses. The latter are held down at

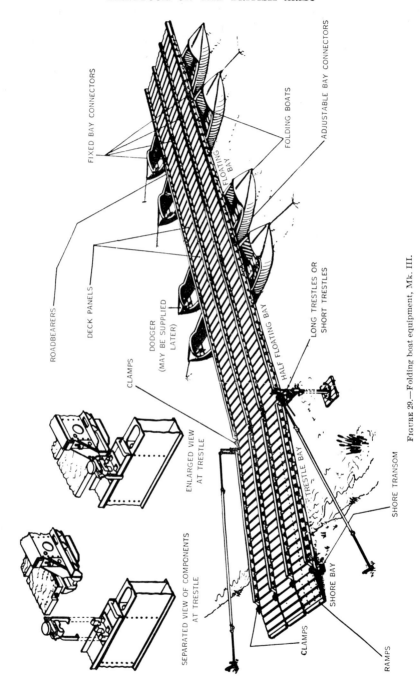

FIXED BAY CONNECTORS

FLOATING BAY

FOLDING BOATS

ADJUSTABLE BAY CONNECTORS

ROADBEARERS

DECK PANELS

DODGER
(MAY BE SUPPLIED
LATER)

CLAMPS

ENLARGED VIEW
AT TRESTLE

SEPARATED VIEW OF COMPONENTS
AT TRESTLE

HALF FLOATING BAY

LONG TRESTLES OR
SHORT TRESTLES

TRESTLE BAY

SHORE TRANSOM

CLAMPS

SHORE BAY

RAMPS

FIGURE 29.—Folding boat equipment, Mk. III.

58

their ends by steel ribands which also serve as wheel guides and are secured to the pontons by means of racking bolts.

(*b*) To get from the end of the floating portion of the bridge to the shore, a long landing bay, or a sliding bay and a trestle bay, are normally required. The long landing bay provides a substitute for trestle, trestle bay, and sliding bay. It avoids the difficulties and uncertainties attendant upon erecting trestles on an imperfectly reconnoitered site. It is of box-girder construction with special decking and

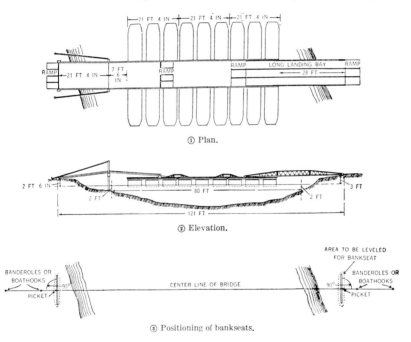

① Plan.

② Elevation.

③ Positioning of bankseats.

FIGURE 30.—Example of ponton bridge layout.

permits loads to travel straight from the shore to the first raft of the ponton bridge. The sliding bay is a normal-length bay used in standard load-bearers and chesses. One end is positioned on the deck of the floating portion, the other end supported on the trestle saddle, or shore transom. The trestle bay is the same as the sliding bay and is used between trestle and shore. The trestle, trestle bay, and sliding bay are used when long landing bays are not available or when conditions on the shore do not permit their use. The ponton equipment is shown in figures 30 and 31.

FIGURE 31.—Long landing bay.

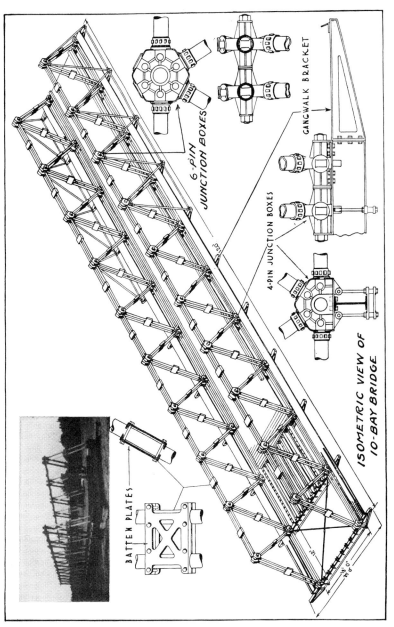

6-PIN JUNCTION BOXES

GANGWALK BRACKET

4-PIN JUNCTION BOXES

ISOMETRIC VIEW OF 10-BAY BRIDGE

BATTEN PLATES

FIGURE 32.—Inglis bridge, Mk. III.

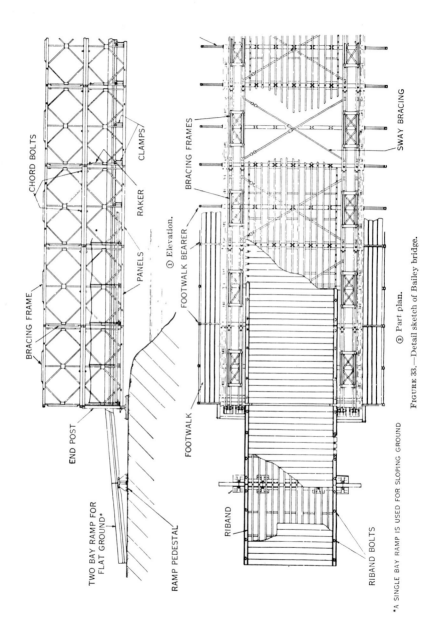

CHORD BOLTS

BRACING FRAME

CLAMPS

RAKER

PANELS

① Elevation.

END POST

TWO BAY RAMP FOR FLAT GROUND*

RAMP PEDESTAL

BRACING FRAMES

FOOTWALK BEARER

FOOTWALK

RIBAND

RIBAND BOLTS

SWAY BRACING

② Part plan.

*A SINGLE BAY RAMP IS USED FOR SLOPING GROUND

FIGURE 33.—Detail sketch of Bailey bridge.

(7) *Inglis bridge, Mk. III.*—The Inglis bridge (fig. 32) is a through-type Warren truss with tubular members connected in equilateral triangles of 12-foot sides and is designed to be capable of carrying any military load over spans ranging from 36 to 192 feet. For long spans and heavy loads the trusses can be double- or triple-tubed; the depth of the trusses can be doubled by building them in two stories, or various combinations of these arrangements can be used, such as a single-tubed truss with double-tubed center bays, a double-tubed truss with single-tubed second story, etc. Experiments are being carried out in the use of this bridge as a tank-assault bridge and also, with floating piers, as the superstructure of a ponton bridge.

(8) *Bailey bridge.*—The Bailey bridge (fig. 33) is made up of rectangular panels 5 feet high and 10 feet long. The panels are made up of angle irons about 3 by 1¾ inches placed back to back with welded joints. Knee-brace members and end panels, all bolt-connected, serve to join the panels into a sort of a box-girder type of construction. These 10-foot built-up box-girder sections fasten together longitudinally by a pin connection at the bottom and top of each panel. The panels may be pinned together in various combinations, according to the span and load-carrying capacity desired. It is believed that the bridge will carry loads up to 90,000 pounds over a 170-foot span, and loads up to 150,000 pounds over a 120-foot span. The use of the bridge with floating piers is being tested.

(9) *Hamilton bridge.*—The Hamilton bridge is a permanent type of bridge which may be carried in normal service vehicles but which is usually held at the base. This bridge will take all military loads (except railroad loads) over the following limiting spans:

> Single-truss girders, 80 feet.
> Double-truss girders, 140 feet.

c. Bridge policy.—(1) Present British policy is to carry only sufficient bridging equipment with divisions for unforeseeable minor obstacles; the remaining bridging equipment is to be concentrated in the corps bridge company (RASC) under direct control of the corps commander. The present interim scale of bridging equipment is as follows:

	Recn boats	Assault boats	Kapok	Small box-girder (SBG)	Folding-boat equipment (FBE)	Inglis or Bailey	Ponton	Remarks
Inf Div	32	- - - - -	- - - - -	Two sets	240 feet	- - - - -	- - - - -	- - - - - - - -
Armd Div	31	- - - - -	- - - - -	One set (special)	- - - - -	- - - - -	- - - - -	Armd Div has four track-bridges (20 feet).
Corps Br Co	30	72 per Div	585 feet	Two sets	480 feet	40-ton load over one 120-foot span per Div	420 feet	- - - - - - -

It is proposed to readjust this scale ultimately as follows:

(a) Reconnaissance boats will be allotted to divisional engineers on the basis of 1 to each officer, with a reserve of 12 in the field park company. They will also be carried in the bridge company (RASC).

(b) Assault boats will be carried in the bridge company (RASC) on a scale of 60 for each division in the corps.

(c) The Inglis bridge, Mk. III (60 feet of single-tubed bridge), will be carried by (infantry) divisional engineers and by armoured divisional engineers to deal with minor obstacles. Each bridge company (RASC) will carry 480 feet of double-tubed bridge. Floating piers for use with the bridge will be carried in the bridge company, provided experiments and design now in progress are successful.

(d) *Bailey bridge.*—This bridge may supplant the Inglis bridge as divisional equipment.

(e) The Kapok assault bridge (520 feet) will be carried in each bridge company (RASC).

(*f*) Tank-assault bridging will be carried in the divisional field park squadron of the armoured division. The type of bridging has not been determined.

(2) It is contemplated that folding-boat equipment and ponton equipment will be retained in the bridge company (RASC) until a floating pier suitable for use with the Inglis (or Bailey) bridge has been designed. The small box-girder (SBG) bridge is standard divisional equipment but may be replaced by the Inglis (or Bailey) bridge. This and the large box-girder bridge (obsolescent), the Hamilton bridge, and stock spans will be kept at railheads and engineer store (base) depots for semipermanent bridging on the lines of communication.

SECTION XI

ROYAL CORPS OF SIGNALS

46. General.—*a.* The Royal Corps of Signals (R Sigs), which corresponds to the Signal Corps in the U. S. Army, is responsible for all army communications down to headquarters of infantry battalions, artillery batteries (U. S. battalions), and units of other arms on a similar level. It is also responsible for wire communications between army formations and such units of the Royal Air Force as may be allotted for support of the army, and for all wire communications for the RAF, these being effected by air formation signals. It will be noticed from this that R Sigs is responsible for communications further down in the army organization than is the U. S. Signal Corps. But, on the other hand, the U. S. Signal Corps embraces a wider field, for R Sigs confines its responsibilities solely to ground methods of communication and is not responsible for such duties as aerial photography.

b. Infantry battalions and artillery batteries and troops have their own signalers for communications below company level. These personnel are not members of the Royal Corps of Signals.

c. Higher formations are responsible for communication with next lower formations and for lateral communication between adjacent lower formations.

d. If a formation or unit is supported by another unit, such as artillery, the supported formation or unit is responsible for the communication with the supporting unit.

e. The following is a list of some British signal terms and their U. S. equivalents:

British	United States
Signal office	Message center
Cable	Field wire
Drum	Reel
Wireless-telegraphy (W/T)	Radio (key)
Radio-telephony (R/T)	Radio (voice)
Valve	Tube
To superpose	To simplex
Teleprinter	Teletype
Quad cable	Spiral four (cable)
Despatch rider (D/R)	Messenger

f. The senior R Sigs officer at GHQ is the Signal Officer-in-Chief (Chief Sigs),[20] and is a major-general. At army headquarters the senior R Sigs officer is the Chief Signal Officer (CSO) of the army concerned, and is a brigadier; at corps headquarters he is the Chief Signal Officer (CSO) of the corps concerned, and is a colonel; at divisional headquarters he is the Officer Commanding, Divisional Signals (OC Div Sigs), and is a lieutenant-colonel; at brigade headquarters he is the Brigade Signal Officer (Bde SO), and is a captain; at field regimental headquarters he is the Regimental Signal Officer (Regt SO), and is a subaltern.

g. Each unit or formation has a signal office (message center), which is the terminal of all lines of communication emanating from and ending at the unit or formation concerned. Every message to and from personnel normally resident at a unit or formation will be routed through its own signal office. Thereafter responsibility for delivery rests with R Sigs personnel. In charge of each signal office is the Signalmaster, who is directly responsible to the commanding officer for the administration, operation, change of reliefs, and general efficient handling of the signal personnel at the formation or unit signal office. This duty is performed in turn by those junior officers in charge of wireless sections, operating sections, and line sections.

h. Communications personnel, when on duty, may be distinguished by a blue and white signals arm band, which is worn on each upper arm by the following officers and men:

(1) Officers of the R Sigs.

---

[20] Formerly known as SO-in-C.

(2) Regimental signaling officers.

(3) Noncommissioned officers of all arms employed in message centers or in charge of artillery battery signalers.

(4) Messengers of all arms while employed on dispatch riding duties.

(5) R Sigs personnel engaged in the construction and maintenance of wire and cable.

47. Hq signals.—*a.* This corresponds to the U. S. Army signal battalion. Its organization varies according to circumstances, and it provides communications for the Hq of a higher formation such as GHQ or army.

b. The unit consists essentially of a headquarters and three companies and is commanded by a lieutenant-colonel. No. 1 company is the construction company; Nos. 2 and 3 companies are operating and maintenance companies and are identical. Companies are subdivided into sections, the number of which varies according to requirements. No. 1 company contains line (i. e., line-laying) sections and a line-maintenance section. Nos. 2 and 3 consist of teletype operating sections, wireless sections, messenger sections, and a technical maintenance section.

48. Corps signals.—*a.* The corps signal unit (known, for example, as (12) Corps Signals), also corresponds to the U. S. Army signal battalion.

b. It is organized into a headquarters and three companies and is commanded by a lieutenant-colonel. No. 1 company is the construction company, No. 2 company is the operating company, and No. 3 company is the corps artillery company. Companies are subdivided into sections as follows:

> No. 1 (Construction) Co:
> > 4 line sections.
> > 1 line-maintenance section.
>
> No. 2 (Operating) Co:
> > 3 operating sections.
> > 3 wireless sections.
> > 2 messenger sections, each of 1 sergeant and 24 messengers.
>
> No. 3 (Artillery) Co:
> > Signal sections for corps artillery units.

c. If the number of formations and units of the corps is increased or decreased, the number of sections is altered accordingly.

49. Divisional signals.—*a.* Within an infantry division the signal unit corresponding to the divisional signal company in the U. S.

Army is known, for example, as (38th) Divisional Signals. It is commanded by a lieutenant-colonel and is considerably larger than the U. S. company, for it includes the equivalent of the U. S. infantry regiment and artillery battalion communication platoons. Divisional signals is responsible for all communications within the division, down to infantry battalions and artillery batteries. It maintains all radio sets in the division and carries out first-line repairs to signal equipment. It is also responsible for lateral communication between its infantry brigades (U. S. regiments) and, in general, for communications with the division on its left flank, where this is not provided by corps signals.

b. Divisional signals is divided into a headquarters, a headquarters company, and four companies:

(1) *Unit Hq.*—Executive office of the Officer Commanding, Divisional Signals (OC Div Sigs) (2–O and 8 EM).

(2) *Hq Co.*

Hq (1–O and 5 EM, captain commanding).

Q Section—pay, welfare, equipment provision, and general administration (1–O and 35 EM).

M Section—tactical maintenance of all signal equipment in the division (1–O and 25 EM).

(3) *No. 1 Co.*—Provides communications at divisional headquarters and to infantry brigades, artillery regiments, and the army tank brigade. The company consists of—

Hq (1–O and 6 EM, major commanding).

A Section—radio (2–O and 36 EM).

B Section—cable (wire) (1–O and 28 EM).

C Section—radio (1–O and 37 EM).

D Section—dispatch rider (messenger) (24 EM, company quarter-master sergeant commanding); includes a cipher sub-section, with a captain commanding.

O Section—operating (3–O and 64 EM).

(4) *No. 2 Co.*—Provides communications for artillery regiments, including anti-tank, from regimental headquarters down to batteries. The company consists of—

Hq (1–O and 5 EM, major commanding).

E Section ⎫
F Section ⎬ One section attached to each field artillery regiment (1–O and 37 EM each).
G Section ⎭

H Section—divisional artillery Hq staff section (1–O and 34 EM).

(5) *No. 3 Co.*—Provides communications for infantry brigades (U. S. regiments), from brigade headquarters down to infantry battalions; also for the reconnaissance regiment, down to reconnaissance squadrons, and for the Commander, Royal Engineers, down to engineer companies (known as field companies, RE).

Hq (1–O and 5 EM, major commanding).

R Section—reconnaissance regiment section (17 EM, company quarter-master sergeant commanding).

J Section ⎱ One section attached to each infantry brigade (2–O
K Section ⎰ and 59 EM each; also 7 infantrymen attached to
L Section ⎰ each).

(6) *No. 4 Co.*—Provides communications from the army tank brigade to the tank battalions; also furnishes a section to each tank battalion for communications down to squadrons. The company consists of—

Hq (2–O and 19 EM, major commanding).

W Section—army tank brigade section (1–O and 48 EM).

X Section ⎱ One section attached to each tank battalion (18
Y Section ⎰ EM each, company quarter-master sergeant com-
Z Section ⎰ manding each).

c. Attached to divisional signals is a light aid detachment (LAD), which is responsible for the recovery and repair of damaged vehicles.

50. Armoured divisional signals.—*a.* Armoured divisional signals provides communications within the armoured division down to and including headquarters of armoured regiments, infantry (motorized) battalions, artillery batteries (U. S. battalions) engineer squadrons, motor companies, and armoured car squadrons. The unit corresponds to, but is considerably larger than, the U. S. armored signal company, and is commanded by a lieutenant-colonel.

b. Normally communication is almost entirely by voice. There are over 500 radio sets in the division, including 1 in every armoured vehicle, and there are more than 50 different radio nets.

c. Armoured divisional signals is divided into a headquarters, a headquarters squadron, and four squadrons.

(1) *Unit Hq.*—Executive office of the Officer Commanding, Armoured Divisional Signals (OC Armd Div Sigs) (4–O and 25 EM).

(2) *Hq Sq.*—Administers the provision of stores, and deals with technical maintenance both mechanical and radio. The squadron consists of—

Hq (1–O and 4 EM, captain commanding).

Q Troop—quarter-master (1–O and 24 EM).

M Troop—maintenance and repair (1–O, who is the Technical Maintenance Officer (TMO), and 31 EM).

(3) *No. 1 Sq.*—Provides communications between rear and advanced Hq, and also between the two armoured brigades and any other supporting arms whose communications are not supplied by Nos. 2, 3, and 4 Squadrons. The squadron is divided into two groups: advanced divisional headquarters group and rear divisional headquarters group. Each group consists of a headquarters and three troops.

Hq (1–O and 12 EM, major commanding).

(*a*) *Advanced Group.*—Provides communications to those formations and units stationed in the forward areas.

Hq (1–O and 2 EM, captain commanding).

A Troop—Adm Div Hq troop (1–O and 54 EM).

C Troop—radio (1–O and 30 EM).

D Troop—messenger (24 EM, company quarter-master sergeant commanding).

(*b*) *Rear Group.*—Provides communications to the services and reserve units of the division.

Hq (1–O and 2 EM, captain commanding).

U Troop—rear divisional troop (1–O and 36 EM).

B Troop—wire (1–O and 28 EM).

O Troop—operating (2–O and 32 EM, captain commanding).

(4) *No. 2 Sq.*—Provides communications down to the Royal Horse Artillery (mechanized) regiments (U. S. battalions) and within the RHA regiments down to batteries. The squadron consists of—

Hq (1–O and 7 EM, major commanding).

H Troop—divisional artillery commander's troop (1–O and 33 EM).

E Troop⎤One troop attached to each RHA regiment (1–O and
F Troop⎦ 41 EM each).

(5) *No. 3 Sq.*—Provides communications within the infantry brigade, the armoured car regiment (U. S. battalion), and the engineer battalion down to the infantry battalion, the armoured car squadron, and the engineer squadron, respectively. The squadron consists of—

Hq (1–O and 7 EM, major commanding).

J Troop—infantry brigade (2–O and 66 EM, captain commanding).

R Troop—armoured car regiment (33 EM, company quarter-master sergeant commanding).

N Troop—engineer battalion (1–O and 20 EM).

(6) *No. 4 Sq.*—Provides communications within the armoured brigade down to armoured squadrons. The squadron consists of—

Hq (2–O and 23 EM, major commanding).

W Troop—armoured brigade (1–O and 51 EM, captain commanding).

X Troop ⎫ One troop attached to each armoured regiment (15
Y Troop ⎬ EM each, company quarter-master sergeant com-
Z Troop ⎭ manding each).

V Troop—motor battalion (19 EM, company quarter-master sergeant commanding).

51. Standard procedures.—*a. Phonetic alphabet.*

A. Ac	J. Johnnie	S. Sugar
B. Beer	K. King	T. Toc
C. Charlie	L. London	U. Uncle
D. Don	M. Monkey	V. Vic
E. Edward	N. Nuts	W. William
F. Freddie	O. Orange	X. X-ray
G. George	P. Pip	Y. Yorker
H. Harry	Q. Queen	Z. Zebra
I. Ink	R. Robert	

When it is necessary to spell a word, the word itself is first spoken, followed by the phonetic spelling; for example, "Two: T for Toc, W for William, O for Orange."

b. Pronunciation of figures (numbers).—The word "figures" will always precede any number; 10 will be spoken "Figures Wun Owe." Pronunciation of numbers is similar to U. S. usage except for numbers such as 11, 22, 33, etc. For instance, 11 may be pronounced "Wun Wun" or "Double Wun"; 22 is "Too Too" or "Double Too," etc. Should the pronunciation of figures fail to make the figures clear to the listener, the speaker will say each figure and then count up to it as in the following table:

0. "Owe"	--- ---	*O-w-e*
1. "Wun"	--- ---	Owe — *One*
2. "Too"	--- ---	One — *Two*
3. "Th-r-ree"	--- ---	One — Two — *Three*
4. "Foer"	--- ---	Two — Three — *Four*
5. "Fife"	--- ---	Three — Four — *Five*
6. "Six"	--- ---	Four — Five — *Six*
7. "Sev-en"	--- ---	Five — Six — *Seven*
8. "Ate"	--- ---	Six — Seven — *Eight*
9. "Niner"	--- ---	Seven — Eight — *Nine*

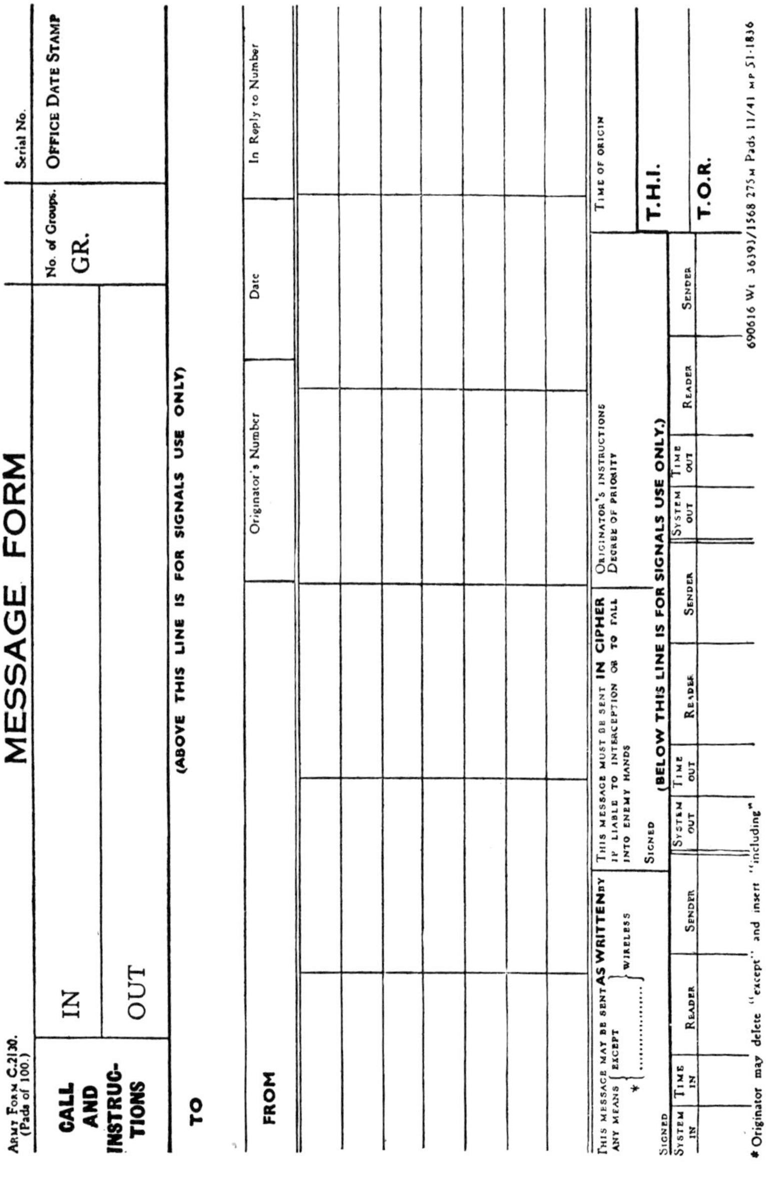

MESSAGE FORM

Army Form C.2120.
(Pads of 100.)

CALL AND INSTRUC- TIONS	IN		No. of Groups. GR.	Serial No. OFFICE DATE STAMP

OUT

(ABOVE THIS LINE IS FOR SIGNALS USE ONLY)

TO

FROM	Originator's Number	Date	In Reply to Number

THIS MESSAGE MAY BE SENT AS WRITTEN BY ANY MEANS { EXCEPT .... } WIRELESS

THIS MESSAGE MUST BE SENT IN CIPHER IF LIABLE TO INTERCEPTION OR TO FALL INTO ENEMY HANDS

ORIGINATOR'S INSTRUCTIONS DEGREE OF PRIORITY

TIME OF ORIGIN

T.H.I.

SIGNED

(BELOW THIS LINE IS FOR SIGNALS USE ONLY.)

SYSTEM IN	TIME IN	READER	SENDER	SYSTEM OUT	TIME OUT	READER	SENDER	SYSTEM OUT	TIME OUT	READER	SENDER

T.O.R.

* Originator may delete "except" and insert "including"

690616 Wt 36393/1568 275m Pads 11/41 mp S1·1836

FIGURE 34.—Message blank.

Example: 26019 will be spoken as follows (*with emphasis on the figure (number) to be transmitted*): "Figures Too—Six—Owe—Wun—Niner: Too, Wun—*Too;* Six, Foer—Fife—*Six;* Owe, *O-w-e;* Wun, Owe—*Wun;* Niner, Sev-en—Ate—*Niner.*"

c. Writing a message for transmission.—Messages are normally composed on a message form (blank) similar to that shown in figure 34. Spaces should be filled in as follows:

(1) "To": the name of the unit to receive the message or its code sign.

(2) "From": the name of the unit sending the message or its code sign.

(3) "Originator's Number": writer's identification number (see par. 165).

(4) "Date": day of the month only (e. g., December 7 is written 7).

(5) "In Reply to Number": the identification number of the message, if any, to which reference is being made.

(6) The text is written from left to right with one word in a box. It may consist of plain language, cipher, or code. A period, or "stop," is indicated by a circle with a dot in the center.

(7) The originator signs his name and rank in one of the two spaces at the bottom, thus giving instructions regarding cipher.

(8) "Originator's Instructions, Degree of Priority": the degree of priority, if any, is given. The various degrees of priority are as follows:

Degree of priority	*Used by—*
Most immediate	Commander-in-Chief or his chief staff officer only.
Emergency	Commanders and senior staff officers [21]; only for messages of the utmost importance having a direct bearing on operations.
Immediate	Regimental commander or senior staff officers; for messages of special importance.
Important	Any officer; for messages requiring priority above ordinary routine messages. Signal officers may use this priority. Any other instruction, such as "To await arrival," may be put in this space.
No indication	For routine messages.
Deferred	For messages of minor importance.

---

[21] Priority lists, showing in detail which officers may use each priority, are issued by the General Staff.

(9) "Time of Origin": the time at which the writer signs the message (the 24-hour clock is used, and local time).

(10) All other blanks on the message are filled in by R Sigs personnel. (T. H. I.=time handed in; T. O. R.=time of receipt.)

(11) If an acknowledgement is required, "Ack" is written at the end of the text.

d. Procedures for sending message.—There are several procedures in use:

(1) *"Written message" procedure.*—The message is written out as above and sent exactly as written, together with various signal procedures used by R Sigs.

(2) *"VE" procedure.*—The message may be given orally to the operator to transmit, or may be written down simply as a text without the address or references required in a written message. This is used for quick questions and answers.

(3) As regards actual transmission of the message the following procedures are used:

(*a*) *"Normal" method.*—The message is sent straight through.

(*b*) *"SR" (send replies) method.*—Each group is answered by the receiver before the new group is sent. This method is very slow and is used only when communication is difficult.

(*c*) *"F" procedure.*—The message is sent through twice at slow rate, no answers being given. This method is used when the receiver must not, or cannot, reply.

(*d*) *"G" procedure.*—The whole message is repeated back by the receiver.

(*e*) *"DC" procedure.*—Difficult communication (DC) procedure is used in cases where interference is strong. The sender sends each group twice instead of once.

e. Strength of signals.—The strength of signals received by radio is described as follows: strength 3 means "scarcely readable"; strength 6, "fair"; strength 7, "good"; strength 9, "very strong."

f. Transmission of a message.—A message may be sent as a telegram by one of the procedures described above, or may be sent as a phonogram. In the case of a phonogram the sending operator telephones the message and the receiving operator writes it down on a message form.

52. Equipment.—*a. Wire and associated stores.*—In general, these are very like those in the U. S. Army, the principles of operation being exactly the same. The principal instruments used in forward areas are—

(1) *Telephone "D," Mk. V.*—Calls by buzzer; responds to buzzer calls or by bell to magneto calling; speech and Morse code (buzzer).

(2) *Telephone "F."*—Calls by buzzer or magneto generator; responds to buzzer calls or by bell to magneto calling; speech—no Morse code key.

(3) *Fullerphone.*—A portable DC telegraph instrument of high sensitivity—signals practically immune from interception.

(4) *Switchboard universal call (UC).*—Ten-line or six-line; portable switchboard, with lamp indicators, which will respond to and call buzzer or magneto instruments.

(5) *Superposing unit.*—Corresponds to the simplex unit; designed primarily for use with switchboard universal call; simplexes a series fullerphone on a telephone circuit (twin line or ground return); simplexes a phantom to ground fullerphone or telephone on a twin line; simplexes a fullerphone or telephone phantom on two twin lines; further development of phantom circuits.

(6) *Line labels (wooden tags).*—These are of various shapes and are attached to wires at points where identification difficulties might arise. Linemen, by feeling the tags, can tell in the dark which unit owns the line. Tags are clearly marked to make identification simple; for example, BW–A means a line laid by The Black Watch (see par. 167*g*) to "A" Co. If there is more than one line between the same stations, a figure is added; for example, BW–A2. (See fig. 35.)

(7) *Wire.*—(*a*) *"D," Mk. III.*—A thin braided steel and copper wire used by infantry and artillery; single generally, but twisted is available; range, 10 miles.

(*b*) *"D," Mk. VIII.*—A larger but similar wire used by divisional signals; single and twisted; range, 15 miles.

(*c*) *Quad cable.*—Used in rear of the division; rubber-covered and rubber-insulated; contains two twisted pairs; range, 45 miles.

(*d*) *7-pair india rubber vulcanized (IRV).*—Used in rear areas and also, in short lengths, at Hq's, where it is usually buried to conceal approaches; range, 60 miles.

b. Radio (as used in forward area).—British radio differs in one main aspect from U. S. radio equipment of pre-war design in that British sets have a larger frequency coverage and tend to make one set do for many different arms of the service, whereas U. S. sets are more specialized, each arm having its own type.

(1) *No. 18 set (Nos. 38 and 48 sets being developments).*—Used by infantry and for general patrol work:

    Output: .5 watt.

    Frequency band: 6.0 to 9.0 megacycles (mc/s).

Range:
    Mobile—voice, 2 miles; cw, 6 miles.
    Stationary—voice, 5 miles; cw, 8 miles.
Weight: 30 to 35 pounds for No. 18 set; the others are lighter.
(2) *No. 38 set.*—Used by infantry and paratroops:
Output: .5 watt.
Frequency band: 7.3 to 8.3 mc/s.
Range: voice, 4 miles maximum.
Weight: 12 pounds (batteries carried separately).
(3) *No. 11 set (and No. 21 set).*—Used by infantry and artillery:
Output: high power, 7 watts; low power, 1.5 watts (No. 21
    set: on higher band, .8 watt; on lower band, 1.5 watts).
Frequency band: 4.2 to 7.5 mc/s for both sets (No. 21 set has
    also 19 to 31 mc/s).
Range:
    Mobile—voice, 4 miles; cw, 10 miles.
    Stationary—voice, 6 miles; cw, 15 miles.
Weight: 47 pounds.
(4) *No. 19 set.*—Primarily an armoured force set, but has many
other uses for general purposes:
Output: 15 watts.
Frequency band: 2.1 to 8 mc/s and 230 to 250 mc/s.
Range:
    Mobile—voice, 10 miles; cw, 15 miles.
    Stationary—voice, 15 miles; cw, 20 miles.
Weight: 192 pounds.
(5) *No. 22 set.*—Middle-distance set, division to brigade:
Output: 20 watts.
Frequency band: 2 to 8 mc/s.
Range: voice, 20 to 40 miles; cw, 50 miles; mcw, 40 miles.[22]
Weight: three pack loads of about 30 pounds each.
(6) There are many other radio sets in use. When a radio set is
replaced, the new set is generally numbered ten ahead of the old set.
For instance, the No. 13 set was replaced by the No. 23, which, in
turn, was replaced by the No. 33. Other sets which may be found
are as follows:
    No. 5 set—very-high-power set for strategical use.
    No. 9 set—obsolescent, replaced by No. 19 or No. 22 set.
    No. 12 set—high-power set for Royal Armoured Corps and
        army use.

_____

[22] CW, or cw (continuous wave), corresponds to U. S. A1; MCW, or mcw (modulated continuous wave), to U. S. A2 (tone); voice, to U. S. A3.

No. 17 set—very small portable very-high-frequency (VHF) set for anti-aircraft use.

No. 26 set—high-power VHF multi-channel directional set for use in rear areas.

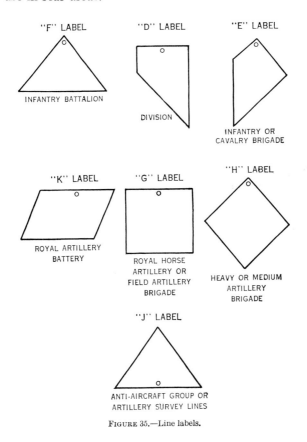

FIGURE 35.—Line labels.

No. 33 set—high-power set for army and corps Hq's.

No. 34 set—headquarters intercommunication set (very low power).

No. 36 set—high-power VHF set for anti-aircraft gun control.

No. 46 set—specially designed, portable low-power set for combined operations.

c. Maintenance and repair.—(1) (*a*) The Royal Corps of Signals is responsible for first-line repair to all signal equipment in use by units of all arms included in the formation. Whenever possible, units return equipment requiring repair or adjustment to the signal unit responsible, such as divisional or corps signals. If it is beyond first-line repair, it is turned over to the formation ordnance unit, and an immediate replacement is made if available. Normal replacements and issues are sent straight forward from the base ordnance depot to the brigade ordnance company, and issued from there direct to the unit. (Many of these functions are to be taken over by the Royal Electrical and Mechanical Engineers (REME)—see p. 80, note 23.)

(*b*) A small dump of cable and line stores is maintained by the CSO's of armies and corps for issue to meet some emergency or specific operation. These stores are obtained direct from the base ordnance depot, and are issued by R Sigs and not through ordnance channels.

(2) The general definition of a first-line repair carried out by R Sigs tradesmen is a repair or replacement which can be effected without the use of machine tools. Anything which is a definite workshop job is passed on to the ordnance workshops.

Section XII

ROYAL ARMY SERVICE CORPS

53. General.—Certain terms used in connection with supply in the British Army require preliminary explanation.

a. Supplies.—This term includes food, forage, gasoline, lubricants, disinfectants, hospital supplies, fuel for cooking and heating, and illuminants.

b. Stores.—This term includes war material other than supplies. It is divided into—

(1) *Ordnance stores.*—These include personal and unit equipment, armament and small arms, ammunition, explosives, engineer and signal stores, tanks, armoured cars and carriers, tractors, clothing and personal accessories, camp equipment, office supplies, materials for workshops, and all mechanical transport vehicles other than those which are the direct responsibility of the Royal Army Service Corps (RASC) (see par. 54).

(2) *Engineer stores.*—These consist of material and equipment required for engineer work of all kinds, whether carried out by engineers or by other arms. The term includes permanent line signal stores, but not explosives.

(3) *Transportation stores.*—These embrace material and equipment which are peculiar to the transportation services but are not provided by other services.

(4) *RASC stores.*—These include mechanical transport vehicles or the RASC, spare parts, and the material and equipment for their repair.

(5) *Medical and veterinary stores.*—These include drugs, dressings, medical and veterinary instruments, and appliances.

c. Transportation.—This term refers to administration of the movement of troops, stores, and supplies.

d. Transport.—This term is used—

(1) In a general sense to denote the driver, vehicle, and such equipment as is necessary to render the vehicle mobile.

(2) To denote that portion of an organized unit, formation, or service the primary duty of which is the transportation of troops, stores, and supplies.

54. Function.—The RASC is charged with the responsibility for the storage and issue of supplies, for certain phases of their transportation, including the vehicles assigned for that purpose, and for the administration of barracks and quarters. It supplies the daily needs of the soldier, that is, supplies him with food, gasoline, and lubricants, and brings him his ammunition. The RASC is also responsible for transporting his blankets and reserves of anti-gas clothing.

55. Organization.—*a. General.*—(1) The RASC is organized into two branches, supply and transport, which are coordinated under a directorate, the head of which is a major-general known as the Director of Supplies and Transport (DST).

(2) In war the supply and transport services, under the direction of DST, are under the control of the Quarter-Master-General (QMG).

(3) The supply branch is charged with the supply of food, forage, fuel, light, disinfectants, medical comforts, and gasoline and oils for vehicles.

(4) The transport branch is charged with the provision, issue, operation, and inspection of all vehicles in RASC units or driven by RASC personnel, and with the provision of spare parts, miscellaneous mechanical transport stores (MT stores), and materials, equipment, and tools required in the operation and maintenance of these vehicles. The maintenance and repair of these vehicles is to be shared by the RASC and the Royal Electrical and Mechanical Engineers (REME).[23]

b. Personnel.—(1) *Officers.*—RASC officers are organized on a regimental basis, are interchangeable, and are trained in all branches of RASC duties.

(2) *Supply branch.*—The personnel of this branch are organized by trades. They are bakers, butchers, issuers, and clerks. The clerks section of this branch provides the clerical personnel required for commanders and staffs at headquarters of formations in addition to those required by the RASC itself.

(3) *Transport branch.*—(*a*) The personnel of this branch are organized into drivers, qualified tradesmen trained in the trades associated with automobiles (e. g., coppersmiths), MT storekeepers, and technical mechanical transport clerks (TMT clerks).

(*b*) The animal transport branch, which is composed of drivers and tradesmen trained in pertinent trades (e. g., harnessmakers), is one of the typical small divisions of the transport branch.

56. Units.—*a. Supply personnel.*—(1) These are organized into supply companies, which are usually dispersed into detachments of varying size and attached to the nearest RASC transport unit.

(2) It is the responsibility of the transport unit commander to train supply personnel attached to his unit.

(3) Supply companies, RASC, are lettered companies (e. g., "A" Company), and are responsible for butchering meat and baking bread, the issue of all supplies, and the clerical duties in connection with supply accounts, etc.

---

[23] It is intended that this newly formed corps will eventually take over all maintenance and repairs, behind the first echelon, of all items. The procurement and storage of all items (including repair parts) will remain in the hands of the appropriate service. All troops engaged in maintenance and repair work, excepting those of the first echelon, will eventually belong to this corps.

b. Transport personnel.—(1) The basic organization is the transport company, which consists of a headquarters and operating sections (the number dependent upon the tasks assigned the company).

(2) Operating sections are normally commanded by an officer—captain or subaltern—and consist of a section headquarters and a number of sub-sections each in charge of a noncommissioned officer.

(3) The normal sub-section consists of five vehicles and is the smallest unit in the transport branch.

57. Transport.—Transport generally is organized into—

a. First-line transport.—This is organic transportation in battalions and below. It is divided into "A" and "B" echelons: "A" echelon moves with the unit in combat; "B" normally follows with the trains.

b. Second-line transport.—Second-line transport is normally operated by the RASC between refilling points (RP's), which are usually selected by divisional headquarters, and delivery points (DP's), which are selected by unit commanders.

c. Third-line transport.—This is normally operated by the RASC between railheads (RH's) and refilling points. The second- and third-line RASC transport is known as field transport.

d. Reserve transport.—This reserve undertakes general transport duties and provides a reserve of transport.

e. Technical transport.—Technical transport consists of specially equipped vehicles, as, for example, mobile workshop lorries and ambulance car companies.

58. Operation (figs. 36 and 37).—*a. Second-line transport.*—(1) *General.*—Second-line transport forms an integral part of the formation which it serves, and, in the case of divisions, it is grouped under the command of a Commander, RASC (CRASC). Each transport holds on wheels a fixed reserve of ammunition and gasoline.

(2) *Organization.*—Second-line transport in both the infantry and the armoured divisions consists of a headquarters of a Commander, RASC, who can administer and command from two to five companies. In the infantry division these companies are as follows: one tank brigade company, two infantry brigade companies, and one divisional troops company; in the armoured division: one armoured brigade company, one infantry brigade company, and one armoured divisional troops company.

(3) *Supplies.*—(a) In the case of supplies, the transport provided may be called a combination of second- and third-line in that it operates from railhead to delivery points. The unit is the company, RASC, which is provided on the basis of one to each brigade, division,

and corps troops. The supply columns are organized into two echelons which carry out deliveries every alternate day to the formations they serve. These units receive from railhead, and carry and deliver

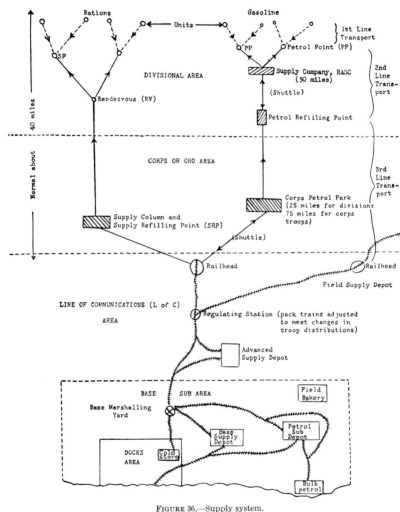

FIGURE 36.—Supply system.

supplies, mails, and engineer and ordnance stores. In addition, they normally hold a reserve of rations.

(b) Although separate channels of supply are shown in figure 36 in the divisional area for each item, delivery of all types of supply is accomplished by brigade or divisional troops companies for their respective units.

b. Third-line and reserve transport.—Third-line and reserve transport operates behind second-line transport, draws ammunition, gasoline, and other supplies from railhead, and delivers to refilling points the

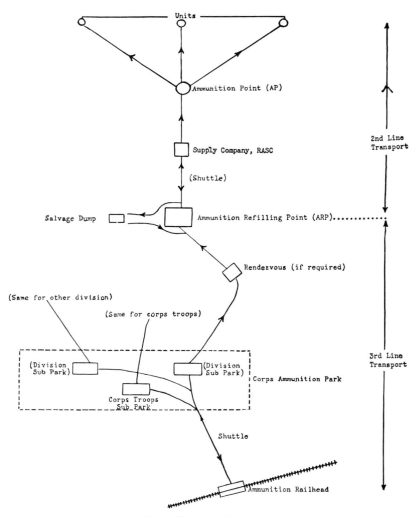

FIGURE 37.—Ammunition supply.

quantities required to keep the second-line transport filled. A pool of RASC general transport companies is placed at the disposal of the formation commanders, who must see to it that the reserves of ammunition, gasoline, and supplies held on wheels are sufficient to cover all their actual tactical requirements. Each general transport company is composed of three or four platoons, each operating thirty 3-ton trucks. These platoons are used for carrying ammunition, troops, and supplies according to the immediate needs of the situation.

c. Technical transport.—This comprises such units as bridge companies and ambulance car companies. The latter are normally used in the line of communications (L of C) area for clearing casualties from ambulance trains to hospitals and from hospitals to ships; and they are also formed into motor ambulance convoys, which are usually employed for clearing casualties from field ambulances (see pars. 65 and 67) to casualty clearing stations and from casualty clearing stations to ambulance trains.

59. L of C installations.—The RASC provides a staff and operates the following installations:

a. Mechanical transport stores depots (MTSD's).

b. Motor transport vehicle reception depots (VRD's).

c. Heavy repair shops (HRS's).

d. Base supply depots (BSD's).

e. Field bakeries.

f. Advanced supply depots (if formed).

g. Field supply depots (if formed).

h. Detail issue depots (for the reception of surpluses from trains at railhead, making up deficiencies, and for issue of supplies in detail to local troops).

60. Principles of supply.—*a. Supplies.*—(1) There is a regular delivery of required supplies to all units daily at a time and place convenient to them.

(2) In addition to one emergency ration, all units must have 2 days' supplies with them at all times. These stocks are replenished by the daily delivery of 1 day's supplies.

b. Gasoline.—(1) At the beginning of the march all vehicles are filled and all reserves made complete.

(2) An adequate reserve is maintained on wheels in front of railhead (sufficient for 75 miles, carried by petrol companies).

(3) Replenishment will normally take place on completion of the march.

61. Location of supplies.—The supply situation on any one day is as follows:

a. First day's supply.—(1) On the man—an emergency ration.

(2) On first-line transport—the unconsumed portion of the current day's ration.

b. Second day's supply.—In one echelon of the supply column ready for delivery that evening.

c. Third day's supply.—In the supply pack train, at or approaching the railhead, or in the other echelon of the supply column for delivery the following evening.

62. Transport to railhead.—*a.* This is normally done by means of what is known as a "pack" train. Pack trains are run on daily schedules and contain the 1-day requirements of one or more formations in supplies and in engineer and RASC stores.

b. Trains are loaded at the various depots and marshaled into pack sections at the base marshalling yard for dispatch to railhead.

c. A section pack number is allotted to each formation served, each railroad truck (freight car) destined for a particular formation being labeled with this number. In the marshalling yard, therefore, all trucks bearing the same number are put together to form the pack section, which contains 1 day's requirements for a particular formation.

d. Pack trains are classified as "standard" or "variable." The standard pack train is loaded on a fixed basis for each formation served, thus facilitating the work of the base depots. Any surpluses or deficiencies on arrival at railhead can usually be adjusted by the railhead supply officer from his store. Variable pack trains are restricted to the minimum and are normally adopted for army or corps troops when demands are subject to considerable fluctuation.

e. A third type of train, known as a "bulk" train, is also used. These trains carry one or more commodities in bulk and normally run from base depots to regulating stations or advanced depots.

Section XIII
ROYAL ARMY MEDICAL CORPS

63. General.—The Royal Army Medical Corps (RAMC) provides the medical service in the British Army. Under its jurisdiction come the various nursing services, the principal one of which is Queen Alexandra's Imperial Military Nursing Service (QAIMNS).[24] The general responsibilities of the RAMC are—

---

[24] Members of the QAIMNS rank with the officers of the Army as follows:
Matron-in-chief—colonel.
Principal matron—lieutenant-colonel.
Matron—major.
Sister or staff nurse—lieutenant.

a. The evacuation, care, and treatment of sick or injured troops and of gas casualties in all situations. The RAMC is not responsible for "cleansing" men contaminated with blister gas unless they are rendered unfit by the gas to continue in action. The "cleansing" of men who are not rendered unfit is a unit responsibility.

b. Advice and initiation of measures to insure the health of troops.

c. Supply and replenishment of medical equipment and supplies.

d. Advice with regard to the location of medical units.

64. Tactical considerations.—*a. Principle of operation.*—Medical units in the field take some time to open and, once opened, cannot be moved quickly, on account of tentage and stores that have to be packed up, and the sick and wounded who must be evacuated.[25] Consequently, in principle, no more units should be opened up than are required to deal with anticipated casualties. This is especially important in mobile operations.

b. Medical plan.—(1) When preparing the medical plan for a specific operation, "G" (General Staff) gives a forecast of anticipated casualties. On this basis, the medical staff and "A" (Adjutant) are in a position to estimate transport requirements by calculating the probable percentages of killed and of lying, sitting, and walking wounded.

(2) If the calculations show the need for more transport than is available, "A" must obtain it from "Q" (Quarter-master). Since the calculation is based on an arbitrary expectation of casualties by "G," a reserve of transport to meet unexpectedly heavy casualties is usually provided.

(3) For a divisional operation the Assistant-Director of Medical Services (ADMS), having made his calculations, submits his plan for evacuation of casualties, showing what proportion of his resources he proposes to open and what he will keep in reserve. If the plan is approved by "A," it is then put into effect by ADMS.

(4) As they are a matter of general interest, the locations and times of opening and closing the forward evacuating centers are inserted in the administrative paragraph of the operation order (OO). (See par. 122*a*(4).)

c. Organization for evacuation of casualties.—The organization for the evacuation of casualties (fig. 38) is based on a system of three zones:

(1) *Collecting zone.*
> Regimental medical establishments (RAP's, ADS's, WWCP, and MDS).

---

[25] A fully established advanced dressing station requires 1 hour to open and 1 hour to close. A fully established main dressing station requires 2 hours to open and 2 hours to close. These times are in addition to that required to clear casualties.

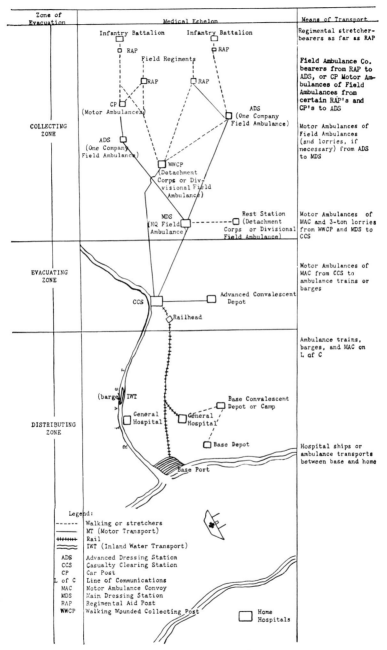

FIGURE 38.—System of evacuation.

Field ambulances.
Motor ambulance convoys.

(2) *Evacuating zone.*
Casualty clearing station.
Motor ambulance convoys.
Ambulance trains.
Ambulance barges (if on water).
Ambulance airplanes.

(3) *Distributing zone.*
General hospitals.
Convalescent depots.
Hospital ships and carriers.
Ambulance transports.
Home hospitals.

65. Medical resources of formations and units.—*a. Division.*—In the infantry division there are 2 field ambulances [26] (battalions), 2 field dressing stations, and 1 field hygiene section, with a total of 691 officers and enlisted men. In the armoured division there are 1 light field ambulance, 1 field ambulance, 1 field dressing station, and 1 light field hygiene section, with a total of 559 officers and enlisted men.

b. Infantry battalion.—In the infantry battalion there are 1 medical officer, 1 medical orderly, medical equipment in a 15-cwt truck, stretcher-bearers, 1 sergeant, and 20 enlisted men. The stretcher-bearers collect casualties and bring them to the regimental aid post (RAP).

c. Other units.—Several other units have a medical officer and orderly in their organization; but although stretchers are sometimes provided, no special stretcher-bearers are allowed. Casualties from units without any medical resources will be treated by the nearest unit in the chain of evacuation.

d. Armoured fighting vehicles (AFV's).—A medical kit is carried in each AFV, and personnel are trained in its use. If the situation permits, casualties are evacuated from the tank, with an attached field medical card indicating the nature of the injury and the first aid already given. Casualties are then collected by medical personnel.

e. Regimental aid post (RAP).—Regiments provided with a medical officer open an RAP in battle. Its site is the responsibility of the commanding officer in consultation with the medical officer. Evacuation from the RAP is a responsibility of the field ambulance

---

[26] The actual vehicles are called "motor ambulances."

(company). At the RAP the first field dressing is applied or adjusted.

66. Collection.—*a. Bearer relay post.*—This is established as a turn-over point from one squad of stretcher-bearers to the next, when the ground precludes the use of motor ambulances.

b. Main dressing station (MDS).—The MDS is formed by the headquarters of the field ambulance (company). Records and particulars are taken for the first time. Anti-tetanus serum is injected; but here also only urgent treatment is attempted. Rifles and any ammunition are collected from the wounded at the MDS.

c. Walking wounded collecting post (WWCP).—The object of this post is to relieve pressure on the advanced dressing station (ADS) in battle. Walking wounded are directed to the WWCP, whence they are taken direct to the casualty clearing station (CCS) by transport (usually lorries) provided specially by "Q" of corps headquarters. The WWCP is formed only when heavy fighting is expected. It should be located 2 to 5 miles from forward troops at a convergence of roads or tracks from the front. It may be formed by corps field ambulance or by divisional field ambulance.

67. Field ambulance (battalion).—*a. Divisional troops.*—There is one field ambulance for each infantry brigade.

b. Organization.—(1) A field ambulance is organized into a headquarters and 2 companies. Each company can furnish 1 advanced dressing station (ADS). Headquarters can furnish an MDS with a capacity for 100 to 150 casualties. Thirty-six stretcher-bearers from each company and 8 motor ambulances from headquarters field ambulances are available for collecting casualties from the RAP's and for transporting them to the ADS and from there to the MDS.

(2) Not all the personnel of field ambulances are carried in unit motor transport. Three extra 3-ton lorries are required if all personnel are to be carried.

c. Method of operation.—(1) Field ambulance personnel establish contact with the RAP's, and field ambulance stretcher-bearers remove casualties to the ADS or to the car post (CP), if it is formed, in front of the ADS.

(2) Evacuation from the ADS to the MDS is by motor ambulances of field ambulances.

(3) Evacuation beyond the MDS is the responsibility of motor ambulance convoy (MAC), a corps unit.

d. Ambulance stations.—(1) *Advanced dressing station (ADS).*— This is a collecting center from the RAP's in the forward zone. During mobile operations only one company of the field ambulance generally opens at a time; the other is held in reserve ready to move to the next location. At the ADS only exceptionally urgent treatment is attempted. Dressings are adjusted and hot drinks are available. The location of the ADS depends on whether or not motor ambulances can work up to, or near, the RAP. If they can, and if the road communications are good, the ADS may be located some distance behind the forward troops, but it must be within a few minutes' run by motor ambulance to and from the RAP or the CP.

(2) *Car post (CP).*—This is the forward point to which motor ambulances work if they cannot work for the RAP's. Bearers from the various RAP's bring lying cases to the CP, whence they are taken to the ADS by motor ambulance of field ambulance. As soon as a motor ambulance arrives at the ADS from the CP, it is replaced at the CP by another one. Since 1,000 yards is the practical limit of the stretcher-bearers' carrying capacity, either a CP or a bearer relay post must be established when the ADS is more than 1,000 yards from the RAP's.

Section XIV

ROYAL ARMY ORDNANCE CORPS

68. Function.—The procurement and issue of ordnance stores are the responsibility of the Royal Army Ordnance Corps (RAOC), but all of these stores are eventually to be maintained and repaired by the Royal Electrical and Mechanical Engineers (REME). However, throughout this handbook the RAOC is discussed prior to the organization of the REME, since details on the latter are not complete (see p. 80, note 23). At present, the RAOC supplies combat troops with all the ordnance stores that they may require and recovers and repairs their equipment. The RAOC also has the responsibility for provision of laundries and officers' clothing depots, for decontamination of clothing, and for protecting its own units and installations from enemy attack.

69. Ordnance stores.—Ordnance stores comprise armament and ammunition, including RAF bombs; all fighting vehicles such as tanks and armoured cars; unit transport (as differentiated from RASC vehicles driven and maintained by RASC personnel); radio, electrical, and optical equipment; clothing, including shoes; and general stores, such as tables, buckets, and cordage. (Food, gasoline, lubricants, and expendable medical supplies are not included in ordnance stores.)

70. Line of communications (L of C) area.—*a.* Typical examples of RAOC units and installations, distributed as required in the line of communications area (fig. 36) with representatives attached to headquarters of various sub-areas, are as follows:

(1) Base ordnance depots (BOD's), and advanced ordnance depots if ordered.

(2) Base ordnance workshops (BOW's), and advanced ordnance workshops if ordered.

(3) Base ammunition depots (BAD's), and advanced ammunition depots if ordered.

(4) Detachments of RAOC personnel at each regulating station (fig. 36).

(5) Small production factories with ammunition repair factory.

b. The personnel for base depots and workshops are provided for by War Establishments, and consist chiefly of the following classes of tradesmen: clerks, storemen, drivers, armament artificers and artisans, and ammunition examiners. RAOC personnel may be reinforced by military or civilian labor units.

71. Personnel in forward areas.—RAOC personnel in the forward areas are disposed as follows:

a. At headquarters of services at field GHQ.—DOS—Director of Ordnance Services.

b. At army headquarters.—(1) DDOS—Deputy Director of Ordnance Services.

(2) DDOS (E)—Deputy Director of Ordnance Services, Engineering.

(3) DADOS (O)—Deputy Assistant-Director of Ordnance Services, Operations, for ordnance services in connection with army troops.

c. At corps headquarters.—(1) DDOS—Deputy Director of Ordnance Services.

(2) ADOS (A)—Assistant-Director of Ordnance Services, Administration.

(3) ADOS (E)—Assistant-Director of Ordnance Services, Engineering.

(4) DADOS (O)—Deputy Assistant-Director of Ordnance Services, Operations, for ordnance services in connection with corps troops.

d. At divisional headquarters.—(1) ADOS—Assistant-Director of Ordnance Services, Administration. ADOS is located at divisional headquarters with a small staff which deals with the indents (requisitions) submitted by units for ordnance stores. In addition, he has four warrant officers (one for each brigade and one for divisional troops). These warrant officers visit all units at frequent intervals to assist them in the preparation of requisitions.

(2) DADOS (A)—Deputy Assistant-Director of Ordnance Services, Administration.

(3) DADOS (E)—Deputy Assistant-Director of Ordnance Services, Engineering.

e. At supply and ammunition railheads, with RAOC detachments.— OO—Ordnance Officer.

72. Disembarkation area.—The typical organization for the RAOC in a disembarkation port area usually includes an Ordnance Officer, Docks (OO Docks); a detachment attached to dock services; a port workshop detachment; and a vehicle convoy section, for stock vehicles only.

73. Repair installations (fig. 39).—The following types of repair installations are engaged in the field in repairing and replacing warlike ordnance stores:

a. First-echelon repairs.—(1) *Light aid detachments (LAD's).*—(a) Each infantry brigade, artillery regiment, engineer field park company, divisional signals, reconnaissance regiment, machine-gun battalion, and light anti-aircraft regiment, has attached a LAD under the command of an ordnance mechanical engineer officer (OME) or a technical warrant officer (armament sergeant-major). These detachments vary slightly in composition, depending on the unit to which they are attached, but generally comprise 13 to 15 tradesmen, 1 break-down lorry (wrecker), fairly comprehensive hand tools, a lightweight welding outfit, and 1 or 2 store lorries to carry small-vehicle and armament spares for first-line maintenance. There are 15 LAD's in the infantry division, and 14 in the armoured division.

(*b*) The function of the LAD is to assist the combat units in first-line maintenance and recovery and to keep them in operation. Such a detachment, therefore, does not handle jobs requiring extensive repair but confines its attention to repairs which can be completed in 4 hours.

(2) *Light anti-aircraft ordnance workshop sub-sections.*—These are allotted to corps and divisions on the scale of one for each light anti-aircraft battery (battalion).

b. Second-echelon repairs.—(1) *Brigade ordnance companies.*—These companies undertake work on warlike ordnance stores which the LAD's have found to be beyond their facilities or to require too much time for repair. There is one ordnance company for each infantry, armoured, and tank brigade. Both repairs and storage of spare parts and assemblies are carried out by these companies.

(2) *Non-divisional ordnance workshops.*—The workshops undertake work which the brigade ordnance companies have found to be beyond their facilities or to require too much time for repair. They are allotted on the basis of one to each corps.

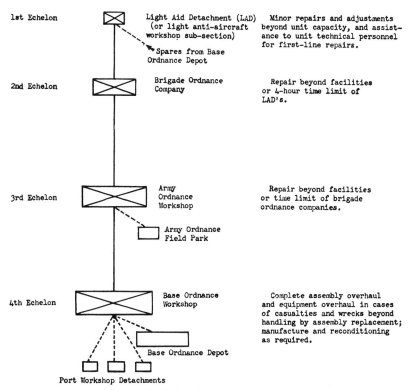

FIGURE 39.—System of repair for ordnance stores.

c. *Third-echelon and L of C repairs.*—(1) *Army ordnance workshop.*— Third-echelon repairs are carried out in army ordnance workshops, which are mobile units considerably larger than the brigade ordnance companies and proportionately better equipped to carry out repair and overhaul. In view of their mobility, they do not undertake jobs estimated at more than 48 hours, but arrange for such jobs to be done by the base ordnance workshops. An army ordnance field park supplies the necessary stores and spares and also carries a number of replacement vehicles.

93

(2) *Base ordnance workshop.*—L of C repairs are carried out in base ordnance workshops, which are static units and require covered accommodation. They are equipped to carry out major repairs and overhauls, and, when necessary, to manufacture small spares. Like the army ordnance workshops, they are variable in size. Their organization is such that, by the addition of certain specialist sections of standard design, a workshop can be established to service whatever force may be formed. Spares and stores for the base ordnance workshop are obtained from the base ordnance depots.

74. Supply of ammunition.—*a.* The main difference between ammunition supply and the supply of other ordnance stores is that, in the case of ammunition, wide and unpredictable fluctuation of expenditure occurs. RAOC installations in forward areas include ammunition detachments with army corps ammunition dumps. An effort is made to keep the flow of ammunition from rear to front automatic and adequate. Each echelon is replenished from the next rearward echelon.

b. The General Staff decides on the quantities of ammunition required in the field in rounds per gun and its distribution at depot and railhead. It then requests the necessary quantities from the War Office. Ordnance is responsible for the provision of spare components and the maintenance of L of C warlike stocks, and it must at all times be able to tell the General Staff in detail what is held. Ordnance is also responsible for bringing to the attention of the General Staff any anticipated shortages of any nature, and for distributing fresh supplies among the base depots to maintain appropriate stocks at each.

c. Units do not requisition ammunition. Expenditure is reported daily by the fighting units, and formations submit consolidated reports to GHQ with forecasts of any anticipated abnormal expenditure. GHQ orders the necessary train loads of ammunition forward from base depots to ammunition railhead, from which automatic replacement of expenditure is made to the RASC for distribution (fig. 37).

d. Ordnance responsibility for general supply of ammunition ceases at railhead, or at corps or GHQ dumps when these are formed, except for any inspection work that may be required. Thereafter the RASC handles all ammunition and delivers it to the units in the field.

75. Supply of other stores.—*a.* The normal system of meeting ordnance requirements is by direct supply to the units from the BOD in response to detailed indents (requisitions) received from ADOS of the division, except for certain classes of replacement items supplied by ordnance field parks.

b. Packages are vouchered and consigned from the BOD direct to he individual units and dispatched to supply railheads by the daily)ack train, and carried from there by RASC supply columns working)n a double-echelon system to delivery points. Under stabilized conlitions, however, certain stores in universal demand, such as clothing, nay be supplied in bulk from the BOD to ADOS, who will arrange he issue in detail to meet demands.

Section XV

OTHER ARMS AND SERVICES

76. General.—The following branches of the service either are 1ot discussed or are discussed only with occasional reference to other)ranches:

> Reconnaissance Corps.
> Royal Army Chaplains' Department.
> Royal Electrical and Mechanical Engineers.
> Royal Army Pay Corps.
> Royal Army Veterinary Corps.
> Army Educational Corps.
> The Army Dental Corps.
> Pioneer Corps.
> Army Catering Corps.
> Army Physical Training Corps.
> Corps of Military Police.
> Military Provost Staff Corps.
> Queen Alexandra's Imperial Military Nursing Service.
> Officers' Training Corps.

For a brief discussion of the Intelligence Corps, see paragraphs 141 and 142.

77. Women in the Army.—*a. General.*—Her Majesty the Queen is Commandant-in-Chief of the three principal women's auxiliary services:

(1) The Women's Royal Naval Service (WRNS), popularly known as the "Wrens".

(2) The (Women's) Auxiliary Territorial Service (ATS), an auxiliary of the Army, popularly known as the "Ats."

(3) The Women's Auxiliary Air Force (WAAF), popularly known as the "Waffs".

b. Auxiliary Territorial Service (ATS).—(1) *General.*—(*a*) Aside from the nursing services, which form part of the Royal Army Medical Corps, the ATS, a direct descendant of the Women's Army Auxiliary Corps of the First World War, is the official women's organization of the British Army. Originally organized to train women so that they could release men for fighting duties, the ATS became technically subject to military law under the Army Act in 1941. Accordingly, it is now subject to a modified Army discipline, including court-martial for offenses such as desertion.

(*b*) The ATS is the largest women's organization of a military character and its present 250,000 members have full military status, wear uniforms and insignia of rank, and are entitled to all privileges accorded to soldiers. They are enlisted for 4 years or for the duration of the war, but they may obtain their release on such grounds as ill health, or they may be discharged for cause. Members of the ATS may volunteer for service in theaters of war abroad.

(2) *Organization and duties.*—(*a*) The ATS is organized on the lines of the Regular Army. At the head of the organization is the Director of the Auxiliary Territorial Service (DATS), a woman, in rank a chief controller, the corresponding rank to a major-general. The largest administrative unit is a "Group," which may consist of any number of companies, depending on the geographical location. Each company is normally composed of two or three platoons. The organization of a company depends on its role. Broadly speaking, companies may be designated as motor (driving) companies, clerical companies, signal companies, kine-theodolite (aircraft height- and range-finding) companies, and general duties companies.

(*b*) The kine-theodolite companies have now taken over operational roles in the Anti-Aircraft Command (see par. 36*e*) as members of anti-aircraft gun crews, as communications experts, and as operators of precision fire-control instruments.

(*c*) The general duties companies are composed of cooks, orderlies, storekeepers, and clerks.

(3) *Ranks.*—(*a*) The enlisted women in the ATS are ranked like soldiers in the Army, and the officers carry the King's Commission.

The ranks of the commissioned officers and the corresponding ranks in the Army are as follows:

ATS	*Army*
Chief controller.	Major-general.
Senior controller.	Brigadier.
Controller.	Colonel.
Chief commander.	Lieutenant-colonel.
Senior commander.	Major.
Junior commander.	Captain.
Subaltern.	Lieutenant.
Second subaltern.	Second-lieutenant.

(*b*) Women address their superior officers as "Ma'am" and call each other by their surnames.

(*c*) In general the pay of the ATS is two-thirds that of the corresponding ranks in the Army.

(4) *Uniforms.*—The regular ATS uniform (fig. 40) is a khaki full-panel skirt with belted tunic (coat), fastened with brass buttons stamped with the Royal Arms cipher. A khaki overcoat similar to a soldier's greatcoat is provided for winter. The headgear is a service-dress cap with a soft visor or a chocolate-brown field-service cap piped with green, with a gusset of beech color and the ATS badge on the left-hand side. Officers wear the Sam Browne belt.

c. First Aid Nursing Yeomanry (FANY).—(1) *General.*—The FANY is a branch driving section of the ATS. At the beginning of the war it was an independent organization, but after a few months it was amalgamated with the ATS and became subject to the regulations governing the administration of the latter.

(2) *Uniforms.*—The standard ATS uniform is worn by the FANY; for identification purposes, however, members of the FANY put the cap strap over the top of the service-dress cap instead of across the front, and wear the FANY badge across the top of the coat sleeves.

d. Other women's organizations.—(1) *General.*—The following women's organizations are attached to the Army in a voluntary capacity and are not under the Army Act: the (Women's) Motor Transport Corps (MTC); the American Women's Ambulance Corps; the Women's Legion.

(2) The MTC uniform (fig. 40) is a variation of the ATS officer's uniform; the field-service cap is styled differently and is piped with blue; the coat buttons are bronze instead of brass; and the Sam Browne belt is worn.

78. Navy, Army and Air Force Institutes (NAAFI).—*a.* The NAAFI, which is known abroad as the Expeditionary Force Institutes (EFI),[27] is a non-profit-making corporation governed by representatives from each of the British fighting services with a civilian board of management. Its duties are to serve kitchen supplies and bulk-issue stores, if necessary, to the three fighting services in any theater of war throughout the world and to British forces situated in the British Isles. In effect, this corporation is a cooperative insti-

Members of the A.T.S. Left to right: Private, subaltern, sergeant. Where applicable the badge of the corps or unit was worn on the left breast of the tunic, as illustrated by the sergeant.

FIGURE 40.

tution run by the forces for the benefit of the forces. In time of war it has the full backing of the British Treasury, which has a representative on the board of management.

b. In theaters of war the employees of the NAAFI are incorporated in the armed forces.

[27] The invaluable service of the NAAFI to the armed forces is illustrated by a quotation from Lord Gort's *Despatches* in the *Supplement to the London Gazette*, 2nd despatch (War Office, March 1941), page 21: "The supply situation was * * * bad, and on 21st May [1940], Corps had only 2 days RASC supplies in the forward area. Matters might, at any time, have become serious had it not been for the success of the measures taken between 23rd and 26th May, to organize the supplies in Lille belonging to the Expeditionary Force Institutes * * * ."

c. The policy of the NAAFI is to sell goods at retail prices, and profits accruing are returned to units in the form of rebates and other services such as entertainments and sports goods.

FIGURE 40A (ABOVE). – Members of the Women's Transport Service (FANY) – subaltern and private.

FIGURE 40B (LEFT). – Members of the Women's Motor Transport Corps (MTC).

Chapter 4

RANKS, UNIFORMS, AND INSIGNIA

SECTION I

RANKS

79. Royal Navy.—*a. Commissioned officers.*—In the British armed forces the Royal Navy takes precedence over the Army and the Royal Air Force. The following lists show the corresponding ranks of those holding the King's Commission in the three services:

Royal Navy	Army	Royal Air Force
Admiral of the Fleet.	Field-Marshal.	Marshal of the Royal Air Force.
Admiral.	General.	Air Chief Marshal.
Vice-Admiral.	Lieutenant-General.	Air Marshal.
Rear-Admiral.	Major-General.	Air Vice-Marshal.
Commodore (1st and 2nd class).	Brigadier.	Air Commodore.
Captain.	Colonel.	Group Captain.
Commander.	Lieutenant-Colonel.	Wing Commander.
Lieutenant-Commander.	Major.	Squadron Leader.
Lieutenant.	Captain.	Flight Lieutenant.
Sub-Lieutenant and Commissioned Warrant Officer.	Lieutenant.	Flying Officer.
	Second-Lieutenant.	Pilot Officer.

b. Enlisted men.—Enlisted men in the Royal Navy are called "ratings," and are graded upwards from boy, 2nd class, to chief petty officer.

c. Royal Marines.—The Royal Marines ("Jollies") were originally boarding parties used by the Royal Navy to carry out the hand-to-hand fighting between ships which was a feature of sea battles a century or so ago. They are now primarily used as sea soldiers; and although they are a part of the Royal Navy, they still retain the Army names of rank. Their ranks correspond to naval ranks (as above) except that when afloat a major of marines is equal to a naval commander.

d. Women's Royal Naval Service (WRNS).—(1) *General.*—The WRNS was originally formed in November 1917, and was demobilized in October 1919. It was revised in April 1939 to replace in time of war officers and men in certain naval shore establishments. The WRNS has not been accorded naval status, and is not subject technically to naval discipline. Its officers do not hold the King's Commission. The woman at the head of the organization is called a director, the corresponding rank to a rear-admiral. The chief duties of the "Wrens" include confidential clerical work, bookkeeping, storekeeping, telephone operating, motor driving, cooking, and stewarding, as well as many mechanical jobs requiring a high degree of dexterity.

(2) *Ranks.*—The ranks of the officers and the enlisted women and their corresponding ranks in the Royal Navy are as follows:

WRNS	*Royal Navy*
Director.	Rear-admiral.
Deputy director.	Commodore (1st and 2nd class).
Superintendent.	Captain.
Chief officer.	Commander.
First officer.	Lieutenant-commander.
Second officer.	Lieutenant.
Third officer.	Sub-lieutenant and commissioned warrant officer.
Chief wren.	Chief petty officer.
Petty officer wren.	Petty officer.
Leading wren.	Leading seaman.
Wren.	Seaman.

80. Army.—*a. Commissioned officers.*—(1) The ranks of commissioned officers and the corresponding ranks of those in the U. S. Army are as follows:

British	United States
Field-Marshal.	- - - - - - - - - - - -
General.	General.
Lieutenant-General.	Lieutenant General.
Major-General.	Major General.
Brigadier.	Brigadier General.
Colonel.	Colonel.
Lieutenant-Colonel.	Lieutenant Colonel.
Major.	Major.
Captain.	Captain.
Lieutenant.	First Lieutenant.
Second-Lieutenant.	Second Lieutenant.

(2) In the Royal Navy, the Army, and the Royal Air Force "lieutenant" is pronounced "leftenant."

(3) It will be noted that brigadier is a proper title in the British Army. Although it corresponds to the rank of brigadier general in the U. S. Army, it is improper to address such an officer as "General." The British rank of brigadier-general was abolished in 1920.

(4) Certain designations which may appear to be official ranks are merely temporary assignments that may be held by officers of varying grade. For example, Brigade Major, Staff Captain, and Staff Lieutenant are appointments and not ranks, but they are usually held by officers of the grade indicated by the title.

(5) Lieutenants and second-lieutenants are called subalterns, and are addressed orally as "Mister."

(6) Promotions and appointments are governed as follows: (*a*) The rank of field-marshal is conferred for eminent military services, and the bearer of it remains on the active list for life.

(*b*) Generals command armies; lieutenant-generals, corps; major-generals, divisions. Commanders of artillery and engineer formations of large commands as well as senior officers in the auxiliary services may also hold general rank.

(*c*) The brigadier is temporary for the job, holding the appointment only while commanding a brigade or performing other duties for which the appropriate rank is that of brigadier. Major-generals are usually appointed from brigadiers and colonels.

(*d*) Vacancies are not permitted; normally they are filled at once, either by transfer of an officer of appropriate rank or by the promotion of a junior. If an officer occupies a job calling for higher rank for even as little as 3 days, he must be given acting rank for that time. The first 21 days in acting rank are unpaid. After 21 days, if the officer retains acting rank, he is paid on the higher scale, including the difference in pay for the 21-day period. In the case of junior officers, acting rank automatically becomes temporary rank after 3 months; in the case of lieutenant-colonels and colonels, after 6 months and 9 months, respectively.

(e) An officer holding temporary rank who is for any reason, including illness, but not recuperation from wounds, unable to perform his duties for a period of 21 days reverts to what is known as "war substantive" rank, a rank which is one grade lower than the former temporary rank and below which the officer will not go for the duration of the war.

(f) Brevet rank, which is not given in wartime, is the rank held by promotion to a higher grade for distinguished service whether a vacancy exists or not. For example, a captain promoted by brevet to the rank of major acts as a captain while serving with his regiment during peacetime, but on active service he takes precedence as major from the date of his brevet.

b. *Enlisted men.*—(1) Enlisted men are called "other ranks" (OR). The grades of the most essential, from highest to lowest, are: regimental sergeant-major [2] (RSM), regimental quarter-master sergeant (RQMS), company sergeant-major (CSM), company quarter-master sergeant (CQMS), staff-sergeant (S/Sgt), sergeant (Sgt), lance-sergeant (L/Sgt), corporal (Cpl), lance-corporal (L/Cpl), and private (Pte).

(2) The regimental sergeant-major holds a warrant appointing him to his grade and is ranked as warrant officer, class I. The regimental quarter-master sergeant and the company sergeant-major hold similar warrants and are ranked as warrant officers, class II. The grade of warrant officer, class III, was discontinued soon after the outbreak of the Second World War.

(3) The company sergeant-major corresponds to the U. S. first sergeant. The senior sergeant of a platoon is the platoon sergeant.

(4) Various specialist grades of sergeant exist in the different arms and services.

(5) Lance-sergeants and lance-corporals are appointments, not ranks, and are given to corporals and privates, respectively, who have

---

[2] The spelling "sergeant," as in the Royal Air Force, rather than "serjeant" is used for the sake of uniformity.

qualified and been recommended for further promotions when vacancies occur.

(6) In the different arms of the service equivalent ranks often bear different names. For example, in the Royal Artillery a corporal is called a bombardier. The private is variously styled, as follows:

Normal: Private.	Infantry:
Cavalry: Trooper.	Brigade of Guards: Guardsman.
Artillery: Gunner.	Fusiliers: Fusilier.
Engineers: Sapper.	Rifle Battalion: Rifleman.
Signals: Signalman.	

Any private who drives a motor vehicle (excluding motorcycles) is ranked as "driver."

c. Salutes and honors.—(1) The right-hand salute is used as a sign of loyalty and respect for the King's Commission, and is never given by a soldier without headgear. The extended arm is raised sideways to the horizontal; then the forearm is brought smartly to the forehead. The palm of the hand faces to the front, the wrist, four fingers, and thumb being straight, with the forefinger coming to rest 1 inch above the right eye.[3] The open hand originally symbolized the absence of any weapon that could be used against the holder of the King's Commission.

(2) When the national anthem ("God Save the King") is played during ceremonial parades, all ranks in uniform not under the orders of the officer commanding the parade stand at attention and commissioned officers salute. If indoors where headdress is not worn, all ranks and civilians stand at attention.

(3) At any time, when the King's Colour (a square of silk bearing the King's Arms) and the Regimental Colour are displayed, and the Colour Party marches across the direct line of vision, civilians uncover and they and all ranks stand at attention and all ranks salute.

(4) Salutes are normally exchanged as in the U. S. Army, except that neither the second-lieutenant nor the lieutenant is required to salute his superior below the rank of major unless on parade or when reporting officially.

(5) In paying compliments to senior officers, the senior member of a party of soldiers will call the others to attention, and he alone will salute. In returning a salute given to one or more officers, only the senior officer will return the compliment by saluting.

---

[3] The right-hand salute of the Royal Air Force is the same as that of the Army; that of the Royal Navy is similar to that of the U. S. armed forces.

(6) Officers and enlisted men when boarding or leaving any of His Majesty's ships, or a foreign man-of-war, salute the quarterdeck.

(7) When in uniform, officers and enlisted men salute their superiors of the Royal Navy, the Royal Air Force, and the armed forces of foreign nations who would be saluted by them if they held corresponding ranks in their own service. All men in the armed forces in civilian clothes salute by raising their hats.

81. Royal Air Force.—*a. Commissioned officers.*—(1) The commissioned officers are listed in order of rank in paragraph 79.

(2) Air officers, or officers of air rank, are officers of the rank of air commodore and above.

(3) Except for a limited scheme of time promotion in the junior ranks, all promotion of officers is by selection.

(4) When addressing officers orally, the custom of the RAF is to say the rank in full; for example, "wing commander" is not abbreviated to "commander," and "group captain" is not abbreviated to "captain," etc. Flying officers and pilot officers are addressed orally as "Mister."

b. Enlisted men.—(1) The term "airmen" is used to describe personnel below commissioned rank. The main grades of these, from highest to lowest, are: warrant officer (the grade of warrant officer, class II, has been abolished), flight sergeant, sergeant, corporal, leading aircraftman, aircraftman, 1st class, and aircraftman, 2nd class.

SECTION II

UNIFORMS AND INSIGNIA

82. General.—Ranks are indicated in the Royal Navy, the Army, and the Royal Air Force in several ways: by sleeve insignia; by insignia on shoulder straps; or by cap decorations (or by one or more of the three in combination). Duties are indicated by sleeve insignia; by armlets (arm bands, brassards); or by miscellaneous badges. Both ranks and duties are indicated in the Army by tabs, or gorget patches.

83. Royal Navy.—Naval uniforms and insignia are discussed briefly for purposes of identification only.

a. Commissioned officers.—(1) Full-dress uniforms and cocked hats are not worn during wartime. The usual naval uniform to be met with is of navy blue; the tunic (coat) is double-breasted, and with it is worn a white shirt and black necktie. White uniforms, with the coat buttoned up at the collar, are worn in the Tropics or wherever the climate makes it suitable. The white-topped cap may be worn with either the navy-blue uniform or the white, but is usually worn during the summer months. (Khaki uniforms are worn ashore on special duties or assignments.)

(2) The rank of naval officers is shown by sleeve insignia on navy-blue uniforms and by insignia on the shoulder straps on white uniforms and on overcoats. In plate I the illustrations show both the left sleeve insignia and the left shoulder straps of executive officers.[4] (The warrant officer is accorded the respect paid to commissioned ranks. The midshipman, who is next below the sub-lieutenant and the commissioned warrant officer in rank, is in all respects an officer, although he is actually a cadet in training prior to being commissioned a sub-lieutenant. He is also accorded the respect paid to commissioned ranks.)

(3) The branch to which a naval officer belongs is shown by the strips of colored cloth between the gold stripes (one strip below in the case of one gold stripe), as follows:

Executive—No colored cloth.	Instructor—Light blue.
Engineer—Purple.	Shipwright—Silver gray.
Surgeon—Scarlet.	Electrical—Dark green.
Dental—Orange.	Ordnance—Dark blue.
Paymaster—White.	Wardmaster—Maroon.

(4) The peaks (visors) and badges of officers' caps are partial indications of rank. The visors of both the blue and the white cap are of black (patent leather). The visor for all officers up to and including lieutenant-commander is plain; for commodores, 2nd class, captains, and commanders, it has one row of gold oak leaves; and for flag officers (rear-admirals and above) and commodores, 1st class, it has two rows of gold oak leaves. (See fig. 41.)

(5) Commissioned officers of the Royal Naval Reserve (RNR) wear insignia of rank similar to that of commissioned officers in the Royal Navy, but in zigzag stripes. Those of the Royal Naval Volunteer Reserve (RNVR) wear the same, but in wavy stripes.

---

[4] Tone plates of uniforms and insignia follow page 120.

b. Enlisted men.—Chief petty officers and petty officers wear distinctive cap badges. Insignia on sleeves of various grades of enlisted men indicate appropriate ranks and duties. (See fig. 42.)

c. Royal Marines.—The Royal Marines wear navy-blue uniforms as well as khaki (similar to the Army style). The only difference between their shoulder-strap insignia and those of the Army is that the letters "RM" are worn at the bottom of the strap nearest the arm (fig. 43). Commissioned officers' caps differ from those of noncommissioned officers by having a different badge and red piping round the crown of the cap.

d. Fleet Air Arm.—The Fleet Air Arm was originally under the control of the Air Ministry, but since 1939 it has been controlled entirely by the Admiralty. For this reason, officers of the Fleet Air

① Flag officers and commodore, 1st class. ② Commodore, 2nd class, captain, and commander. ③ Other commissioned officers.

FIGURE 41.—Royal Navy caps.

Arm wear naval uniforms, but are distinguished from naval officers by the letter "A" in the circle surmounting the sleeve stripes (fig. 44). Those officers who are actual pilots wear their wings on their sleeves, and not on the left breast as in the Royal Air Force (see plate VII and fig. 51).

e. Women's Royal Naval Service (WRNS).—The uniform of the "Wrens" is a navy-blue coat and skirt. Officers wear black tricorne hats (see fig. 40), and "ratings" simple blue hats in winter and white in summer.

84. Army.—*a. Uniforms.*—(1) *General.*—There are two dress uniforms which are not worn during wartime: full dress (for daytime use on special ceremonial occasions) and mess dress [5] (for use of officers only at official dinners, guest nights, or when ordered in mess by the president of the Mess Committee). Undress uniforms [5] for all ranks (those of officers being of a finer quality), usually of dark blue and buttoned up to the throat with a high collar, may be worn during the evening in peacetime for duty or dining, and may also be worn as an evening uniform during wartime. During wartime, however,

---

[5] Wellington boots are worn with mess-dress and undress uniforms.

CHIEF PETTY OFFICER'S
CAP BADGE

PETTY OFFICER'S
CAP BADGE

PETTY OFFICER'S
SLEEVE INSIGNIA

OTHER SLEEVE INSIGNIA

GUNNER'S MATE

GUNLAYER
FIRST CLASS

QUARTERS RATING
FIRST CLASS
GUNNERY BRANCH

PETTY OFFICER
TELEGRAPHIST

RANGETAKER
FIRST CLASS

RANGETAKER
SECOND CLASS

TORPEDO GUNNER'S
MATE

TORPEDO
COXSWAIN

CHIEF
ARMOURER

CHIEF
SHIPWRIGHT

DIVER

FIGURE 42.—Royal Navy enlisted men's insignia.

CHIEF YEOMAN AND
YEOMAN OF SIGNALS

VISUAL SIGNALMAN,
TRAINED OPERATOR

REGULATING
PETTY OFFICER

SICK BERTH
RATING

SUBMARINE DETECTOR
INSTRUCTOR

TELEGRAPHIST
AIR GUNNER

LEADING SEAMAN

ACTING OBSERVER'S
MATE

COOK

OFFICER'S
STEWARD

OFFICER'S
COOK

FIGURE 42 (continued).— Royal Navy enlisted men's insignia.

the usual dress for officers is service dress for evening wear and battle
dress for daytime. Battle dress was adopted in 1939. The uniform
is exactly the same for both officers and enlisted men, and is at the

present time the only official dress for enlisted men (plate II and figs. 45 and 48). (See also figs. 50, 61, 67, and 81.)

(2) *Service dress.*—(*a*) In wartime this uniform is worn only by officers, for office duty, for "walking out," for evening wear, and for ceremonials (fig. 46). Normally made of barathea or a high quality of serge or twill, the single-breasted tunic (coat) may be belted and has shoulder straps and four pockets, usually patched. The sleeves generally have pointed cuffs and no buttons, although most mounted regiments and some infantry regiments wear them without points and with two or more buttons. Underneath the coat a khaki shirt with a khaki necktie is worn. The trousers, of the same material as the coat, are long and cuffless. Only mounted officers, staff officers, officers of field rank (major and above), or officers of units that were formerly horsed may wear breeches (of cavalry twill) and field boots (see the colonel in fig. 46). Officers of Scottish regiments wear rounded jackets and trews (trousers) of the regimental tartan. In addition, officers of Highland regiments, when not on parade with troops, may wear the kilt with service dress.

FIGURE 43.—Shoulder strap of a lieutenant of the Royal Marines.

FIGURE 44.—Sleeve insignia of a lieutenant of the Fleet Air Arm.

(*b*) Both the service-dress (U. S. service) cap (fig. 46) and the field-service, or forage (U. S. garrison), cap—popularly called the "fore and aft"—are worn with service dress. The service-dress cap is normally khaki-peaked (i. e., the visor is of plain khaki) for all ranks. But in this case,[6] as in the case of the field-service cap; the greatcoat (overcoat); the sleeves, pockets, and general style of the coat; and many other matters of dress, there are countless variations from regiment

---

[6] For example, during peacetime officers often wear with service dress the blue undress cap, but with a khaki cover. The visor of the cap is of black (patent leather), and for officers of the rank of colonel and above is adorned with gold oak leaves, as follows: brigadiers and colonels, one row (corresponding to the visor of the regular cap of commodores, 2nd class, captains, and commanders in the Royal Navy, and to that of group captains in the Royal Air Force); field-marshals and general officers, two rows (corresponding to the visor of the regular cap of flag officers and commodores, 1st class, in the RN, and to that of air officers in the RAF). See paragraph 83a(4) and figure 41, and paragraph 85b(1)(e) and plate VII.

to regiment and from corps to corps (fig. 45 ① and ②, and plate III).

(c) Officers in service dress usually wear brown kid gloves and may carry canes, riding crops, or swagger sticks (fig. 46).[7]

① Roll call order ('Tam o' Shanter — as above— or other regimental headgear worn in place of the regular field-service cap where required).

② Drill order (showing rifle, bayonet, and skeleton web belt).

FIGURE 45.—Sergeant in various orders of battle dress.

(d) The service-dress uniform for enlisted men in peacetime consisted of a coat buttoned up to the throat (see figs. 84 and 85), and breeches and puttees for horsed units and long trousers for other units. It is issued at the present time only to members of The Brigade of Guards and the Corps of Military Police.

---

[7] A short stick is often called a "kosh," and the word is also used loosely in this respect.

111

(3) *Battle dress.*—(*a*) This uniform is a two-piece khaki serge (plate II and figs. 45, 48, 58, 61, 67, and 81). The trousers are long and some-what baggy, with web anklets worn at the bottom. The rather full blouse (so-called, but more like the U. S. shirt), which fastens up to the

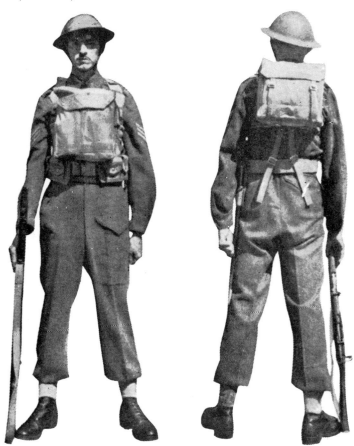

③ Battle order (showing rifle, bayonet, skeleton web belt, gas mask haversack, and haversack).

FIGURE 45 (*continued*).—Sergeant in various orders of battle dress.

throat, is of waist length and of the same material as the trousers. It has two breast pockets.[8] The blouse buttons onto the top of the trou-sers on the inside and is taken in at the waist by a cloth belt which fastens on the right side. Enlisted men wear the blouse buttoned up at the throat. Both officers and men wear a khaki shirt underneath.

---

[8] Actually, the complete uniform, trousers and blouse, has nine pockets, including a very large one on the front of the left thigh for maps and papers.

for officers, who unbutton the top two buttons of the blouse, the collar of the shirt is visible and is tied with a khaki necktie. There is no special battle-dress overcoat. Pipers in Scottish and Irish regiments may wear the kilt with battle dress at all times.

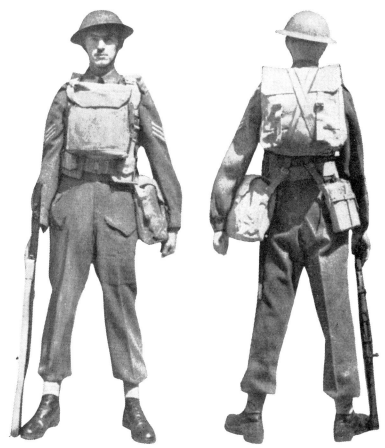

④ Full marching order (showing rifle, bayonet, gas mask haversack, haversack, pack, and other equipment).

FIGURE 45 (*continued*).—Sergeant in various orders of battle dress.

(*b*) The headgear is a field-service cap, but under active service, or when so ordered, the steel helmet. (See figs. 45 ③ and ④, 48, 50, 58, 61, 62, 67, 80, and 81.) The service-dress cap is also worn with battle dress, but this is the exception and not the rule.

(*c*) Washable two-piece or one-piece overalls are worn over the battle dress under certain circumstances, as, for example, in mechanized units (fig. 80).

(4) *Tropical dress.*—(*a*) This uniform is made of a light khaki material. The "walking out" dress for officers is of exactly the same cut as that of service dress, and it may be worn with shirt sleeves.

(*b*) Shorts of the same material and short sleeves may be worn in very hot weather. Ankle puttees (U. S. wrapped leggings or spiral

FIGURE 46.—Colonel and two lieutenant-colonels, Royal Army Medical Corps, in service dress.

puttees) are worn with woolen stockings; full puttees, with hose tops. (See figs. 58 and 62.)

b. Insignia.—(1) *Commissioned officers.*—(*a*) *General.*—In 1920, sleeve badges on officers' uniforms were abolished. Since 1939 the Sam Browne belt has not been required for officers except when on parade.

(b) *Service dress.—1.* Officers' ranks are shown by the metal insignia, usually gilt, on the shoulder straps of their coats and overcoats, as illustrated in plate II.

2. The "star," known in the vernacular as a "pip," is not actually a star, but a diamond-shaped, elliptical, or somewhat square device that may vary also in size according to the regiment or corps. For example, The Brigade of Guards and The South Wales Borderers wear an elongated "pip," whereas very small "pips" and crowns are worn by The Oxfordshire and Buckinghamshire Light Infantry.[9] The standard "pip" is slightly more than ¾ inch square, the crown being of appropriate size. On the base rests a cross patee surmounted by a green-enameled laurel wreath which, in turn, encircles a medallion. The medallion consists of three miters, two above one, surrounded by a motto on red enamel—"TRIA JUNCTA IN UNO," which refers to the union of the United Kingdom. The "pip" is worn with the miters pointing toward the collar. Some regiments wear the crown with a red backing.

3. The coloring of the "pip" also varies, from polished, unenameled to black. Bronze "pips," crowns, and buttons are worn by such regiments as The Hampshire Regiment and The North Staffordshire Regiment, whereas black ones are worn by rifle regiments and by chaplains (see plate II).

4. In some regiments the unit name in metal is worn on the shoulder strap nearest the arm, as, for example, in The Queen's Bays ("BAYS"— see plate II), the 10th Royal Hussars ("XRH"), etc.

(c) *Cap badges, cap bands, and tabs.—1.* All officers up to and including lieutenant-colonel wear buttons, cap badges, and insignia on the collar of the coat peculiar to their regiments or corps. (See plate III and fig. 47 for examples of regimental and corps insignia; see also the two lieutenant-colonels in fig. 46.)

2. Field-marshals, general officers, and brigadiers and colonels of the General Staff wear a scarlet band around the service-dress cap and wear General Staff buttons (embossed with the arms of Great Britain). (See plate II and the regimental sergeant-major's insignia, plate VIII.) On the collar of the coat they wear scarlet tabs, or gorget patches. (See the colonel in fig. 46 for the position of the tabs.)

3. Field-marshals wear as a cap badge cross batons within a laurel wreath surmounted by a lion above a crown (plate III). The tabs have a line of small gold oak leaves down the center (plate II).

---

[9] For the regiments referred to in this chapter, see paragraph 167.

THE LIFE GUARDS

ROYAL REGIMENT OF ARTILLERY

CORPS OF ROYAL ENGINEERS

ROYAL CORPS OF SIGNALS

GRENADIER GUARDS

THE KING'S OWN ROYAL REGIMENT

THE CAMERONIANS

THE SOUTH STAFFORDSHIRE REGIMENT

ROYAL ARMY SERVICE CORPS

ROYAL ARMY MEDICAL CORPS

ROYAL ARMY ORDNANCE CORPS

FIGURE 47.—Regimental and corps insignia.

116

4. General officers wear as a cap badge crossed baton and sword within a laurel wreath surmounted by a lion above a crown (plate III). The tabs have a line of small gold oak leaves down the center (plate II).

5. Brigadiers and colonels wear as a cap badge a crown surmounted by a lion (plate III and fig. 46). The tabs of both have a straight maroon line down the center.

6. Full colonels of the services other than General Staff wear a band around the service-dress cap and tabs colored according to the service, as shown by the following examples:

Corps of Royal Engineers—Bright blue.

Royal Army Chaplains' Department—Purple.

Royal Army Medical Corps—Cherry.

Royal Army Ordnance Corps—Blue.

Royal Army Pay Corps—Yellow.

Royal Army Veterinary Corps—Maroon.

Army Educational Corps—Cambridge blue.

The Army Dental Corps—Emerald green.

7. In the case of the usual field-service cap, the cap badge is worn on the left side roughly 1 inch from the front, but the position varies according to the style of the cap (Tam O'Shanter, Glengarry, beret, etc.). For example, on the beret of the Royal Tank Regiment it is worn in the front center. (See plate III.)

(2) *Enlisted men.*—Since, as stated above, battle dress is at the present time the only official uniform for enlisted men, enlisted men's insignia of rank is discussed in (3)(*g*), below. On the field-service cap enlisted men wear regimental or corps insignia in the same manner as officers. (See plate III and fig. 45 ① and ②.)

(3) *Battle dress.*—(*a*) All insignia worn on the battle dress is of cloth, except in The Brigade of Guards, where officers may wear metal insignia of rank.

(*b*) Officers wear on their shoulder straps cloth insignia of rank surmounted on pieces of cloth (1¼ inches square) the color of which varies according to the arm of the service. Distinguishing marks, or strips of cloth (⅜ by 2 inches), which also vary in color according to the arm of the service, are worn on both sleeves by all ranks 3¼ inches below the shoulder straps. (An exception to this practice is made by The Brigade of Guards,[10] the five regiments of which wear the appropriate regimental name in crescent shape just below the shoulder. See figs. 48, 50, and 61.) The arms of the service with their corresponding colors for the backing to officers' insignia of rank and for distinguishing marks are indicated in plates IV and V.

[10] See paragraph 167*f*.

117

(*c*) In some regiments all ranks may wear the unit name on detachable loops on the shoulder straps nearest the arm.

FIGURE 48.—Grenadier Guards in battle dress.

(*d*) Directly below the shoulder and above the colored strips all ranks wear divisional, army corps, etc., insignia (figs. 48 and 61), and below the strips regimental or corps colors may be worn, as illustrated in figure 49.

118

(e) Regimental or corps colors may be painted on the left side of the steel helmet (fig. 50).

(f) On the service-dress overcoat, which may be worn with battle dress, officers and enlisted men wear only insignia of rank and distinguishing marks. On mackintoshes (raincoats) insignia are not usually worn.

(g) Warrant officers and noncommissioned officers wear their insignia of rank on both sleeves a few inches above the cuff except in the case of the company quarter-master sergeant, the staff-sergeant (fig. 61), the sergeant (figs. 45 and 50), the lance-sergeant, the corporal

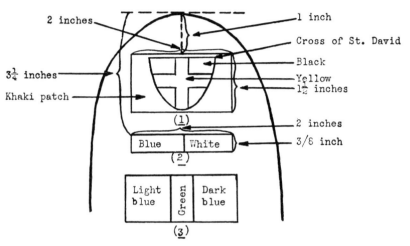

1. Divisional insignia (always worn).
2. Distinguishing marks (always worn).
3. Regimental or corps colors (may be worn).

FIGURE 49.—Design for the left upper-arm sleeve of a member of the 38th Divisional Signals (battle dress).

(fig. 14), and the lance-corporal, who wear theirs on both sleeves above the elbow. Instructors' badges are worn in conjunction with insignia of rank. Thus a sergeant instructor wears both badges above the elbow, whereas a sergeant-major instructor displays both badges together on the cuff. The insignia of the essential grades of noncommissioned officers are illustrated in plate VIII. Other enlisted men's insignia showing duties are worn on both upper sleeves. Chevrons for good conduct are worn point up on the lower left sleeve only, as follows: 1 for 2 years, 2 for 5, 3 for 12, 4 for 16, and 5 for 21. See plate VIII.

(4) *Armlets* (*arm bands, brassards*).—Officers below the rank of colonel holding staff appointments wear, with whatever uniform is

appropriate, a cloth armlet 3½ inches wide on the right arm above the elbow.

(*a*) *Officers on staff at War Office.*—The top half of the armlet is red; the bottom half, black. A gilt crown surmounted by a lion is situated in the center of the top half; the red lettering on the bottom half indicates the branch.

(*b*) *Headquarters, Home Forces, British Expeditionary Force, and Middle East.*—The armlet is similar to that worn by officers attached to the War Office, but without the central crest and with the lettering in yellow.

(*c*) *Command headquarters.*—The armlet is of red, black, and red horizontal strips, with red lettering on the central black strip.

(*d*) *Divisional headquarters.*—The armlet is red with black lettering.

(*e*) *Area, district, and garrison headquarters.*—The armlet is green with black lettering.

(*f*) *Brigade headquarters.*—The armlet is blue with black lettering.

(*g*) *Movement, embarkation, and transport of troops.*—The armlet is white.

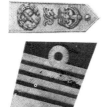

ADMIRAL OF THE FLEET
("GR" (GEORGE REX) INDI-
CATES AIDE-DE-CAMP TO
KING GEORGE VI)

ADMIRAL

VICE-ADMIRAL

REAR-ADMIRAL (1)
AND COMMODORE, 1ST CLASS (2)

COMMODORE, 2ND CLASS

CAPTAIN

COMMANDER

LIEUTENANT-COMMANDER

LIEUTENANT

SUB-LIEUTENANT
AND COMMISSIONED WARRANT OFFICER

WARRANT OFFICER

Gold Braid on Navy Blue cloth

TAB OF A GENERAL
OFFICER

SERVICE-DRESS CAP.
BRIGADIER OR COLONEL,
GENERAL STAFF

TAB OF A BRIGADIER
OR COLONEL,
GENERAL STAFF

FIELD-MARSHAL

GENERAL

LIEUTENANT-GENERAL

MAJOR-GENERAL

BRIGADIER

COLONEL

LIEUTENANT-COLONEL

MAJOR

CAPTAIN

LIEUTENANT

SECOND-LIEUTENANT

CAPTAIN OF RIFLE REGIMENT OR
CAPTAIN, ROYAL ARMY CHAPLAINS'
DEPARTMENT (CHAPLAIN, 4TH CLASS)

COMMISSIONED OFFICER
IN BATTLE DRESS

MAJOR OF THE QUEEN'S BAYS

FIELD-MARSHAL

GENERAL OFFICER

BRIGADIER AND COLONEL

COLONEL AND ABOVE

8TH KING'S
ROYAL IRISH HUSSARS

ROYAL TANK REGIMENT

THE BLACK WATCH

ROYAL ARMY CHAPLAINS'
DEPARTMENT

THE GORDON HIGHLANDERS

PLAIN KHAKI—ALL RANKS IN THE FIELD

INTELLIGENCE CORPS

Arm of service	Color of backing to officers' insignia of rank	Distinguishing marks on sleeves for all ranks
Staff Corps of Military Police	Red	RED 1
Royal Armoured Corps	Yellow	YELLOW—RED 2
Royal Regiment of Artillery	Red	RED—BLUE
Royal Corps of Engineers	Blue	BLUE—RED
Royal Corps of Signals	Blue	BLUE—WHITE 2
Infantry (except rifle regiments) and general list [3]	Scarlet	SCARLET
Infantry (rifle regiment)	Rifle green	RIFLE GREEN
Reconnaissance Corps	Green	GREEN—YELLOW
Royal Army Chaplains' Department	Purple	PURPLE
Royal Army Service Corps	Yellow	YELLOW—BLUE

[1] Worn with the armlet in the case of CMP.
[2] Where two colors are mentioned, the first color will be worn to the front (see fig. 49).
[3] Unattached troops.

Arm of service	Color of backing to officers' insignia of rank	Distinguishing marks on sleeves for all ranks
Royal Army Medical Corps	Dull cherry	DULL CHERRY
Royal Army Ordnance Corps	Blue	BLUE
Royal Army Pay Corps	Yellow	YELLOW
Royal Army Veterinary Corps	Maroon	MAROON
Army Educational Corps	Cambridge blue	CAMBRIDGE BLUE
The Army Dental Corps	Green	GREEN—WHITE
Pioneer Corps	Red	RED—GREEN
Intelligence Corps	Green	GREEN
Army Catering Corps	Gray	GRAY—YELLOW
Army Physical Training Corps	Black	BLACK—RED—BLACK

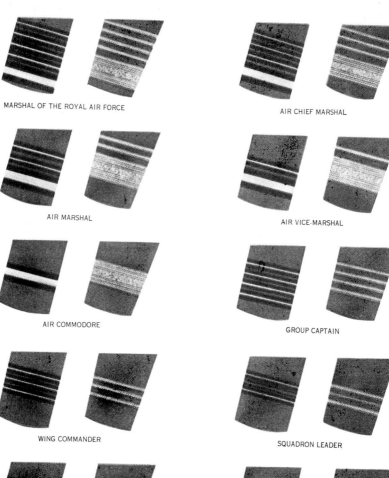

MARSHAL OF THE ROYAL AIR FORCE

AIR CHIEF MARSHAL

AIR MARSHAL

AIR VICE-MARSHAL

AIR COMMODORE

GROUP CAPTAIN

WING COMMANDER

SQUADRON LEADER

FLIGHT LIEUTENANT

FLYING OFFICER

PILOT OFFICER

Dark Blue/Light Blue cloth rings — service dress; Gold Braid rings — full dress

OFFICERS OF AIR RANK

GROUP CAPTAIN

OTHER OFFICERS

FIELD-SERVICE CAP

CHAPLAIN

AIRMAN

PILOT

OBSERVER   AIR GUNNER

PLATE VI

ARMY ENLISTED MEN'S INSIGNIA

REGIMENTAL
SERGEANT-MAJOR
(WARRANT OFFICER, CLASS I)

REGIMENTAL QUARTER-MASTER-
SERGEANT AND COMPANY
SERGEANT-MAJOR
(WARRANT OFFICERS, CLASS II)

COMPANY QUARTER-MASTER-
SERGEANT AND
STAFF-SERGEANT

SERGEANT AND
LANCE-SERGEANT

CORPORAL

LANCE-CORPORAL

GUNNERY INSTRUCTOR

BANDSMAN

SIGNALLER
(Blue/White Flags)

ARMOURER

PIONEER

BOMB
DISPOSAL SQUAD
(Yellow Bomb
on Red Disc)

GOOD CONDUCT CHEVRON

RAF AIRMEN'S INSIGNIA

WARRANT OFFICER

FLIGHT SERGEANT
Gilt Crown

SERGEANT

CORPORAL

SERVICE-DRESS
UNIFORM
(FLIGHT SERGEANT)

LEADING
AIRCRAFTMAN

GOOD CONDUCT
CHEVRON

AIRCRAFTMAN'S
WORKING DRESS

PHYSICAL TRAINING
INSTRUCTOR

WIRELESS
OPERATOR

GEORGE CROSS

VICTORIA CROSS

DISTINGUISHED SERVICE
ORDER

DISTINGUISHED FLYING CROSS

MILITARY CROSS

DISTINGUISHED CONDUCT MEDAL

NSPICUOUS GALLANTRY
MEDAL (REVERSE)

GEORGE MEDAL

MILITARY MEDAL
(REVERSE)

Maroon

VICTORIA CROSS
(1856)

Blue

George Cross image

GEORGE CROSS
(1940)

Light Blue

ORDER OF THE GARTER
(1349)

Green

ORDER OF THE THISTLE
(1687)

Grey

ORDER OF ST PATRICK
(1788)

Red

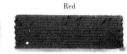

ORDER OF THE BATH
(1399)

Red   Blue

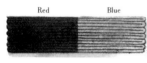

ORDER OF MERIT
(1902)

White/Grey/White

ORDER OF THE STAR OF INDIA
(1861)

Blue/Red/Blue

ORDER OF ST MICHAEL
AND ST GEORGE
(1818)

Brown

ORDER OF THE INDIAN EMPIRE
(1877)

Red/White/Red/Blue/Red/White/Red

ROYAL VICTORIAN ORDER
(1896)

White/Red/White/Red/White

ORDER OF THE BRITISH EMPIRE
(MILITARY - 1917)

Gold on Red

ORDER OF THE COMPANIONS
OF HONOUR
(1917)

Blue/Red/Blue

DISTINGUISHED SERVICE ORDER
(1886)

Red/Blue/Red

IMPERIAL SERVICE ORDER
(1902)

Blue/White/Blue

DISTINGUISHED SERVICE CROSS
(1914)

White/Blue/White

MILITARY CROSS
(1914)

Blue and White

DISTINGUISHED FLYING CROSS
(1918)

Red and White

AIR FORCE CROSS
(1918)

Red/Blue/Red

DISTINGUISHED CONDUCT MEDAL
(1845)

Blue/White/Blue

CONSPICUOUS GALLANTRY MEDAL
(1929)

Blue/White

DISTINGUISHED SERVICE MEDAL
(1914)

Blue/White/Red stripes

MILITARY MEDAL
(1916)

Blue and White

DISTINGUISHED FLYING MEDAL
(1918)

Red and White

AIR FORCE MEDAL
(1918)

Blue and Mauve

GEORGE MEDAL
(1940)

Green/Yellow

AFRICA GENERAL SERVICE MEDAL
(1902)

Green/Blue

INDIA GENERAL SERVICE MEDAL
(1908)

Red and White

NAVAL GENERAL SERVICE MEDAL
(1909 1914)

Red, White, Blue

1914 STAR (MONS)

Red, White, Blue

1914 1915 STAR

Blue, Black, White, Yellow centre

BRITISH WAR MEDAL
(1914 1918)

Blue, Light Blue, Green, Yellow, Red

VICTORY MEDAL[1]
(1914-1918)

Blue, Light Blue, Green, Yellow, Red

VICTORY MEDAL
(1914-1918)

Dark Yellow, Green stripes

TERRITORIAL WAR MEDAL
(1914 1919)

Blue/Green/Blue

GENERAL SERVICE MEDAL
IRAQ MESOPOTAMIA
(1923)

Red and White

MERITORIOUS SERVICE MEDAL (ARMY)[2]
(1845)

Blue and White
Red

MERITORIOUS SERVICE MEDAL (AIR FORCE)
(1919)

Red and White
Blue

KING GEORGE VI S CORONATION
MEDAL

Maroon and White

LONG SERVICE AND GOOD CONDUCT
MEDAL (ARMY)
(1830)

Blue and White

LONG SERVICE AND GOOD CONDUCT
MEDAL (NAVY)
(1831)

Blue and White
Red

LONG SERVICE AND GOOD CONDUCT
MEDAL (AIR FORCE)
(1919)

[1] Oak leaf for citation in dispatches.
[2] Same for the Navy except blue for red.

Soldier in battle dress —
fighting order; he is wearing
1937 pattern ammunition
pouches, more commonly
worn by first-line units than
the 1908 pattern pouches
shown in Fig. 45.

(*h*) *Officers' branch of staff.*—The branch of the staff to which an officer belongs is indicated by the lettering on the armlet, as follows:

A_____ Adjutant-General's.

A (plus drawing of a gun). Royal Artillery.

A & Q_____ Combined Adjutant-General's and Quarter-Master-General's.

FIGURE 50.—Scots Guards in battle dress.

121

ADC_____	Aides-de-Camp.
AD Mn (in gold letters).	Officer in Charge of Administration.
AEC_____	Education Officer's.
BM_____	Brigade Major.
C_____	Chaplain-General's.
CQM_____	Camp Quarter-Master's.
E_____	Royal Engineers.
G_____	General Staff.
GA_____	Garrison Adjutant.
JA_____	Judge-Advocate's.
M_____	Medical.
MS_____	Military Secretary's.
O_____	Ordnance.
P_____	Royal Army Pay Corps.
PM_____	Provost-Marshal's.
PR_____	Director of Public Relations.
Q_____	Quarter-Master-General's.
S_____	Signals.
SC_____	Staff Captain.
ST_____	Supply and Transport.
TA_____	Territorial Army Directorate.

(5) *Dominions Armies.*—Each dominion in the British Commonwealth of Nations has its own Army organized and equipped substantially in the same way as the British Army. The uniforms, insignia of rank, etc., are, with minor differences, the same.

85. Royal Air Force.—*a. Uniforms.*—(1) *General.*—There are two dress uniforms which are not worn during wartime: full dress, of slate blue (for use of officers on ceremonial occasions), and mess dress, of slate blue (for evening wear by officers in mess).

(2) *Service dress.*—The service-dress uniform, of slate blue, for officers and airmen (fig. 51 and plate VIII), is used for wear in cold or temperate climates. The single-breasted coat is belted at the waist and has four pockets (the upper two are patched). The trousers are long and cuffless. A black necktie is worn with the shirt, which is of lighter blue. Overcoats and raincoats are of slate blue, as well as the working dress (plate VIII). Officers and airmen wear a service-dress cap, or on informal occasions they may alternatively wear a field-service, or forage, cap (fig. 51).

(3) *Tropical service dress.*—This uniform, of khaki drill, for officers and airmen may be worn with the coat or with shirt sleeves. The

shirt is of khaki, and with it is worn a black necktie. Shorts and short sleeves may be worn in very hot weather.

(4) *Tropical mess dress.*—This uniform, of white drill, for wear by officers in mess is not obligatory in wartime.

b. Insignia.—(1) *Commissioned officers.*—(*a*) *Dress uniforms.*—The rank is shown by gold bands on both sleeves.

(*b*) *Service dress.*—The rank is shown by blue and white bands on the sleeves of the coat and on the shoulder straps of the overcoat. Both service-dress and dress sleeve insignia ("rings") are shown in plate VI.

FIGURE 51.—RAF officers in service dress (after receiving awards and decorations).

(*c*) *Tropical service dress.*—The rank is shown by blue and white bands on removable shoulder straps, or, if worn with shirt sleeves, on removable shoulder loops.

(*d*) *Tropical mess dress.*—The rank is shown by gold bands on blue removable shoulder straps.

(*e*) *Caps and cap badges.*—The service-dress cap for all officers up to and including the rank of wing commander has a plain (slate blue) cloth visor; for the group captain, a black (patent leather) visor with one row of gold oak leaves; and for air officers, a black (patent leather) visor with two rows of gold oak leaves. The cap badge is also different

123

for air officers and chaplains. (See plate VII.) The field-service cap for air officers is edged with pale blue piping (plate VII).

(*f*) *Other badges.*—The pilot's flying badge ("wings"), and the badges of the observer and the air gunner are worn on the left breast of the coat just above the pockets and above any service ribbons (fig. 51 and plate VII). Chaplains and medical and dental officers wear distinctive badges on the collar.

(2) *Airmen.*—(*a*) The rank of airmen is shown by insignia on both sleeves of the coat and the overcoat. The metal badge of rank of the warrant officer is worn on the cuffs of both sleeves. The insignia of rank of other noncommissioned officers are worn on both upper sleeves, the various chevrons point-down. (See fig. 51 and plate VIII.)

(*b*) Other insignia showing duties are worn on both upper sleeves. The chevron for good conduct is worn point-up on the lower left sleeve only. (See plate VIII.)

(*c*) At the top of both sleeves, all airmen wear a rectangular piece of cloth on which the RAF eagle is embroidered: in blue on the service dress; in red on the tropical service dress.

(*d*) The visor of the service-dress cap for all airmen is of black (patent leather), and the cap badge is distinctive (plate VII).

(3) *Distinguishing shoulder titles.*—During the present war, authority has been given to RAF personnel whose country of origin is a dominion of the British Commonwealth of Nations, or an allied nation, to wear the name of the country of origin in pale blue at the top of both sleeves in service dress. Some care may be needed on occasion not to confuse RAF personnel wearing these distinguishing badges with personnel belonging to the air forces of the dominions.

c. Royal Observer Corps.—The Royal Observer Corps (ROC) is a component of the RAF. Officers wear the RAF uniform with black braid on the cuffs of sleeves and a special cap badge. Other members wear a buttonhole badge.

d. Auxiliary and Volunteer Reserve.—The Auxiliary Air Force (AAF) and the RAF Volunteer Reserve (RAFVR) wear the same uniforms as the RAF. However, members of the Auxiliary wear the letter "A," and members of the Volunteer Reserve wear the letters "VR," in gilt on the collar. Members of the American Eagle Squadron also wear the letters "VR" in gilt on the collar, and a special badge at the top of both sleeves.

e. Dominions air forces.—Each dominion in the British Commonwealth of Nations has its own air force. The Royal Canadian Air Force (RCAF) and the Royal New Zealand Air Force (RNZAF) wear uniforms of the same pattern and color as the RAF uniform, but are to be distinguished by slightly different buttons and by different lettering in the center of the pilot's badge. The Royal Australian Air Force (RAAF) wears a uniform of the same pattern but made of dark blue cloth. The South African Air Force (SAAF) wears a khaki uniform with Army insignia of rank.

86. Decorations and awards.—*a. General.*—Many decorations and awards are available for outstanding performances by civilians and by men and women in the Royal Navy, the Army, the Royal Air Force, and auxiliary services. The Victoria Cross and the George Cross take precedence over all other decorations. Then come the various Orders; other medals for valor or gallantry; campaign medals, in order of date; Coronation and Jubilee medals; long service and good conduct medals; and miscellaneous awards. Service ribbons for various medals are illustrated in order of precedence in plates X and XI.

b. Highest decorations.—(1) *Victoria Cross (VC)* (plate IX).—To all ranks of the three services and to civilians acting under their order, direction, or supervision; instituted in 1856. The VC can be won only "by performing in the presence of the enemy some signal act of valour or devotion to the Country," and when worn, this bronze cross takes precedence over every other decoration. When the service ribbon is worn, a miniature replica of the cross in bronze is affixed to the center of it (plate X). If the recipient wins the award twice, another replica cross is added to the ribbon. Women have been eligible for the VC since 1920.

(2) *George Cross (GC)*[11] (plate IX).—To men and women in all walks of life; instituted in 1940. The military division of the GC permits its award to members of the fighting services who have performed acts coming within the terms of the warrant. When the service ribbon is worn, a miniature replica of the cross in silver is affixed to the center of it (plate X).

c. Orders.—(1) The Most Noble Order of the Garter, the Most Ancient and Most Noble Order of the Thistle, and the Most Illustrious Order of St. Patrick are the three most important Orders of British chivalry, and the recipients of the awards, the Knight of the Garter (KG), the Knight of the Thistle (KT), and the Knight of St. Patrick (KP), represent the three highest Orders of Knighthood in Great Britain. The Garter is awarded, outside the British royal family, only to a few peers of very high rank, to one or two statesmen of

---

[11] The George Medal (plate IX), created at the same time as the George Cross, recognizes civilian bravery, and will be awarded more freely than the GC. The Medal of the Order of the British Empire, for Gallantry, known as the "Empire Gallantry Medal" (EGM), has been replaced by the GM, and all holders of the EGM have been awarded the GM.

particular eminence, and occasionally to members of certain foreign royal families. The Thistle and the Patrick, although awarded to equally eminent personages, are open only to Scotsmen and Irishmen, respectively. The Order of Merit (OM) is limited to a total of 24 eminent people, who may be in any sphere of activity, and is one of the very few distinctions of first rank which does not carry a knighthood. These four Orders are not indicated by any ribbons except when the holder is wearing full dress; and on these occasions the particular Order is indicated by various insignia, including a sash of the appropriate color.

(2) Other outstanding Orders, most of which contain military divisions, are the Most Honourable Order of the Bath, the Most Exalted Order of the Star of India, the Most Distinguished Order of St. Michael and St. George, the Most Eminent Order of the Indian Empire, the Royal Victorian Order, the Most Excellent Order of the British Empire, and the Order of the Companions of Honour. The first three of these Orders have three classes—Knights Grand Cross, Knights Commanders, and Companions. The next two Orders have five classes: the Victorian Order has the three mentioned above, and Members of the fourth and fifth classes; the Order of the British Empire has as its additional classes Officers and Members of the Order. The Order of the Companions of Honour consists of one class only, but ranks after the first class of the Order of the British Empire. The ribbons of these seven Orders are worn immediately after the VC and the GC and before other medals for valor and gallantry.

d. Other medals for valor and gallantry.—(1) *Distinguished Service Order (DSO)* (plate IX).—To commissioned officers in any of the three services. The DSO is awarded to an officer who has been specially mentioned in dispatches for meritorious or distinguished service in the field or in the presence of the enemy. The DSO is the next most important decoration after the George Cross.

(2) *Distinguished Service Cross (DSC)*.—To naval and marine officers of or below the relative rank of lieutenant-commander, and to warrant officers, who have been mentioned in dispatches for meritorious or distinguished service.

(3) *Military Cross (MC)* (plate IX).—To Army officers of or below the rank of captain and to warrant officers, class I, for acts of distinction or gallantry in the field. Its naval counterpart is the DSC.

(4) *Distinguished Flying Cross (DFC)* (plate IX).—To officers and warrant officers of the RAF for valor, courage, or devotion to duty while flying in active operations against the enemy.

(5) *Air Force Cross (AFC)*.—To officers and warrant officers of the RAF, or of the other services, and to civilians for courage or devotion to duty, though not in active operations against the enemy.

(6) *Distinguished Conduct Medal (DCM)* (plate IX).—To enlisted men of the Army for gallantry in action. The DCM is awarded on the recommendation of the Commander-in-Chief, and carries a small pension or gratuity. Its naval counterpart is the CGM.

(7) *Conspicuous Gallantry Medal (CGM)* (plate IX).—To enlisted men of the Royal Navy, the Royal Marines, and the Fleet Air Arm for acts of conspicuous gallantry in action. Its obverse is the same as that of the DCM and the MM.

(8) *Distinguished Service Medal (DSM)*.—To enlisted men of the Royal Navy and the Royal Marines for acts of bravery under fire.

(9) *Military Medal (MM)* (plate IX).—To enlisted men of the Army for individual or associated acts of bravery brought to notice by the recommendation of the Commander-in-Chief in the field. Its naval counterpart is the DSM, and its obverse is the same as that of the DCM and the CGM.

(10) *Distinguished Flying Medal (DFM)*.—To enlisted men of the RAF for the same feats of gallantry for which the DFC is awarded to RAF officers.

(11) *Air Force Medal (AFM)*.—To enlisted men of the RAF, or of the other services, and to civilians for courage or devotion to duty while flying, though not in active operations against the enemy.

e. Campaign medals.—These medals have been awarded to cover campaigns which often extended over a period of years and usually included a number of individual battles. To commemorate these battles, clasps, with the names of the battles engraved on them, were awarded the holders who had taken part in them. These clasps are affixed to the ribbon above the medal, but are not worn when the service ribbon is worn.

f. Other miscellaneous decorations.—Other types of miscellaneous decorations include Jubilee and Coronation medals; commemorative medals struck in honor of special events or performances; and long service and good conduct medals. The Army award for long service and good conduct was instituted in 1830; the Royal Navy, in 1831; the RAF, in 1919.

	Weapon	Caliber (inches)	Approximate weight (pounds)	Rate of fire (rounds per minute)			Maximum effective range (yards)	Remarks
				Rapid	Medium	Slow		
	(a)	(b)	(c)	(d)	(e)	(f)	(g)	(h)
1	Rifle. No. 1, Mk. III. No. 4, Mk. I.	.303	8¾	15		5	1,000	A shoulder-controlled weapon to which can be affixed a bayonet or a discharger cup (see 7, below). Individual fire is rarely effective beyond 600 yards.
2	Pistol	.38	1¾				50	A 6-shot pistol-revolver, carried by officers, dispatch riders, and noncommissioned officers of the rank of sergeant and above.
3	Boys anti-tank rifle	.55	36	9	5		500	A shoulder-controlled weapon.
4	Light machine gun (Bren).	.303	Gun, 23; tripod, 30	120	100	30 to 60	Bipod, 1,000; tripod, 2,000.	An air-cooled gun capable of being fired from the shoulder, with bipod or tripod; it can be laid on fixed lines.
5	Light machine gun (Lewis).	.303	26	120			1,600	A shoulder-controlled weapon with no equipment for laying on fixed lines.
6	Heavy machine gun (Vickers).	.303	Tripod, 56; gun with 10 pounds of water, 42.	250	125	60 to 75	2,000	A water-cooled gun capable of sustained rapid fire. Its heavy mounting admits of laying on fixed lines and of indirect fire. It has an all-around traverse.
7	Hand grenade, HE	2½	1½				By discharger, 80 to 200; by hand, 30.	The grenade can also be fired from a discharger cup attached to the rifle. It is propelled by a blank cartridge filled with ballistite.
8	Smoke grenade	2½	1¼	10	5		250	Fired from a discharger cup.
9	2-inch mortar	2	23½	10	5		470	Each bomb weighs 2¼ pounds; 33 percent of smoke bombs are carried.
10	3-inch mortar	3	Piece, 42; base plate, 37; bipod, sight, box and cradle, 45.	10	5		1,600	Each bomb weighs 10 pounds; 25 percent of smoke bombs are carried.
11	29-mm spigot mortar	29-mm	49¼	12	6		425	A very good short-range AT weapon; throws 14- and 2½-pound bombs.

FIGURE 52.—Characteristics of infantry weapons.

Chapter 5

ARMAMENT AND EQUIPMENT

SECTION I

INFANTRY

87. Characteristics of weapons.—The tabulation in figure 52 gives the characteristics of the principal British infantry weapons.

88. Hand arms.—Riflemen are armed with the Lee-Enfield rifle (fig. 53), caliber .303, weighing, when empty, from 8 pounds 10½ ounces to 8 pounds 14½ ounces, with a sword-type or dagger-type bayonet. Its maximum muzzle velocity is 2,400 feet per second. The standard pistol is a 6-shot revolver (Webley), caliber .38 (fig. 54).

89. Rifle.—*a. General.*—The Lee-Enfield rifle is a breechloading magazine rifle of the bolt type. The No. 4, Mk. I, is now replacing the No. 1, Mk. III. Essentially, both types are like the U. S. rifle, caliber .30, M1903 (Springfield).

(1) Nature of weapon: magazine-fed bolt-action shoulder rifle.

(2) Weight: about 8¾ pounds (No. 1, Mk. III—8 pounds 14½ ounces; No. 4, Mk. I—8 pounds 10½ ounces).

(3) Length: 3 feet 8½ inches.

(4) Effective range: 600 yards; maximum, 2,000 yards.

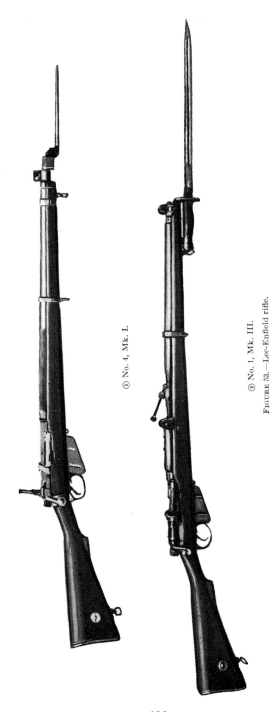

① No. 4, Mk. I.

② No. 1, Mk. III.

FIGURE 53.—Lee-Enfield rifle.

(5) Ammunition: caliber .303 inch; weight of bullet, 175 grains; magazine holds 10 rounds.

(6) Rate of fire: 5 rounds per minute (normal); 15 rounds per minute (rapid).

b. Bayonets.—Two types of bayonets are employed, a sword-type (similar to the U. S. M1905) and a dagger-type (No. 4, Mk. I). The latter (fig. 53 ①), now standard, is 9 inches long, of cruciform section with tapering point. It weighs 10⅝ ounces (bayonet, 7 ounces; scabbard, 3⅝ ounces).

c. Ammunition.—Ammunition comes packed in wooden boxes, either carton-packed for loading into magazines of automatic weapons or bandolier-packed (i. e., in clips) for use with rifles. The type of ammunition is always plainly marked on the box.

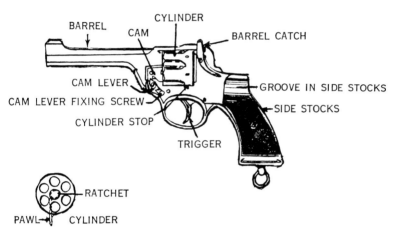

FIGURE 54.—Webley pistol-revolver.

90. Pistol.—The Webley pistol-revolver No. 2, Mk. I, caliber .38, which is replacing the Webley pistol-revolver, No. 1, Mk. VI, caliber .455, is carried by all officers, dispatch riders, and noncommissioned officers of the rank of sergeant or above. The cylinder carries six ball cartridges. Although the maximum effective range is 50 yards, it is most effective at 20 yards and under.

a. Weight: 1 pound 11½ ounces.

b. Length: 10¼ inches (barrel, 5 inches).

c. Depth: 5 inches.

d. Number of chambers: 6.

e. Pitch: 1 turn in 15 inches.

f. Number of grooves: **7.**

91. Machine guns.—*a. Thompson submachine gun.*—The Thompson submachine gun, familiarly known as the "Tommy gun," is used extensively throughout the British Army. The gun, caliber .45, weighs approximately 10 pounds. It is equipped with 2 types of magazine: a box holding 20 rounds and a drum holding 50. It is reasonably accurate up to 50 yards or slightly more. (See the center guardsman in fig. 48.)

b. Sten machine carbine.—This gun is being issued at a rapid rate to air-borne forces, tank crews, reconnaissance units, etc. It can be produced rapidly and at small cost. This fact, together with its light weight, small size, high rate of fire, and great accuracy, has resulted in its use for tasks for which the pistol and the "Tommy gun" have proved inadequate.

(1) Nature of weapon: 9-mm machine carbine.

(2) Weight: 6 pounds 10 ounces.

(3) Length: 30 inches.

(4) Effective range: 200 yards.

(5) Ammunition: 8 magazines, each holding 32 rounds.

(6) Rate of fire: 500 rounds per minute.

c. Bren light machine gun (fig. 55; see also fig. 14).—The .303-inch Bren light machine gun is the basic automatic weapon in the British Army. The trigger mechanism provides for three positions: safety, continuous fire, and single shots (figs. 55 and 56).

(1) Nature of weapon: air-cooled gas-operated magazine-fed machine gun; ordinarily fired from a bipod, but may be mounted on a tripod (fig. 57), an antiaircraft mount (fig. 58), or an armoured automotive carrier (see par. 128). Two guns may also be mounted as a twin.

(2) Weight: 23 pounds.

(3) Length: 45½ inches (barrel, 25 inches).

(4) Traverse: 42° on tripod.

(5) Elevation: 19° on tripod.

(6) Effective range: 600 to 800 yards on bipod; maximum, 2,000 yards.

(7) Ammunition: packed in boxes containing 1,248 rounds per box, and fed into the receiver from a curved magazine, the capacity of which is 30 rounds (26 advisable).

(8) Rate of fire: 450 rounds per minute (maximum); 60 rounds per minute (normal); 120 rounds per minute (rapid).

d. Lewis medium (heavy) machine gun.—The .303-inch Lewis heavy machine gun (called a "medium" MG by the British), although obsolete, is still in use in the Home Guard, but not in the field army except

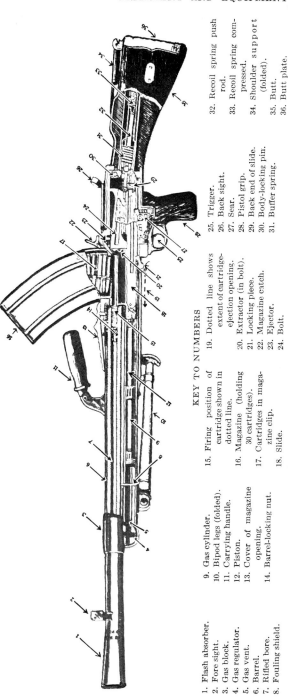

KEY TO NUMBERS

 1. Flash absorber.
 2. Fore sight.
 3. Gas block.
 4. Gas regulator.
 5. Gas vent.
 6. Barrel.
 7. Rifled bore.
 8. Fouling shield.
 9. Gas cylinder.
10. Bipod legs (folded).
11. Carrying handle.
12. Piston.
13. Cover of magazine opening.
14. Barrel-locking nut.
15. Firing position of cartridge shown in dotted line.
16. Magazine (holding 30 cartridges).
17. Cartridges in magazine clip.
18. Slide.
19. Dotted line shows extent of cartridge-ejection opening.
20. Extractor (in bolt).
21. Locking piece.
22. Magazine catch.
23. Ejector.
24. Bolt.
25. Trigger.
26. Back sight.
27. Sear.
28. Pistol grip.
29. Back end of slide.
30. Body-locking pin.
31. Buffer spring.
32. Recoil spring push rod.
33. Recoil spring compressed.
34. Shoulder support (folded).
35. Butt.
36. Butt plate.

To fire the gun when it has been cocked, the trigger (25) is pulled; the sear (27) releases the slide (18), which is forced forward by the push rod (32) set in motion by the recoil spring (33). As the bolt (24) moves forward, it strips the cartridge from the magazine (16) into the firing position (15). Towards the end of its forward movement by the slide (18) rises on beveled lugs and comes to a gradual stop and is locked. The bolt, however, continues its forward movement and its hammer strikes the firing pin and fires the cartridge. As the bullet passes the gas block (3), the expanding powder gases pass through the gas regulator (4) and the gas vent (5) into the gas cylinder (9) and drive back the piston (12). This unlocks the bolt and the slide opens the breech, extracts the spent cartridge, which is drawn back, strikes the ejector (23), and is thrown out through a hole in the base of the gun at 19. The gas, still driving back the piston and slide, compresses the recoil spring (33). When all this has been accomplished, the recoil spring again commences to force the bolt, slide, and piston forward, automatically places the next cartridge in position, and fires it. Then the whole cycle of operations is repeated until all the cartridges in the magazine have been fired. Then the empty magazine is removed and replaced by a charged one. Should the barrel get too hot, it can be replaced by a cool barrel by operating the barrel-locking nut (14).

FIGURE 55.—Diagrammatic sketch of Bren gun.

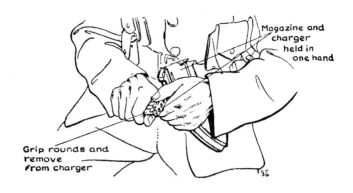

Magazine and charger held in one hand

Grip rounds and remove from charger

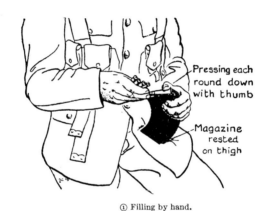

Pressing each round down with thumb

Magazine rested on thigh

① Filling by hand.

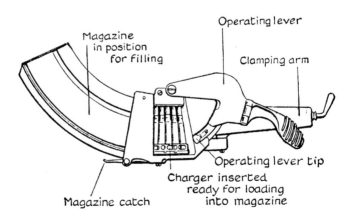

Magazine in position for filling

Operating lever

Clamping arm

Operating lever tip

Magazine catch

Charger inserted ready for loading into magazine

② Filling by magazine filler.

FIGURE 56.—Operation of Bren gun.

134

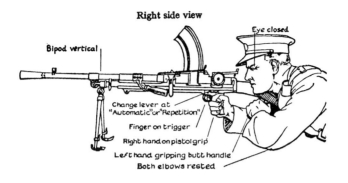

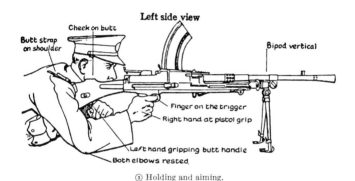

③ Holding and aiming.

④ Correct aim.

FIGURE 56 (*continued*).—Operation of Bren gun.

135

FIGURE 57.—Bren gun mounted on tripod, showing bipod.

FIGURE 58.—Bren gun on anti-aircraft mount.

occasionally as a weapon for ground defence.　In the Home Guard it is used extensively for beach defence, and can be mounted on an anti-aircraft mount for use against low-flying airplanes.

(1) Nature of weapon: air-cooled gas-operated machine gun.
(2) Weight: 26 pounds.
(3) Length: 50½ inches.
(4) Length of barrel: 26¼ inches.
(5) Ammunition: fed by a circular steel cylinder.
(6) Rate of fire: 150 rounds per minute (maximum).

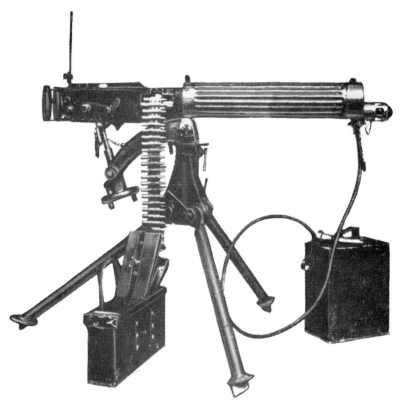

FIGURE 59.—Vickers .303 medium (heavy) machine gun.

e. Vickers medium (heavy) machine gun (fig. 59).—The .303-inch Vickers heavy machine gun (called a "medium" MG by the British) is the basic weapon of the (heavy) machine-gun battalion. The mounting consists of a crosshead elevating gear and a socket mounted on three legs. Cartridges are held in a web belt which passes from right to left through the feed block.

137

(1) Nature of weapon: water-cooled recoil-operated machine gun.

(2) Weight: approximately 32 pounds; including water, 42 pounds.

(3) Length: 43¾ inches.

(4) Traverse: 360°.

(5) Elevation: −25° to +13°; by using adjustable legs, −55° to +43°.

(6) Effective range: 400 yards; maximum, 2,000 yards.

(7) Ammunition: web belt holds 250 rounds.

(8) Rate of fire: 500 to 600 rounds per minute (maximum); 125 rounds per minute (normal); 250 rounds per minute (rapid).

The caliber .303 Vickers is also mounted in tanks (see fig. 87). For other tank-mounted machine guns, see paragraph 110c.

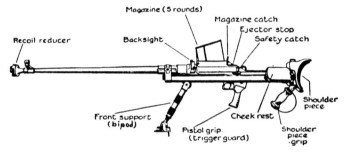

① Left-side view.

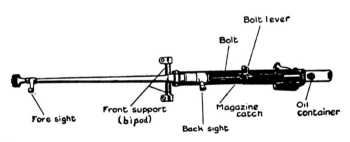

② Top view.

FIGURE 60.—Boys anti-tank rifle.

92. Anti-tank rifle.[1]—*a. General.*—The Boys anti-tank rifle (fig. 60) is an ordinary bolt-action magazine rifle, caliber .55, firing a 930-grain armour-piercing bullet at an undisclosed muzzle velocity, probably about 3,000 feet per second. It will penetrate 24-mm armour at normal angle of incidence at 100 yards, and 9-mm armour at a 40° angle at 500 yards. Its rate of issue is one to each platoon

---

[1] Since the British consider anti-tank guns as part of the artillery, the 2-pounder and 6-pounder anti-tank guns are discussed under section II; anti-tank grenades are discussed in paragraph 94b.

FIGURE 61.—2-inch mortars.

or similar unit commanded by a subaltern, including those employed in rear areas.

b. Characteristics.—The shoulder rest has a quickly replaceable rubber pad. Neither it nor the left-hand support is adjustable, however. The bipod support is adjustable for height, the adjustment being made by the left hand. It is intended that the weapon be carried upside down by using the bipod as a handle. Both front and rear sights are offset to the left in order to clear the magazine, which projects vertically above the receiver. Both sights are of the ring type; the front is fixed and the rear is adjustable to two positions corresponding to 300 and 500 yards. The rifle has a hand-operated bolt. Recoil is absorbed by a muzzle brake and spring buffer.

(1) Nature of weapon: bolt-action magazine rifle, fired from bipod.

(2) Weight: 36 pounds.

(3) Length: 5 feet 4 inches.

(4) Effective range: 200 yards; maximum, 500 yards.

(5) Ammunition: magazine holds 5 rounds; weight of round, 1,994 grains.

(6) Rate of fire: 9 rounds per minute (for trained soldier).

93. Mortars.—*a. General.*—Infantry battalions are equipped with 2-inch and 3-inch trench mortars, and a 4.2-inch is being introduced. The 2-inch mortar weighs about 23½ pounds and fires a 2½-pound HE

FIGURE 62.— 3-inch mortar.

or smoke projectile a maximum of 470 yards.   The 3-inch mortar fires a 10-pound HE or smoke projectile with a maximum range of 1,600 yards. It is transported in three loads with a total weight of 124 pounds.

140

b. 2-inch mortar.—This weapon (fig. 61), with some ammunition, can be carried in action by one man, but it is usually carried in a truck.

(1) Nature of weapon: smooth bore, muzzle-loading, high-angle fire.

(2) Weight: 23½ pounds.

(3) Length: 25 inches.

(4) Traverse: 60°.

(5) Elevation: 68°.

(6) Effective range: 470 yards.

(7) Ammunition: HE or smoke bomb; weight of shell, 2 pounds.

(8) Rate of fire: 5 rounds per minute.

c. 3-inch mortar (fig. 62).—On the move this mortar is carried in a specially constructed carrier box in a truck. When brought into action, it is carried by man-harness and is a load for three men. The ammunition is transported for short distances in three-round bomb carriers, but for long transit, or when the battalion is on the march, it is carried in steel ammunition boxes.

(1) Nature of weapon: smooth bore, muzzle-loading, high-angle fire.

(2) Weight: 124 pounds (weight of mortar, 42 pounds; mounting, 45 pounds; base plate, 37 pounds).

(3) Length: 51 inches.

(4) Traverse: 36°.

(5) Elevation: 45° to 80°.

(6) Effective range: 1,600 yards.

(7) Ammunition: HE or smoke bomb; weight of each, 10 pounds.

(8) Rate of fire: 5 rounds per minute.

d. 29-mm spigot mortar.—The 29-mm spigot mortar throws 14- and 20-pound bombs, which are very effective against 3½-inch armour. Other details are given in figure 52.

94. Grenades.—*a. General.*—(1) *Types.*—(*a*) There are three types of grenades: HE (fig. 63), smoke, and signal. The HE grenade can be thrown by hand a distance of 25 to 35 yards. The HE and smoke grenade can be fired from a rifle by means of an attachment called the "discharger" (see figs. 64 and 65). When fired from the rifle, both grenades have an approximate maximum range of 200 yards and a minimum of 80 yards.

(*b*) The weight of the HE grenade is about 1½ pounds, and that of the smoke grenade 1¼ pounds. The probable danger area of the HE grenade may be taken to be 20 yards in all directions from the point of burst. Large fragments may, however, have sufficient velocity to inflict wounds at distances of 100 yards or more. Mechanically the grenade is very similar to the U. S. Mk. II grenade.

(2) *Operation.*—The grenade should be held firmly with the lever under the fingers while the safety pin is withdrawn. So long as the

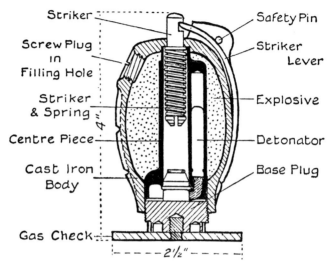

FIGURE 63.— High-explosive grenade.

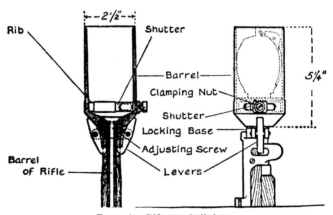

FIGURE 64.—Rifle grenade discharger.

lever is held, the grenade is safe. When the grenade leaves the hand or discharger, the lever flies off, and the striker is forced down onto the cap of the igniter-set by the spring and ignites the fuze, which burns for 7 seconds.

(3) *No. 69 bakelite hand grenade.*—This grenade, which weighs about 8 ounces, has been introduced with the object of providing a light

142

hand percussion grenade for offensive action. The area of burst is very restricted, and it may be thrown from a standing position in the open with impunity to the thrower. The material effect of the grenade is very small and local, but the moral effect is considerable. It is of particular value for patrols in a clash with the enemy. The No. 69 is replacing the heavier No. 36.

  b. Anti-tank grenades.—There are several types of anti-tank grenades:

  (1) *Phosphorus grenade, or AW (Albright & Wilson) grenade, an improved type of "Molotov cocktail."*—This grenade produces an

FIGURE 65.—Firing the rifle grenade discharger.

incendiary mixture and a dense cloud of smoke. A special mortar for throwing AW grenades, known as the Northover projector, has been developed.

  (2) *No. 68 anti-tank grenade (rifle).*—(a) This grenade, which weighs about 1¾ pounds, is fired from the discharger fitted to the service rifle, a 30-grain ballistite cartridge being used. Since it is essential for the grenade to hit the vehicle, a rough sight is provided. Because the use of the sight requires a low trajectory, the effective range is from 75 to 100 yards. On impact, the armour of light, medium, and, in some cases, heavy tanks will be penetrated.

  (b) The ballistite cartridge used with this grenade gives a considerable recoil; and because the rifle must be held at a flat angle, it is essential to place the butt of the rifle against a sandbag or similar object. If possible, the muzzle of the rifle should also be supported on a sandbag.

  (3) *No. 73 anti-tank grenade (hand).*—The object of this grenade is to damage armoured fighting vehicles, the best effect being attained when it is used against the track or suspension of a tank. Because of

its weight (about 4 pounds) and shape, it can be thrown only short distances (10 to 15 yards); and because of its powerful nature, it is absolutely essential that the thrower be behind cover. The use of it, therefore, is limited to static defence or to road blocks.

(4) *ST* (*sticky type*) *anti-tank grenade* (*hand*).—(*a*) This grenade has been introduced for use against light AFV's (armoured force vehicles). It is designed to stick to a suitable target, thus insuring that the HE has its maximum effect. The grenade will not stick if the surface is wet or muddy.

(*b*) The ST grenade is suitable for use at road blocks and in positions of ambush, or for dropping from upstairs windows onto tanks.

(*c*) Although the effect of the explosion is localized, the thrower must take cover because of the blast.

(*d*) For night raids on tank parks, this grenade is an ideal weapon. It can be regarded as a portable demolition charge and planted by hand instead of thrown, so long as the operator retreats in such a direction that he is protected from the explosion. With practice and training, the grenade can be thrown up to about 20 yards.

(5) *Hawkins anti-tank grenade-mine* (*hand*).—This grenade really amounts to a hand-thrown AT mine. It consists of an oval-shaped tin 4¾ by 3¾ by 2¼ inches, filled with 1½ pounds of HE and bound with wire.

95. Rifle grenade discharger (fig. 64).—*a. To fire.*—In order to fire the grenade, the discharger is attached to the rifle, which is then loaded with a ballistite cartridge, and the grenade placed in the discharger. A ballistite cartridge only should be used; half of its length is blackened to distinguish it from other cartridges. In firing (fig. 65) HE or smoke grenades, the barrel of the rifle must be kept at an angle of 45°. In the case of signal grenades, the rifle will be held at an angle of 70°, with the gas port closed. Longer or shorter ranges will be obtained by adjustments of the gas port. To obtain extreme range, the gas port will be fully closed, whereas for the shortest range the gas port will be fully opened.

b. Range.—The following range table shows the average distances that the grenade will be fired according to the various adjustments made to the gas port with the rifle at 45°:

Gas port	Range (yards)
Fully open	80
¾ open	110
½ open	140
¼ open	170
Fully closed	200

FIGURE 66.— Some of the infantry soldier's individual equipment.

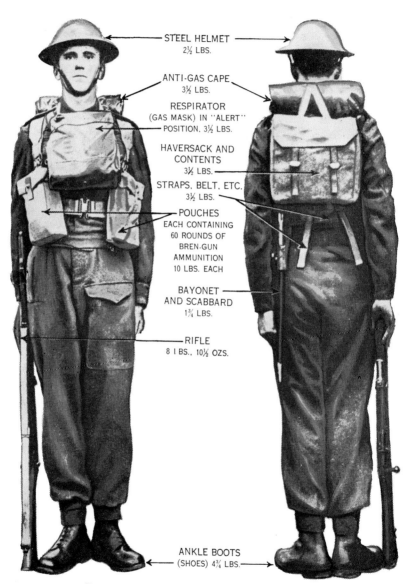

STEEL HELMET
2½ LBS.

ANTI-GAS CAPE
3½ LBS.

RESPIRATOR
(GAS MASK) IN "ALERT"
POSITION, 3½ LBS.

HAVERSACK AND
CONTENTS
3½ LBS.

STRAPS, BELT, ETC.
3½ LBS.

POUCHES
EACH CONTAINING
60 ROUNDS OF
BREN-GUN
AMMUNITION
10 LBS. EACH

BAYONET
AND SCABBARD
1¾ LBS.

RIFLE
8 1 BS., 10½ OZS.

ANKLE BOOTS
(SHOES) 4¾ LBS.

FIGURE 67.—Infantry soldier in some of his equipment.

146

96. Individual equipment.—*a.* The infantry soldier equipped for active service carries a caliber .303 rifle, a bayonet, 50 rounds of ammunition, rations in a ration bag, and the articles pictured in figure 66. These include (from left to right, back row, then front row): ground sheet; greatcoat (overcoat); pay book and identity disk; kit bag; service respirator (gas mask); socks; overalls; haversack; pack; water bottle (canteen); steel helmet; canvas shoes (sneakers); gloves; underclothes; hold-all containing jackknife, shaving brush, tooth brush, spoon, fork, knife, razor, etc.; five brushes; towel; soap and tooth powder; pull-over (sweater); cap-comforter; housewife (a roll of cloth containing cotton, needles, buttons, etc.); shirt; and spare shoes. The overcoat is usually carried in unit transport. The weight of equipment worn and carried is 55 pounds. A mess tin (not shown in the illustration) is also carried.

b. The illustrations in figure 67 show a soldier dressed in some of this equipment. However, when in full marching order he carries a valise (pack) on his back in place of the haversack, the latter being transferred to the left hip above the bayonet (see fig. 45③ and ④). The equipment of the officer differs from that of the enlisted man in that the officer carries a caliber .38 revolver and 12 rounds of ammunition.

SECTION II

ARTILLERY

97. General.—*a.* The tabulation in figure 68 contains data pertaining to the principal British field artillery weapons. These are the 2-pounder, the 6-pounder, and the 17-pounder antitank guns; the 25-pounder field gun-howitzer, (the standard field gun of the British); the 3.7-inch howitzer; the 4.5-inch gun; the 5.5-inch gun-howitzer; and the 7.2-inch howitzer.

b. Instead of mils the British use degrees, minutes, and tenths of minutes, and their instruments are so graduated.

98. Ammunition.—*a. General.*—Artillery ammunition falls into two categories: QF (quick-firing) and BL (breechloading, or U. S. separate loading). In turn, quick-firing is subdivided into "fixed," which is the same as U. S. "fixed," and "separate," which is approximately equivalent to U. S. "semifixed." Breechloading ammunition s always shipped in four parts, as follows:

4.5-inch howitzer.

7.2-inch howitzer.

Weapon	Employment	Maximum range	Traverse	Elevation	Weight in firing position	Muzzle velocity (foot-seconds)	Caliber	Length in calibers	Transport	Trail	Weight of projectile
		Yards	Degrees	Degrees	Pounds	Foot-seconds	Inches				Pounds
18-pounder (3.3-inch gun)	Miscellaneous	9,400	50	38	3,450	1,615	3.3	30	Motorized	Split	18.5
25-pounder (3.45-inch gun-howitzer)	Division	12,500	1 8¹	40	3,968	1,470 to 1,747	3.45	20.65	do	Box	25
3.7-inch howitzer	do	6,000	40	42½	1,860	971	3.7	12.6	do	Split	20
4.5-inch howitzer	do	6,600	60	45	3,464	1,006	4.5	15.5	do	Box	35
4.5-inch gun	Corps	20,500	60	45	16,048	2,265	4.5	42.8	do	Split	55
5.5-inch gun-howitzer	do	16,000	60	45	12,768	1,235 to 1,340	5.5	31.2	do	do	100
6-inch howitzer	do	11,400	8	45	10,088	1,235 to 1,352	6	13.3	do	Box	100
6-inch gun	Army	20,000	7	45	29,750	2,500	6	45	do	do	100
7.2-inch howitzer	do	16,900	8	45	22,750	1,700	7.2	23.7	do	do	200
9.2-inch howitzer	do	13,000	60	50	34,227	1,500	9.2	18.5	do	do	290

¹ 360° on firing platform.

FIGURE 68.—Characteristics of field artillery weapons.

(1) Tubes (equal U. S. primers).

(2) Cartridges (equal U. S. propelling charges).

(3) Shells.

(4) Fuzes.

b. Markings.—(1) *Basic colors.*—The following basic colors are used to denote the four main classes of ammunition:

(*a*) Yellow—High-explosive (HE).

(*b*) Green—Smoke.

(*c*) Grey—Gas.

(*d*) Black—Powder-filled ammunition of armour-piercing (AP) shot.

(2) *Filled shells.*—A red ring around the nose of the shell denotes that the shell is filled. In the case of filled HE shells suitable for tropical climates, the red ring is replaced by a band of red crosses.

(3) *HE shell.*—The various HE fillings are denoted as follows:

(*a*) *Lyddite.*—Yellow shell.

(*b*) *TNT.*—Yellow shell with a green band on the shoulder, stenciled "TNT" in black on the band.

(*c*) *TNT beeswax.*—As above, but stenciled "TNT/BX" with the fraction "93/7" in black below the green band.

(*d*) *Amatol 80/20.*—Yellow shell with a green band on the shoulder; if the mixture of ammonium nitrate and TNT is other than 80/20, the fraction is stenciled in black below the green band.

(*e*) *Pentolite.*—Yellow shell with a green band on the shoulder and a thin black line superimposed on the green band.

(*f*) *Research Department X beeswax.*—Yellow shell with a green band on the shoulder and "RDX/BX" stenciled in black on the band.

(4) *Smoke ammunition.*—The markings for smoke ammunition are as follows:

(*a*) *Phosphorus (burster container).*—Green shell stenciled "PHOS" in black on the shoulder.

(*b*) *Base ejection type.*—Green shell with two white rectangular patches and the number of smoke composition stenciled on each patch.

c. Additional markings.—The following additional markings are commonly encountered:

(1) *Shrapnel.*—Black shell, with a red tip.

(2) *AP shot.*—Black shell, with a double white ring around the nose.

(3) *Star shell.*—Black shell, with a white circle on the shoulder containing a red star.

(4) *AP shell.*—White ring on either side of the red filling ring.

(5) *HE shell with smoke box.*—Markings as already indicated with the addition of two diametrically opposed green disks.

(6) *Shell fitted with economy driving bands.*—Markings as already indicated with the addition of two stripes on opposite sides of the shell extending from the shoulder to the driving (rotating) band.

(7) *Projectiles fitted with tracer.*—"T" indicates tracer, and "TF" tracer combined with fuze; the markings are stenciled on the body of the shell.

(8) *Projectiles suitable for gun and howitzer.*—If a gun or howitzer of the same caliber exists, the letters "GUN" or "HOW" are stenciled after the caliber and a 2-inch black or white band is painted above the driving band of the shell suitable for use.

d. Base ejection smoke shell.—A bursting charge in the forward end forces, by means of steel baffle plates, three smoke canisters out of the rear. As extreme accuracy is not essential, a combination fuze with powder-train elements is used.

99. Anti-tank guns.—*a. 2-pounder.*—(1) *Characteristics.*—The Vickers-Armstrong 2-pounder AT gun, Mk. I, is a semiautomatic caliber 40-mm (1.58-inch) weapon with a muzzle velocity of 2,616 feet per second. It has a $\frac{5}{16}$-inch armour-plate shield and is carried on two rubber-tired wheels, towed by a $\frac{3}{4}$-ton truck. For firing, it is lowered to three outriggers (figs. 69 and 70). It may also be installed in the turret of a tank. Its effective range is not more than 500 yards.

(*a*) Nature of weapon: high-velocity AT cannon.

(*b*) Weight: 1,848 pounds.

(*c*) Length: 11 feet 2 inches (bore, 78.75 inches).

(*d*) Traverse: 360° (if placed on legs).

(*e*) Elevation: −13° to +15°.

(*f*) Ammunition: fixed, AP with tracer (practice), weighing 4.5 pounds complete, the projectile alone weighing 2 pounds 6 ounces; 14 rounds carried on the carriage and 98 in the truck.

(*g*) Rate of fire: 22 rounds per minute.

(2) *Operation.*—(*a*) The gunner's position is on the seat to the left of the gun, as in figure 70. The vertical handwheel on the left controls elevation. The trigger control is attached to this handwheel. Traversing is accomplished by a horizontal handwheel to the right of the gunner. For rapid traverse, a throw-out clutch at the right foot of the gunner allows the NCO gun commander to traverse the gun, pedestal, and gunner together by pressing on the shoulders of the gunner.

(*b*) Three independent sights are provided. The first, a simple ring and bead type, is used by the NCO gun commander for approximate setting. The other two sights are used by the gunner. The

FIGURE 69.—Vickers-Armstrong 2-pounder (anti-tank gun), Mk. I (rear view).

FIGURE 70.—Vickers-Armstrong 2-pounder (anti-tank gun), Mk. I (left view).

telescopic sight has a field of approximately 20°, and a magnification of approximately four times. There is a fixed vertical line and a movable horizontal line with range marks at the left for 300, 600, 900,

1,200, and 1,500 yards. A small knob directly above the sight, provided with a click, permits movement of the horizontal line by increments of 100 yards. This operation is performed by the NCO gun commander after initial setting by the gunner in accordance with oral instructions of the commander. Mounted on and above the telescopic sight is a forward bead sight and a rear notch-type sight, adjustable in training and elevation. Attached to the left side of the pedestal is a receptacle for a spare telescopic sight.

(3) *Portee.*—In order to increase the mobility of the 2-pounder anti-tank gun, the British have been employing it portee on a 30-cwt truck. A recent development has been light self-propelled or assault artillery in which the 2-pounder anti-tank gun is mounted on

FIGURE 71.—6-pounder anti-tank gun.

the Loyd carrier. The regular shield of the 2-pounder is utilized for protection against small-arms fire from the front, and additional protection is provided by armour shields on the two sides of the gun.

b. 6-pounder.—The 6-pounder anti-tank gun (fig. 71), with a muzzle velocity of 2,700 feet per second, has been designed by the British for use against enemy armoured vehicles which are not vulnerable to the 2-pounder at distances of over 200 or 300 yards. A 57-mm gun the 6-pounder will be able to engage tanks at much greater ranges than the 2-pounder, although the latter will still be important to the anti-tank defence of individual formations and units. The 6-pounder is normally mounted on a low 90-degree split-trail wheeled carriage but it is also being installed in certain tanks. In order to facilitate the quick adoption of the proper gun for the circumstances, the wheeled carriage of the 6-pounder is so designed that the 2-pounder may be mounted alternatively. It is intended that the 6-pounder be standard in corps and army anti-tank organization.

(1) Nature of weapon: high-velocity AT cannon.

(2) Weight: 2,471 pounds.

(3) Length: 15 feet 5 inches.

(4) Traverse: 90°.

(5) Elevation: −5° to +15°.

FIGURE 72.—25-pounder field gun-howitzer, Mk. II, on 25-pounder carriage, Mk. I (traveling position).

(6) Ammunition: weight of projectile, 6 pounds 4 ounces.

(7) Rate of fire: 20 rounds per minute.

100. Field guns and howitzers.—*a. 25-pounder field gun-howitzer.*—The 25-pounder (3.45-inch) field gun-howitzer is the basic

FIGURE 73.—25-pounder field gun-howitzer, Mk. II, on 25-pounder carriage, Mk. I (firing position, left rear view).

field piece of the British Army (figs. 72 and 73). It has been replacing both the 18-pounder (fig. 74) and the 4.5-inch howitzer of the last war. The tube has a removable liner which can be changed in the field. The gun can be placed in firing order on its platform in 1 minute. From its steady and easily worked mount it is capable of all-around fire and of more effective close-in defence and anti-mechanized action than any U. S. field piece. The firing platform is in the form of a wheel which is carried either under the trail or on the back of the prime mover. To place the piece in action, the platform is lowered to the ground and the carriage is then manhandled or tractor-drawn over it and coupled to its center. To permit easy maneuvering of the trail, the spade has been imbedded in a "box" commonly called a "banana," which functions very effectively and prevents the trail from digging in. The muzzle velocity with normal charge is 1,470 feet per second, and with supercharge 1,747 feet per second.

(1) Nature of weapon: field gun-howitzer.

(2) Weight: 3,968 pounds.

(3) Length: 25 feet 11 inches, including trailer (barrel, 92.5 inches).

FIGURE 74.—18-pounder field gun, Mk. IVP, on firing platform (left rear view).

(4) Traverse: 360° on firing platform, 8° without platform.

(5) Elevation: −5° to +40°.

(6) Maximum range: 12,500 yards; 13,400 yards with supercharge.

(7) Ammunition: projectiles: armour-piercing (20 pounds), HE (25 pounds), and smoke (base-ejection type, 21.8 pounds); charges: 3 and supercharge.

(8) Rate of fire: 4 rounds per minute (normal).

b. 3.7-inch howitzer.—The 3.7-inch howitzer is the standard pack artillery weapon, and it is also planned for use with the air-borne division. For other details, see figure 68.

c. 4.5-inch gun and 5.5-inch gun-howitzer.—(1) *General.*—The 60-pounder has been converted and replaced by the 4.5-inch gun; the 6-inch howitzer is being replaced by the 5.5-inch gun-howitzer as the latter becomes available. The two new weapons are mounted on the

154

same carriage, which has a split trail and is simple and easy to get into and out of action. While the guns are being fired, the three points of support are the center of the axle and the two trail spades. When the trails are closed, a simple locking mechanism automatically locks in traveling position the carriage proper, the traveling axle, and the trails. Although the trunnions are well to the rear and equilibrators are provided, the recoil mechanism is variable. In addition, the carriage has a quick-release elevating mechanism which permits the tube to be placed in the horizontal position for loading while the elevating rack remains properly laid for the desired target.

(2) *4.5-inch gun* (fig. 75).—This medium artillery gun fires a 55-pound shell and has a muzzle velocity of 2,265 feet per second.

(*a*) Nature of weapon: medium gun.

(*b*) Weight: 16,048 pounds.

(*c*) Length: 16 feet.

(*d*) Traverse: 60°.

(*e*) Elevation: −5° to +45°.

(*f*) Maximum range: 20,500 yards.

(*g*) Ammunition: HE.

(*h*) Rate of fire: 2 rounds per minute.

(3) *5.5-inch gun-howitzer.*—This medium artillery gun-howitzer (fig. 76) fires a 100-pound shell and has a muzzle velocity of from 1,235 to 1,340 feet per second.

(*a*) Nature of weapon: medium gun-howitzer.

(*b*) Weight: 12,768 pounds.

(*c*) Length: 24 feet 8 inches.

(*d*) Traverse: 60°.

(*e*) Elevation: −5° to +45°.

(*f*) Maximum range: 16,000 yards.

(*g*) Ammunition: BL type HE shell.

(*h*) Rate of fire: 2 rounds per minute.

d. 6-inch howitzer.—This is a medium artillery howitzer (figs. 77 and 78) with a muzzle velocity of from 1,235 to 1,352 feet per second. It is made of steel (wire construction) and has a calibrating sight. The breech mechanism is of the Asbury single-motion type, having a parallel breech screw of the Welin pattern.

(1) Nature of weapon: medium howitzer.

(2) Weight: 10,088 pounds.

(3) Length: 17 feet 6 inches.

(4) Traverse: 8°.

(5) Elevation: 0° to 45°.

(6) Maximum range: 11,400 yards.

(7) Ammunition: separate, HE, two marks of shell weighing 100 pounds and 98½ pounds, respectively, the propellant charges being contained in serge cloth bags.

(8) Rate of fire: 2 rounds per minute.

101. Heavy artillery.—*a. 7.2-inch howitzer.*—The 7.2-inch (183-

FIGURE 75.—4.5-inch gun on 4.5-inch gun–5.5-inch howitzer carriage (firing position).

FIGURE 76.—5.5-inch gun-howitzer on 4.5-inch gun–5.5-inch howitzer carriage (traveling position).

mm) howitzer is planned as the largest standard field piece. The 8-inch (203-mm) howitzer is obsolete, and is being converted to the 7.2-inch. The mounting of the 7.2-inch is that of the original 8-inch, modernized for high-speed transport, with low-pressure tires. On this is mounted a modern 7.2-inch piece firing a boat-tailed shell of the same weight as the original 8-inch shell and at 4,500 yards longer range. This 7.2-inch howitzer was developed as a result of the experience of the British in Flanders in 1940. They found the 9.2-inch howitzer much too slow and cumbersome for war of movement.

b. Other artillery.—Figure 79 illustrates a 6-inch gun. For details

FIGURE 77.—6-inch howitzer. (Note calibrating sight.)

FIGURE 78.—6-inch howitzer, with medium dragon tractor.

FIGURE 79.—6-inch gun, Mk. XIX, on Mk. VIIIAP carriage.

concerning the 6-inch gun and the 9.2-inch howitzer, see figure 68. Heavier models are the 9.2-inch gun, the 12-inch howitzer, and the 15-inch howitzer.

SECTION III

ANTI-AIRCRAFT

	Paragraph
Light guns	102
Medium (heavy) guns	103
Fire-control equipment	104
Rockets	105
Detection devices	106

102. Light guns.—*a. Sten 20-mm gun.*—This light anti-aircraft (AA) gun, known as the "Polish Sten," or the "Polsten," with a muzzle velocity of 2,700 feet per second, is similar to the Oerlikon gun of the Royal Navy. It is designed to replace the caliber .303 Bren AA equipment (see par. 91c). The maximum effective ceiling of the gun is 7,500 feet.

(1) Nature of weapon: 20-mm anti-aircraft automatic cannon.

(2) Weight: 121 pounds.

(3) Length: 7 feet 1¾ inches.

(4) Ammunition: magazine holds 60 rounds.

(5) Rate of fire: 460 to 475 rounds per minute (maximum).

b. Bofors 40-mm gun.—Light AA batteries are equipped with the Bofors 40-mm light AA gun (figs. 80 and 81) some of which were purchased in Sweden, Poland, Hungary, and Belgium, and the remainder manufactured under patent in Great Britain. This automatic cannon has an elevation of from −5° to +90° and a 360° traverse, and fires an HE tracer shell weighing 2 pounds at a muzzle velocity of 2,952 feet per second. The shell is equipped with a percussion and self-destroying fuze. The possible automatic rate of fire is 120 to 135 rounds per minute, but single-shot firing at 1 round per second is normally used to facilitate observation of tracers. The maximum effective ceiling of the gun is 7,500 feet.

103. Medium (heavy) guns.—*a. 3.7-inch gun.*—Although there is in use a large number of 3-inch AA guns, the 3.7-inch heavy AA gun is the standard equipment of mobile anti-aircraft heavy-gun batteries for home defence and with the field forces. It has an elevation range from −5° to +80° and a 360° traverse, and fires a 28-pound HE projectile, equipped with a mechanical time fuze, at a muzzle velocity of 2,600 feet per second. The gun weighs 21,280 pounds in the traveling position. Its maximum effective ceiling is 30,000 feet. A considerable number of these guns are emplaced on concrete platforms.

FIGURE 80.—Bofors 40-mm light anti-aircraft gun.

FIGURE 81.—Bofors 40-mm light anti-aircraft gun being prepared for action.

b. 4.45-inch gun.—The 4.45-inch heavy AA gun, known to the service as the 4.5-inch, has an elevation range of from −5° to +80° and a 360° traverse, and fires a 55-pound HE projectile, equipped with a mechanical time fuze, at a muzzle velocity of 2,410 feet per second. It has a firing rate of from 8 to 10 rounds a minute. This gun can be jacked onto 2 two-wheeled bogies for movement from one position to another, but must be fired from a previously prepared concrete base. In the firing position it weighs about 30,000 pounds. Its maximum effective ceiling is 30,000 feet.

104. Fire-control equipment.—Vickers and Sperry directors are both standard equipment. Sperry units manufactured in the United States have been delivered continuously since May 1938. The standard height-finder is a self-contained instrument of the coincidence type. A number of different makes, on bases of 9 feet, 16¼ feet, and 18 feet, are in service.

105. Rockets.—A new type of AA weapon is an unrotating HE shell projected on the rocket principle. The projectors from which the rockets are fired are of different design. Some can fire only 1 projectile, while others can fire up to 20 projectiles, at a single loading.

106. Detection devices.—*a. Searchlights.*—The 90-cm (35.5-inch) AA searchlight is standard, and is provided in two types, one for hand and one for remote control. There are also a number of 120-cm (47.38-inch) and 150-cm (59.1-inch) searchlights in service, as well as many U. S. type Sperry 60-inch lights. The 90-cm model is mounted on four small caterpillar tracks; the 150-cm model is mounted on its own four-wheeled trailer. Reflectors are almost invariably of glass, although a few metal ones are in use.

b. Sound locators.—At least three types of sound locators are standard. Each of the two latest types has four paraboloid horns arranged for electric or stethoscope listening. They are equipped with visual indicating equipment and course-finding sights. Acoustic correctors and a system of remote control of the searchlight make the use of intermediary comparators unnecessary.

c. Radio.—Radio detection devices are used extensively in conjunction with AA equipment.

Section IV

DEFENCE AGAINST CHEMICAL WARFARE

107. General.—*a.* The British Government has ratified an international agreement to prohibit the use of toxic gas in war. Its policy is to provide adequate protection of the military and civilian population against gas attack.

b. Chemical warfare groups are included in Royal Engineer establishments. Experimental work is carried out through the Chemical Defence Committee and the Chemical Defence Research Department under the general supervision of the War Office. Chemical warfare groups are trained to carry out all branches of field engineering except bridging (see par. 40*d*).

c. Each battalion or equivalent unit has a unit gas officer who is detailed from the personnel of the unit and is a graduate of one of the several anti-gas schools maintained by the British Army. The staff of each division and higher unit includes a General Staff Officer (GSO (CW)—see par. 21*a*(1)(*e*)) who is specially qualified in chemical warfare and is adviser to the commander and staff in all matters pertaining to his specialty. This General Staff Officer, who usually has other staff duties, is assisted at the headquarters of a corps or higher unit by a technical officer (chemist—see fig. 3). Gas protective training is a responsibility of unit commanders and is carried out in accordance with the provisions of training manuals.

108. Individual protection.—*a. General.*—British provisions for the protection of its armed forces are thorough and include numerous items of individual and organizational anti-gas equipment. Anti-gas schools provide courses for officers and noncommissioned officers. Troop training in the use of the gas mask, gas-chamber exercises, first aid, and identification of gases is generally similar to U. S. Army practice. British troops are provided with a number of special items of protective equipment for defence against spray or other forms of gas attack. Each battalion or similar unit has one or more squads specially trained for decontamination work. For prompt identification of gas and development of emergency measures for protection, field chemical laboratory units and first aid and cleansing centers are provided.

b. Equipment.—(1) *Gas mask* (fig. 82).—The gas mask has a fully moulded facepiece made of rubber which is connected to the canister by a short corrugated hose tube. The canister contains activated charcoal, an efficient smoke filter. The mask is carried in a haversack, which is slung over the shoulder by a shoulder strap. For use, the mask haversack is brought to a position on the chest and held in place by means of a body cord. (See figs. 84 and 85; see also figs. 45 ③ and ④, 48, and 67.)

(2) *Eye shields.*—Each British soldier carries in his mask haversack several simple eye shields made of plastic material. The purpose of these shields is to protect the eyes from chemical spray from aircraft pending adjustment of the gas mask.

(3) *Protective ointment.*—Several tubes of ointment, designed for protection against mustard gas and lewisite, are also carried in the mask haversack.

(4) *Impregnated protective clothing.*—Provisions are made for impregnating uniforms so as to protect the wearer against vesicant gas

Facepiece, Mk. V.   Container, type E.
Haversack, Mk. V.   Anti-dimming outfit.
FIGURE 82.—Service respirator (gas mask).

vapor. Impregnated clothing is being issued to all troops in Great Britain as other articles wear out and must be replaced.

(5) *Impervious protective clothing* (figs. 83, 84, 85, and 86).—Garments made of oil-treated fabric are provided for individual protection where liquid vesicants are likely to be encountered. These garments consist of the following items: cape, trousers, jacket, hood, overshoes, canopy, and gloves. The cape is issued to each soldier (see also figs. 48 and 67), whereas the other items are issued as specially required.

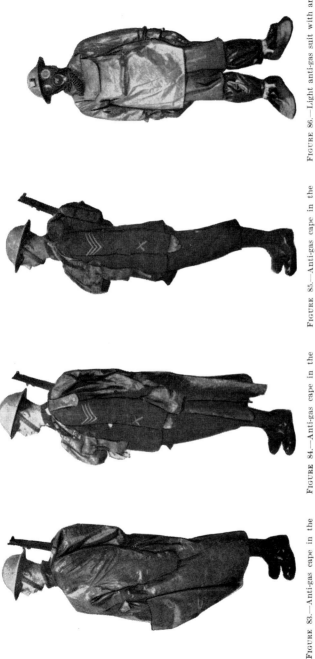

FIGURE 83.—Anti-gas cape in the "worn" position. (The front is fastened back for marching.)

FIGURE 84.—Anti-gas cape in the "alert" position.

FIGURE 85.—Anti-gas cape in the "rolled" position.

FIGURE 86.—Light anti-gas suit with anti-gas overshoes and gloves as worn by certain specialists. (For decontamination work the coat would be inside the trousers, in order to provide maximum protection against vapor, and in strong concentrations a hood would be worn.)

(6) *Gas detectors.*—Each soldier is provided with paper arm bands which change color upon contact with blister gases.

109. Collective protection.—British collective protection devices include the following:

a. Anti-gas pathways, consisting of rolls of specially treated paper which may be laid down over contaminated areas to allow the safe passage of men.

b. Decontamination materials.

c. Clothing bags, made of specially treated fabric and used to collect contaminated clothing.

d. First aid and cleansing centers.

e. Gas alarms.

f. Gas sentries.

SECTION V

ARMOURED FIGHTING VEHICLES

110. Tanks (fig. 87).—*a. General.*—(1) British tanks fall into two categories: cruiser tanks and army, or infantry ("I"), tanks. Cruiser tanks (figs. 88 and 89), the armoured fighting vehicles of the armoured brigades, are relatively fast and maneuverable, and sacrifice armour to speed and armament. Infantry tanks, which are slower and more heavily armoured, are designed to support infantry attacks on field fortifications, preceding the infantry and attempting to over-run the enemy defences. The role of British infantry tanks is one which is not normally envisaged by U. S. armored tactics, although in unusual circumstances U. S. heavy tanks might be called upon to perform a similar mission. See figure 90 for one type of infantry tank. Light tanks are considered by the British to be obsolete from the fighting point of view, although special types are produced for various special operations, including reconnaissance, mountain war-fare, air transportation, and airdrome defence.

(2) In addition to the tanks listed in figure 87, the British are also using a new Mk. VII cruiser tank, popularly known as the Crom-well, and the following U. S. tanks:

> Light M3 (General Stuart).
> Medium M3 (General Lee).
> Medium M3 with British turret (General Grant).
> Medium M4 (General Sherman).

(3) British light tanks are generally lighter than U. S. light tanks, and are not designed for the same role. British cruiser tanks vary

164

considerably in weight, certain models weighing the same as U. S. light tanks, others weighing the same as U. S. medium tanks. The normal role, however, of British cruiser tanks is similar to that assigned to U. S. medium tanks.

b. U. S. light tanks.—U. S. M3 light tanks have been utilized by the British in both reconnaissance and fighting roles.

c. Armament.—For the armament of various British tanks, see figure 87. The caliber .50 Vickers medium (heavy) machine gun is similar in action and general design to the caliber .303 Vickers, but is generally larger owing to the increased size of the cartridge. It weighs approximately 63 pounds and has a rate of fire of 500 to 600 rounds per minute. The 7.92-mm Besa medium (heavy) machine gun weighs 42 pounds and has an actual rate of fire of 650 rounds per minute, or 800 rounds with an accelerator. This gun is also designed in a 15-mm model weighing 115 pounds and firing 400 rounds per minute.

d. Communications.—External communications are usually by radio, lamp, and flag, and internal communications are by voice tube or loud speaker.

111. Armoured carriers.[3]—There are two main types of armoured carriers, the Universal (figs. 91, 92, and 93) and the Loyd (fig. 94). Although there were formerly several models of the Universal carrier, each designed and equipped for a particular type of work, there is now only one. The Universal carrier fitted with rests for a Bren gun and a Boys anti-tank rifle is now what is commonly known as the Bren gun carrier. The Universal carrier can transport three or four men, depending upon the amount of equipment. The Loyd carrier is primarily a personnel and mortar carrier, holding nine men including the driver. The fact that the Loyd carrier has four bogie wheels, whereas the Universal carrier has only three, provides the easiest method of distinguishing between these two types. The following table shows the characteristics of these two carriers:

	Universal	*Loyd*
Weight_____	4 long tons.	3.8 long tons.
Length_____	12 feet.	13 feet 6 inches.
Width_____	7 feet.	7 feet.
Height_____	4 feet 10 inches.	4 feet 8 inches.
Armour_____	Front: 10 mm.	Front: 10 mm.
	Sides: 7 mm.	Sides: 7 mm.
Speed_____	Cross-country: 20 miles per hour.	Cross-country: 20 miles per hour.
	Road: 30 miles per hour.	Road: 30 miles per hour.
Radius of action_	110 miles (approximately).	110 miles (approximately).

---

[3] For tactics of armoured carriers, see paragraph 128.

Name	Popular name	Crew	Weight	Radius	Speed (miles per hour)		Armament	Armour	Dimensions						Remarks
					Cross country	Roads			Length		Width		Height		
			Tons[1]	*Miles*					*Feet*	*Inches*	*Feet*	*Inches*	*Feet*	*Inches*	
Light tank, Mk. VI a, b, and c.		3	6.27	150	23	30	1 caliber .50 Vickers MG; 1 caliber .303 Vickers MG.	Basis, 0.50 inch	13	6	6	8	6	9	Obsolete; unsteady as a gun platform; used in the Western Desert for reconnaissance. The Mk. VIc light tank substitutes the 7.92-mm Besa machine gun for the caliber .303 Vickers.
Light tank, Mk. VII.	Tetrarch	3	7	250			1 40-mm gun; 1 7.92-mm Besa MG.	Front, 0.63 inch; sides, —; turret —.	14	3	8	4	7	0	One of the latest types of light tank; excellent riding qualities.
Light tank, Mk. VIII.	Harry Hopkins	3	8.6	160		25	1 40-mm gun; 1 7.92-mm Besa MG.	Front, 1.5 inches; sides, 0.79 inch; turret, 1.5 inches.	14	3	8	3	6	8	The latest type of light tank.
Cruiser tank, Mk. V A13.	Covenanter	4	18	130	20	25	1 40-mm gun; 2 MG's; 1 submachine gun.	Front, 1.57 inches; sides, 1.18 inches; turret, 1.57 inches.	19	6	9	1	7	3	1.57-inch armour to be replaced by 2.36-inch armour.
Cruiser tank, Mk. VI A15.	Crusader	5	19	140	23	25	1 40-mm gun; 2 7.92-mm Besa MG's.	Front, 1.57 inches; sides, 1.18 inches; turret, 1.57 inches.	19	3	8	8	7	2	Operates best at governed speed not greater than 27 miles per hour; 1.57-inch armour to be replaced by 2.36-inch armour.

							Armour—thickness	Armament							1-inch armour on skirt.	Narrow track.
Mk. II.		20.5	92	8	9	19	Basis, 2.56 inches	1 40-mm gun; 1 7.92-mm Besa MG.	10	8	9	8	6	7	9	6
Infantry tank, Mk. III. Valentine	3	16.4	198	9	6	18	Front, 2.36 inches; sides, —; turret, 2.75 inches.	1 40-mm gun; 1 7.92-mm Besa MG; 1 2-inch mortar.	12	9	1	7	1	7	1	
Infantry tank, Mk. IV. Churchill	5	37	100			23	Front, 3.5 inches; sides, 3 inches; turret, 3.5 inches.	1 40-mm gun; 1 3-inch howitzer; 1 7.92-mm Besa MG; 1 caliber .303 Bren MG; 2 submachine guns.		6	10	8	8	8	1	1

¹ Long tons (see par. 161a).

Light tank Mk. VI

Light tank Mk. VII, Tetrarch

FIGURE 87.—Characteristics of tanks.

Infantry tank Mk. IV, Churchill IV

M3 Medium tank, Grant (U.S. built)

167

FIGURE 88.— Front view of cruiser tank, Mk. VI (Crusader).

FIGURE 89.—Side view of cruiser tank, Mk. VI (Crusader).

112. Armoured cars.—*a. General.*—Although comparatively lightly armoured, British armoured cars are used extensively for reconnaissance and patrol work. Some of the types, with their characteristics, are listed in figure 95. More recent types, not listed in figure 95, are the Daimler and the heavily armoured AEC.[4] The Daimler carries a crew of three, and is protected by 14-mm armour. It mounts a 2-pounder and, co-axially, a 7.92 Besa machine gun and a Bren gun. It is powered by a 6-cylinder 106-brake-horsepower motor with a maximum speed of 60 miles per hour and a radius of action of 150 miles.

FIGURE 90.—Infantry tank, Mk. II (Matilda).

b. Armoured command vehicle.—For some mobile command posts of armoured divisions the British use an armoured command vehicle (ACV) known as the AEC Armoured Command Vehicle. Armour is provided on a 12-mm (0.49-inch) basis, and the chassis is that of a normal 5-ton truck. The vehicle normally carries three officers, three radio operators, and two drivers. Equipment includes seats, desks, and lockers for the personnel, three radio sets, a cipher machine, and necessary electrical equipment. Although there are no vehicular weapons, the enlisted men are armed with rifles.

(1) Weight: 11.93 long tons.
(2) Length: 20 feet.
(3) Width: 8 feet 6 inches.
(4) Height: 9 feet 5 inches.

[4] Associated Equipment Company.

① Front and side.

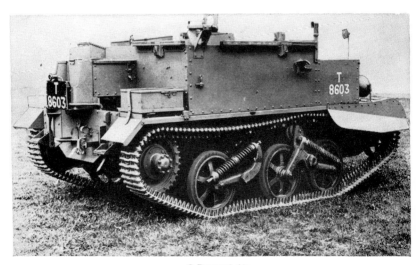

② Rear and side.

FIGURE 91.—Universal armoured carrier.

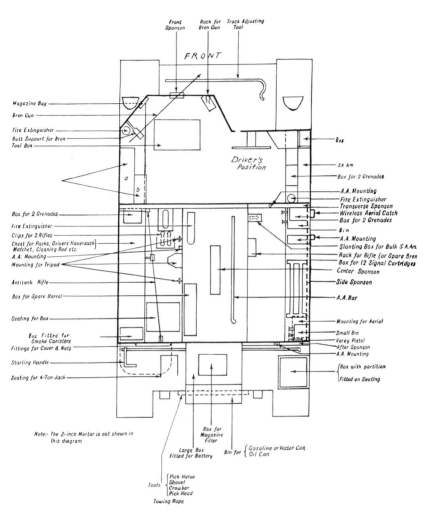

FIGURE 92.—Diagram of Universal armoured carrier.

171

Universal carrier in use as mortar carrier.

① Right side.

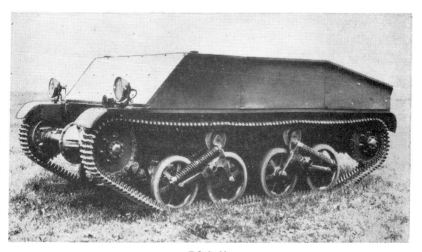

② Left side.

FIGURE 94.—Loyd armoured carrier.

Name	Weight	Crew	Armour	Armament	Dimensions			Speed	Radius of action
					Length	Width	Height		
	Long tons				*Feet Inches*	*Feet Inches*	*Feet Inches*	*Miles per hour*	*Miles*
Scout Car BSA	2.8	2	Upper structure, 1 inch; front, 0.19 inch; sides, 0.25 inch.	One caliber .303 Bren MG; one caliber .55 Boys AT rifle.	10 5	6 7	5 --	Cross-country, 20; road, 35.	200
Humber		3 or 4	Basis, 0.55-inch.	One 7.92-mm Besa MG; one 15-mm Besa MG.			--	Maximum, 45.	250
Morris	4.48	4	Basis, 0.38-inch.	One caliber .303 Bren MG; one caliber .55 Boys AT rifle.			--	Cross-country, 24; road, 45.	240
Guy	5.6	3	Basis, 0.55-inch.	One 15-mm Besa MG; one 7.92-mm Besa MG.	14 6	7 1	8 1	Cross-country,16;road, 24.	200

FIGURE 95.—Characteristics of armoured cars.

Humber armoured car Mk. I

BSA (Daimler) scout car

Dodge 30 cwt truck with cargo trailer

Austin 6 x 4 3 ton truck with office/workshop body

174

113. General.—*a.* With extremely limited exceptions all transportation of the British Army is motorized. The standard motor vehicles are excellent in quality and reasonably adequate in quantity. Various forms of trailers are also provided. (See fig. 96 for characteristics of vehicles. In pars. 114 to 118 only representative types and models are discussed in detail.)

b. In the British Army a distinction is made between trucks and lorries, "truck" being used for any load-carrying vehicle of 1 long ton or less, and "lorry" for a load-carrying vehicle of 30-cwt or more (see par. 161*a*). In addition, the term "van" is used for a truck with a fixed top, and "tractor" for a lorry employed to pull or tow anything. Thus all artillery prime movers are designated as tractors.

c. The present trend in all wheeled vehicles is to design or modify them so that an anti-aircraft sentry, with an all-around field of vision, can be posted in the vehicle. British units in the Middle East have cut holes in the tops of the passenger cars and closed-cab trucks so that sentries can stand on the driver's seat and have their heads and shoulders protrude through the roof of the vehicle. On some of the closed-cab trucks the tops have been removed. On large cargo trucks the sentry is seated on top of the cover.

d. The standard prime movers now being procured are 1½-ton, four-wheeled Morris tractors (or similar tractors manufactured by other firms—see par. 118) for field artillery and 3-ton six-wheeled Scammell tractors for medium artillery (fig. 97). These replaced by 1940 a considerable number of full-tracked tractors, called dragons, were standard. The medium dragon, with a chassis similar to that of a medium tank, was used for medium artillery. Satisfactory performance and the lessened cost caused the change from tracked vehicles to wheeled vehicles.

e. Certain U. S. vehicles are also in use, especially the ¼-ton 4 by 4 truck which the British call a "Blitz Buggy" (the Jeep).

f. British vehicles normally employ right-hand drive. British rules of the road are exactly the reverse of those in the United States; that is, vehicles keep to the left of the road and pull to the right in passing.

Type [1]	Solo motorcycle	2-seater car	4-seater car	8-cwt truck	15-cwt truck	15-cwt truck
Make	(1) Norton; (2) BSA	(1) Austin; (2) Hillman; (3) Morris	(1) Ford; (2) Humber	(1) Morris; (2) Humber; (3) Chevrolet	(1) Bedford; (2) Morris; (3) Chevrolet	(1) Ford; (2) Guy.
Drive		(1) 2; (2) 4	(1) 2; (2) 4	(1)-(2) 2 and 4; (3) 2	(1)-(3) 2	(1)-(2) 2.
Type of engine [2]	500 cc, 1-cyl.	10-hp, 4-cyl.	(1) 30-hp, 8-cyl; (2) 27-hp, 6-cyl.	25 to 29-hp, 6-cyl.	25 to 29-hp, 6-cyl.	(1) 30-hp, 8-cyl; (2) 23-hp, 4-cyl.
Type of body		Utility	Utility	Personnel-carrying	Truck	Truck.
Personnel-carrying capacity.	1 or 2	4	6	5	7	7.
Radius of action (miles)	210	220	(1) 200; (2) 250	220 to 300	230 to 280	250.
Useful load [1]		1,700 lb.			1½ tons	1½ tons.
Units to whom issued	All types in field force.	All types.	Most types.	Some Motor Bns, Arty Regts, Field Cos, Div Sigs, Tk Brigs.	Most types.	Most types.
Remarks	See text for additional material.	See text for additional material on the Austin.	See text for additional material on the Ford.	See text for additional material on the Humber.	May be fitted as an office, water - carrier, compressor, or wireless truck. See text for additional material.	

Type [1]	30-cwt 4-wheeled lorry	4-wheeled AT portee lorry	30-cwt 6-wheeled lorry	30-cwt breakdown lorry
Make	(1) Austin; (2) Bedford; (3) Gen Mot; (4) Chevrolet; (5) Dodge; (6) Ford.	Morris.	Morris	Morris.
Drive	(1)-(2), (6) 2; (3) 2 and 4; (4)-(5) 4	4	4	4.
Type of engine [2]	(1)-(5) 27-hp, 6-cyl; (6) 30-hp, 8-cyl	25-hp, 4-cyl.	25-hp, 4- and 6-cyl.	25-hp, 6-cyl.
Type of body	Load-carrying	Portee with hand winch.	(1) Load-carrying; (2) equipped with 4-ton winch.	1-ton hoist; 4-ton.
Personnel-carrying capacity	2	5	(1) 22; (2) 2.	2.
Radius of action (miles)	(1)-(2) 240; (3) 450; (4) 310; (5) 320; (6) 170.	260.	180.	260.
Useful load [1]	1½ tons		1½ tons	
Units to whom issued	Most types.	Anti-tank regiments.	(1) Light aid detachments; (2) Field Cos and Sqs, Field Park Cos and Sqs, and Tunnelling Cos.	Light aid detachments and anti-aircraft regiment workshops.
Remarks	Obsolescent; see text for additional material.		Obsolescent.	

Type [1]	3-ton 4-wheeled lorry	3-ton 4-wheeled lorry	3-ton 6-wheeled lorry	3-ton 6-wheeled lorry	3-ton 6-wheeled lorry	3-ton 6-wheeled lorry	3-ton 6-wheeled lorry
Make	(1) Austin; (2) Bedford; (3) Karrier; (4) Ford.	(1) Dennis; (2) Ford.	(1) Albion; (2) AFC; (3) Austin; (4) Leyland; (5) Gen Mot; (6) Chevrolet-Thornton.	(1) Guy; (2) Leyland; (3) Gen Mot.	(1) Albion; (2) Leyland.	Leyland	(1) Leyland; (2) Dodge; (3) Guy; (4) Albion.
Drive	(1) 2; (2) 2 and 4; (3)-(4) 4.	(1)-(2) 2	(1)-(6) 4	(1)-(3) 4	(1)-(2) 4	4	(1)-(4) 4.
Type of engine [2]	(1)-(3) 27-hp, 6-cyl; (4) 30-hp, 8-cyl.	(1) 25-hp, 4-cyl; (2) 30-hp, 8-cyl.	(1) 3.89 liters, 4-cyl; (2) 31-hp, 4-cyl; (3) 3.99 liters, 6-cyl; (4) 29-hp, 4-cyl; (5) 33-hp, 6-cyl; (6) 30-hp, 6-cyl.	(1) 5.1 liters, 4-cyl; (2) 5.9 liters, 4-cyl; (3) 33-hp, 6-cyl.	(1) 3.89 liters, 4-cyl; (2) 5.9 liters, 4-cyl.	5.9 liters, 4-cyl	(1) 5.9 liters, 4-cyl; (2) 34-hp 4-cyl; (3) 5.1 liters, 4-cyl; (4) 3.89 liters, 4-cyl.
Type of body	Load-carrying	Hydraulic dump	Detachable hoops and canvas covers.	Flat floor with searchlight projector.	(1) Bridging equipment; (2) Machinery.	House-type body with sound-ranging equipment.	Variously outfitted with derricks, cranes, and superstructure.
Personnel-carrying capacity.	28	2	28	10	2		?
Radius of action (miles).	(1) 280; (2) 230 to 280; (3)-(4) 240.	160 to 180	(1) 170; (2) 180; (3) 210; (4) 195; (5) 372; (6) 140.	(1) 145; (2) 200; (3) 350.	(1) 170; (2) 200	200	(1) 200; (2) 250; (3) 140; (4) 170.
Useful load [1]	3¾ tons	3¾ tons	3¾ tons	3¾ tons			
Units to whom issued	All types	Engineers	All medium and heavy artillery regiments, anti-aircraft regiments, etc.	Searchlight units of ADGB (Air Defence of Great Britain).	Engineer and ordnance units.	Artillery survey units.	Light aid detachments, ordnance units, and engineer units.
Remarks	See text for additional material.						

FIGURE 96.—Characteristics of motor vehicles.

See footnotes at end of table.

177

Type¹	Tractor	Tractor	Tractor	Tractor	18-ton 6-wheeled tank transporter	30-ton 10-wheeled tank transporter
Make	(1) FWD; (2) AEC	Scammell	Morris	(1) Ford; (2) Guy; (3) Chevrolet.	(1) White-Ruxtell; (2) Mack.	Scammell.
Drive			(1), (2) 4	(1)-(3) 4		
Type of engine²	(1) 51-hp, 6-cyl; (2) 7.58 liters, 6-cyl.	8.4 liters, 6-cyl.	(1) 25-hp, 6-cyl; (2) 25-hp, 4-cyl.	(1) 30-hp, 8-cyl; (2) 3.68 liters, 4-cyl; (3) 27-hp, 6-cyl.	(1) 51-hp, 6-cyl; (2) 46-hp, 6-cyl.	8.4 liters, 6-cyl.
Type of body	Flat floor, detachable hoops and cover.	(1) Gun tractor, steel paneled with ½-ton hoist; (2) Heavy breakdown truck with sliding jib and hand winch.	All-metal gun tractor	All-metal gun tractor	Flat floor with ramps	Articulated flat floor with ramps.
Personnel-carrying capacity	12	(1) 12; (2) 3	(1) 7; (2) 6	6	2.	7.
Radius of action (miles)	(1) 700; (2) 360 (towing)	(1) 355 (towing); (2) 535	175 to 180.	(1)-(3) 240; (2) 160	400.	175.
Useful load¹	3⅓ tons.				20⅓ tons.	33⅓ tons.
Units to whom issued	Medium artillery regiments and heavy antiaircraft regiments.	(1) Heavy artillery regiments; (2) Recovery units of armoured formations and brigade ordnance companies.	(1) Light anti-aircraft regiments; (2) Field regiments.	Field regiments	RASC tank transporter companies.	Armoured division recovery sections and army tank brigades.
Remarks		See text for additional material.	See text for additional material.			

¹ In indicating the type of vehicle, British designations and weights have been used (see par. 161a). Approximate U. S. values have been used, however, in the weights given under useful loads.

² British horsepower ratings are used here (see par. 161b).

FIGURE 96 (continued).—Characteristics of motor vehicles.

178

114. Motorcycles.—*a.* The two standard solo motorcycles are the BSA[5] (fig. 98) and the Norton. They will normally carry one rider, with his pack and blanket stored in pannier bags on either side of the rear wheel. A pillion seat is also provided for occasional use. Brakes are mechanically operated, internal expanding. A foot brake operates the rear wheel; a hand brake, the front wheel. Standing orders require that every British Army officer below the grade of colonel be a proficient motorcycle operator. Motorcycles are widely used by dispatch riders (messengers).

(1) Engine: single cylinder.

(2) Speed: 60 miles per hour.

(3) Fuel consumption: 46 miles per gallon.

(4) Gas tank capacity: 3⅗ U. S. gallons (approximately).

(5) Net weight: 310 pounds.

b. The Norton, in a combination passenger-carrying model, is also issued to infantry battalions and armoured regiments, and, in a combination box body, to provost companies.

115. Motorcars.—*a. Austin 10-horsepower two-seater car.*—This is a light two-seater open runabout (fig. 99) with a baggage space behind the seat. It is a convenient vehicle for directing convoys because of its ability to cut through congested traffic where a larger vehicle would be held up.

(1) Engine: 4-cylinder.

(2) Maximum speed: 52 miles per hour.

(3) Fuel consumption: 33 miles per gallon.

(4) Radius of action: 220 miles.

(5) Gas tank capacity: 7 U. S. gallons.

(6) Net weight: 1,512 pounds.

b. Ford V8 30-horsepower four-seater saloon (sedan) car (fig. 100).— This is a standard passenger car, except for the tire equipment (9 by 13 inches) and the special increased clearance between fenders and tires. It has a wheel base of 112 inches and a standard sedan body. The Humber four-seater is similar to the Ford and is also standard.

(1) Engine: Ford, 8-cylinder.

(2) Maximum speed: 76 miles per hour.

(3) Fuel consumption: 13 miles per gallon.

(4) Gas tank capacity: 15 U. S. gallons.

(5) Net weight: 3,136 pounds.

c. Light reconnaissance cars.—Light reconnaissance cars, provided with light armour and with a turret, are issued to reconnaissance regiments (battalions).

---

[5] Birmingham Small Arms (Company).

FIGURE 97.—Scammell heavy breakdown tractor.

FIGURE 98.—Solo motorcycle (BSA).

180

FIGURE 99.—10-horsepower two-seater car (Austin).

FIGURE 100.—30-horsepower four-seater saloon car (Ford).

116. Trucks.—*a. Humber 8-cwt 4-wheeled personnel or wireless vehicle.*—This truck (fig. 101) has a well-type body providing seating accommodations for three men, two facing the off side and one the near side. Lockers are provided for kit and equipment. The whole is protected by a demountable waterproof cover on tubular super-structure. The canopy is removable and can be used on the ground as a shelter.

4 by 2 chassis	*4 by 4 chassis*
(1) *Engine:* 6-cylinder;	6-cylinder.
(2) *Maximum speed:* 55 miles per hour (45 miles per hour governed);	55 miles per hour (50 miles per hour governed).
(3) *Fuel consumption:* 12½ miles per gallon;	11½ miles per gallon.
(4) *Gas tank capacity:* 19 U. S. gallons;	19 U. S. gallons.
(5) *Net weight:* 4,800 pounds;	6,339 pounds.

b. Bedford MW 15-cwt 4-wheeled infantry truck.—When fitted with seats and a canopy, this truck (fig. 102) can be converted into a passenger-carrying vehicle. It is the main transport vehicle for the equipment of an infantry battalion, and often mounts a Bren gun. Its general-service (GS) body has the following dimensions:

Internal length, 6 feet 5½ inches.
Internal width, 6 feet.
Over-all width, 6 feet 7½ inches.

The driver's compartment has a folding detachable canvas top and two adjustable bucket-type seats.

(1) Engine: 6-cylinder.

(2) Maximum speed: 53 miles per hour (40 miles per hour governed).

(3) Fuel consumption: 10 miles per gallon.

(4) Gas tank capacity: 24 U. S. gallons.

(5) Net weight: 4,480 pounds.

117. Lorries.—*a. Bedford OX (30-cwt, general service).*—This lorry (fig. 103) is a semiforward-control vehicle fitted with the standard Bedford steel cab but with the radiator and front end exactly like the 15-cwt Bedford truck, model MW. The internal dimensions of the body are 8 feet 8 inches by 6 feet 6 inches by 2 feet 3 inches. Provision is made for carrying a spare wheel inside the body, at the rear on the near side. The lorry has a standard Bedford all-steel cab with laminated safety glass in the windshield, toughened glass in the doors, and a black light. The windshield wiper—on the driver's side only—is vacuum-operated with reserve tank.

(1) Engine: 6-cylinder.

(2) Maximum speed: 43 miles per hour (40 miles per hour governed).

FIGURE 101.—8-cwt 4-wheeled personnel or wireless truck (Humber).

FIGURE 102.—15-cwt 4-wheeled infantry truck (Bedford MW).

(3) Fuel consumption: 8½ miles per gallon.

(4) Gas tank capacity: 28 U. S. gallons.

(5) Net weight: 5,600 pounds.

b. Bedford OY (3-ton, 4-wheeled, general service).—This lorry (fig. 104) is representative of the type adapted to take special low-pressure tires and to give adequate clearance for moderate cross-country work. This type is the main load-carrier of the Army. The body is a general-service body with a flat floor and with a detachable canopy mounted on hoopsticks. The enclosed steel-paneled cab seats two. The dimensions are: internal length, 11 feet 6 inches; internal width, 6 feet 6 inches; over-all width, 6 feet 6 inches.

(1) Engine: 6-cylinder.

(2) Maximum speed: 43 miles per hour (40 miles per hour governed).

(3) Fuel consumption: 7½ miles per gallon.

(4) Gas tank capacity: 38 U. S. gallons.

(5) Net weight: 5,824 pounds.

118. Tractors.—*a.* The Morris C8 tractor is a 4-wheeled 4-wheel-drive field artillery tractor-lorry used for the "haulage" of field guns (fig. 105). It has a good cross-country performance when towing. The all-metal body carries ammunition and gun stores and holds four men, a driver, and a commander. Lockers are provided for kit and ammunition. Either a spare wheel or a firing platform may be carried at the rear. It has the following dimensions: over-all length, 14 feet 8¾ inches; over-all width, 7 feet 3 inches; over-all height, 7 feet 5 inches.

(1) Engine: 4-cylinder.

(2) Maximum speed: 47 miles per hour (42 miles per hour governed).

(3) Fuel consumption: 6.15 miles per gallon.

(4) Gas tank capacity: 36 U. S. gallons.

(5) Net weight: 7,504 pounds.

b. Light dragon.—The light dragon, Mk. III, has been superseded. The standard prime mover for all field artillery is the Morris C8 tractor described above, or a similar tractor manufactured by other firms.

c. Medium dragon.—The medium dragon, a tank-tractor, was used principally as one of the tractors of medium artillery brigades (fig. 106). It is obsolete but some are used for training

(1) Engine: Armstrong-Siddeley, 8-cylinder, 90 horsepower.

(2) Maximum speed: Road: 15 miles per hour; cross-country, 10; towing: 9 miles per hour.

(3) Fuel consumption: 15 miles per gallon on roads; 2 miles per gallon under service conditions.

(4) Radius of action: 88 miles.

FIGURE 103.—30-cwt general-service lorry (Bedford OX).

FIGURE 104.—3-ton 4-wheeled general-service lorry (Bedford OY).

(5) Gas tank capacity: 44 U. S. gallons.

(6) Net weight: 7.5 long tons.

FIGURE 105.—Morris C8 4-wheeled field artillery tractor.

FIGURE 106.—Medium dragon tractor, Mk. IIIc.

In medium artillery brigades, trucks are used exclusively as tractors.

186

Chapter 6
TACTICS

119. General.—Since British tactical doctrine is generally similar to that of the U. S. Army, it will be discussed briefly.

120. Offensive.—British doctrine of the offensive may be stated as follows:

a. Decisive victory on the battlefield, the ultimate purpose of the Army, can be achieved only by the offensive. Only by attack can a commander get control of the two vital factors in war—time and space—and thereby seize the initiative.

b. The offensive spirit must be shared by all ranks down to the last individual soldier. The most junior commander, rather than wait for orders, must use his initiative to reach his immediate objective, and, in default of a stated objective, must devise one himself.

c. The four basic factors taught by the British in the attack are: surprise, speed, simplicity, and concentration.

(1) Surprise is taught as the most effective weapon in the hand of the attacker, for it enables him to secure superiority of force at the critical moment when he most needs it.

(2) Speed in all stages of the planning and execution of the attack is essential if the initiative is to be gained and maintained. Commanders must make rapid decisions and staffs must insure that the machinery of command works smoothly and efficiently.

(3) A plan should be as simple as possible, for simplicity gives flexibility. The simpler the plan, the more likely it is to succeed, though simplicity must not be made the excuse for carelessness.

(4) The attacker can concentrate his forces at the point that he chooses to attack; the defender, in ignorance of the selected place of attack, must dispose his forces to meet every possible area and point of attack. However, the defender, once the attack is launched, moves his reserves to meet the foe's main effort, and the favorable balance to the attacker begins to disappear. Therefore, the attacker must profit by his initial advantage.

121. Normal operating technique.—The following is the British technique for deployment (development) for combat from a march formation:

a. Organization for deployment.—Before any operation is put into execution, time is necessary for reconnaissance by commanders both for planning and issuing orders and for deploying troops and organizing supporting fire. It is obviously of vital importance to reduce this time to a minimum. This can be done by—

(1) Mental reconnaissance—thinking ahead for possible future action.

(2) Careful organization of the arrangements for reconnaissance.

(3) Rehearsal of deployment.

(4) Carrying out certain preparations concurrently.

b. Stages of deployment.—Deployment drill need not differ materially whether for attack or for defence. It will normally be carried out in the following stages:

(1) *Stage 1.*—(a) Reconnaissance by the commander initiating the plan and by the commanders of the units detailed to support.

(b) Movement of subordinate commanders to a rendezvous to receive orders.

(c) Movement of fighting troops and administrative parts of the force to assembly areas.

(2) *Stage 2.*—(a) Issue of orders by the commander.

(b) Reconnaissance by subordinate commanders and by the commanders of affiliated supporting units.

(c) Movement of fighting troops to unit assembly areas.

(d) Opening of battle Hq.

(e) Administrative preparations.

(The procedures outlined in (b), (c), (d), and (e), above, take place concurrently.)

(3) *Stage 3.*—(a) Issue of orders by subordinate commanders.

(b) Movement of fighting troops to deployment areas.

c. Group system.—The main body or fighting portion of each unit and also the transport not required with the fighting troops (i. e., "B" echelon) are, however, also concerned in deployment and must receive orders. There are, therefore, four main groups concerned in deployment:

(1) The Reconnaissance, or "R," Group, which is the commander's group for reconnaissance and planning.

(2) The Orders, or "O," Group, which is the group for receiving orders. This will normally consist of the subordinate commanders' "R" groups.

(3) The Fighting, or "F," Group, which is the main body of the formation or unit.

(4) The Transport, or "T," Group, which is the transport not required with "F" Group.

This nomenclature saves time when issuing orders. (For the composition of groups, see figs. 107 and 108. Note the "Remarks" column and the fact that such groups may be adapted to circumstances.)

d. System of working.—The principle is that while reconnaissance is being carried out and orders are being issued, there should be a simultaneous and continuous movement forward ending in deployment onto battle frontages by the fighting troops. This process should continue in successive stages from formations down to sub-units. Note also the following:

(1) Need for early issue of warning orders to start groups moving. Assembly areas should be en route to the proposed deployment area.

(2) Reconnaissance by "R" Group must be carefully planned, and the composition of the group, the route to be taken, and the points of observation to be visited must be considered.

(3) Rendezvous for "O" Group should be in the vicinity of a place from which important terrain features within the field of operations are visible. The time fixed for assembly at this rendezvous will depend upon the time that the commander's reconnaissance is estimated to take.

(4) Representatives of supporting arms must be put into early touch with the commanders of units that they are to support.

(5) Arrangements must be made in advance for the supply of food, ammunition, overcoats, blankets, etc., and for the speedy evacuation of casualties.

(6) Orders for "T" Groups (for instance, whether they are to be left under brigade control or released to subordinate units) will depend upon the situation and decisions made under stage 2 (*b*(2), above).

e. Saving time.—This can be done by—

(1) Deciding everything possible at once from the map: for instance, sectors, boundaries, areas, allotment of troops, etc. By this means

Group	Brigade [1]	Battalion	Company	Platoons of rifle and Hq companies	Remarks
Reconnaissance (R)	Brigade Commander. Brigade Major [2] or Brigade Intelligence Officer. Brigade Signal Officer. Brigade Anti-Tank Battery Commander. Brigade Light Anti-Aircraft Battery Commander. No. 11 R/T set. Despatch Riders. Similar "R" Groups of units of supporting arms may accompany Brigade "R" Group (a).	Battalion Commander. Adjutant [2] or Battalion Intelligence Officer. Signal Officer. Despatch Rider. Similar "R" Groups of subordinate units of supporting arms may accompany Battalion "R" Group (b).	Company Commander. Orderly.	Platoon Commander. Orderly.	(a) Equivalent groups, artillery regiment or group, tank battalion, field company, machine-gun company, etc. (b) Equivalent groups, artillery, anti-tank, light anti-aircraft, tank, and machine-gun subunits, sections of field companies, and carrier platoons. (c) Equivalent groups of supporting earms maybe ord red to RV (rendezvous). (d) Certain Hq platoons such as anti-aircraft and pioneer will often receive orders early and be dispersed and in action. (e) In certain circumstances may be with "T" Group.
Orders (O)	Battalion "R" Groups (c).	Company "R" Groups; "R" Groups of Hq Company platoons (d).	Platoon "R" Group.	Section or Detachment Commander.	
Fighting (F)	Brigade Hq and Signal Section. Anti-Tank Battery. Light Anti-Aircraft Battery. 3 Infantry Battalions. Units under command (attached).	Battalion Hq. 4 Rifle Companies. Platoons of Hq Company. "A" echelon transport (e).	Company Hq. 3 Platoons. Platoon trucks (e).	Platoon Hq. Sections or detachments. Platoon trucks (e).	
Transport (T)	Brigade Hq Administrative Transport (if any); "B" echelon of battalions.	"B" echelon, if under battalion control.			

[1] The British brigade is roughly equivalent to the U. S. reinforced regiment.

[2] Neither the Brigade Major from Brigade Hq nor the Adjutant from Battalion Hq should be absent at the same time as the commanders.

FIGURE 107.—Composition of groups in an infantry brigade.

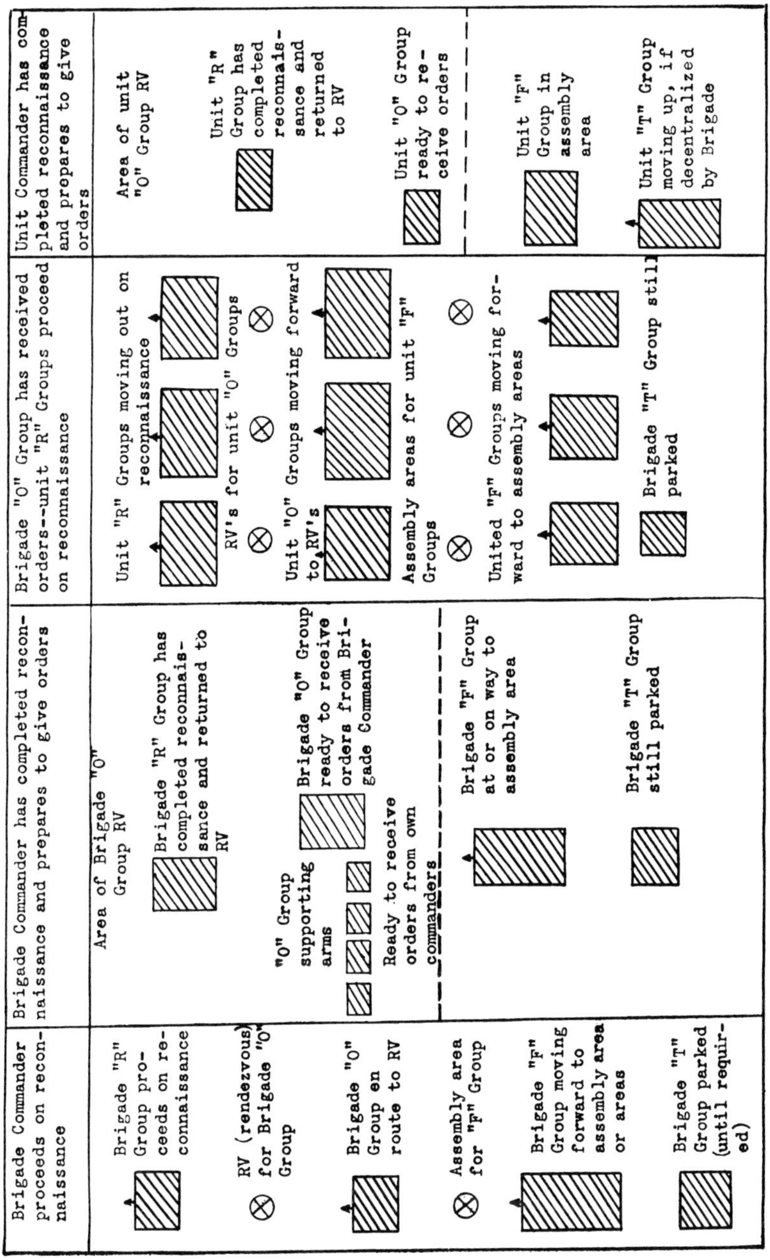

Brigade Commander proceeds on reconnaissance

Brigade "R" Group proceeds on reconnaissance

RV (rendezvous) for Brigade "O" Group

Brigade "O" Group en route to RV

Assembly area for "F" Group

Brigade "F" Group moving forward to assembly area or areas

Brigade "T" Group parked (until required)

Brigade Commander has completed reconnaissance and prepares to give orders

Area of Brigade "O" Group RV

Brigade "R" Group has completed reconnaissance and returned to RV

Brigade "O" Group ready to receive orders from Brigade Commander

"O" Group supporting arms

Ready to receive orders from own commanders

Brigade "F" Group at or on way to assembly area

Brigade "T" Group still parked

Brigade "O" Group has received orders—unit "R" Groups proceed on reconnaissance

Unit "R" Groups moving out on reconnaissance

RV's for unit "O" Groups

Unit "O" Groups moving forward to RV's

Assembly areas for unit "F" Groups

United "F" Groups moving forward to assembly areas

Brigade "T" Group still parked

Unit Commander has completed reconnaissance and prepares to give orders

Area of unit "O" Group RV

Unit "R" Group has completed reconnaissance and returned to RV

Unit "O" Group ready to receive orders

Unit "F" Group in assembly area

Unit "T" Group moving up, if decentralized by Brigade

FIGURE 108.—Stages of deployment of an infantry brigade.

subordinate commanders can carry out some reconnaissance concurrently with the commander's reconnaissance.

(2) Sending a staff officer with oral orders regarding essentials to those subordinate commanders who are most pressed for time. Should adequately trained Motor Contact Liaison Officers be available, these may be used to replace the staff officer.

(3) Having the commander of supporting artillery travel in the commander's car during his reconnaissance. In this case the risk of both becoming casualties must be accepted.

f. Commander's responsibility.—(1) To insure the efficient functioning of all arms in a coordinated plan, the stages outlined for deployment (*b*, above) and illustrated diagrammatically in figure 108 should be carried out in the sequence laid down. Such time as is found necessary to carry out each phase in peacetime, with an ample margin of safety for the many accidents which may occur in wartime, should be allowed.

(2) In proportion as this procedure is condensed, or as parts of it are omitted and as the time allowance is cut down, so the risk of failure, or of success with such heavy casualties as will approximate failure, will steadily increase. Of this there can be no doubt. The question of when and where time can be saved, with and without risk, must therefore be studied continuously. The staff must be prepared at all times to warn the commander if, in their opinion, insufficient time is being allowed. But on every occasion the commander must balance up the pros and cons and gauge the risks. He alone must make the final decisions.

(3) As previously stated, while reconnaissance is being carried out and orders are being issued, there should be a simultaneous and uninterrupted movement forward of all units until final battle development has been completed. While the "R" Group is making its reconnaissance, the "O" Group is assembling at a previously designated point which normally should have good terrain observation characteristics. While each commander of a subordinate unit is moving to his assembly point to receive orders, he should know that his combat units are moving forward to the designated assembly area of a higher command. As soon as he receives his orders, he, in turn, makes his reconnaissance with his subordinate commanders. This whole process is repeated until all units are in position.

122. Operation orders.—*a.* All operation orders adhere to the following form and technique:

(1) *Information.*—(*a*) *Of hostile forces.*—A statement of facts and deductions from all sources, giving a general picture of the situation.

(*b*) *Of friendly forces.*—The intentions of the higher command and of friendly troops, arranged logically (e. g., corps, divisional, and brigade situations).

(*c*) *Of boundaries.*—As laid down by the higher command.

(2) *Intention.*—A brief statement of what the commander issuing the orders intends to achieve (i. e., the decision).

(3) *Method.*—Missions, in logical sequence, allotted to the fighting troops and aircraft.

(4) *Administrative arrangements.*—General instructions for supply, transport, ammunition, medical services, etc.

(5) *Intercommunication.*—Locations of command post's (CP's) lateral lines, etc.

(6) *"Ack" ("Acknowledge").*—Always used in an operation order.

b. A transcript of an actual operation order (involving the 11th Indian Infantry Brigade) follows:

Copy No. —
11 Mar 1941.

11 IND INF BDE OPERATION ORDER NO. 16.

Reference Maps: GIANGHEREN, 1/50,000.
Air Survey Sheets.

1. INFORMATION.
(a) Vide Appendix "A".
(b) Following under comd 11 Ind Inf Bde from 2130 hrs DI-2 day:—
     1 R. F.
     4 Fd Coy S & M.
     4 Raj Rif
     "A" Coy 17 Fd Amb.

2. INTENTION.
11 Ind Inf Bde will capture and hold the line of the high ground incl Mt SANCHIL—BRIGS PEAK feature—HOGS BACK—FLAT TOP (see Appendix "B").

3. METHOD.
The day of attack will be known as DI day and will be notified later.

4. Troops and Objectives.
     2 Camerons—incl Mt SANCHIL—incl BRIGS PEAK feature.
     1 Raj Rif—excl BRIGS PEAK feature—incl HOGS BACK.
     2 Mahrattas—excl HOGS BACK—incl FLAT TOP.

5. ZERO HOUR.
0700 hrs—(Check Zero 0600 hrs).

6. Starting Line.
Present front line from excl Pt 1616 (3586) to 50 yards to WEST of left Coy Posn.
     (Units will be responsible for cutting gaps in the wire before 0500 hours DI day. 1 Raj Rif will cut gaps for 2 Camerons and will provide guides to show 2 Camerons the posn of the gaps).

7. Bde Reserve.

> 1 R. F.
> 4 Raj Rif.

For role of this reserve see Appendix "D".

8. Assembly.

(a) Reliefs on the hill will be carried out (vide 11 Ind Inf Bde No. 0385 dated 10 Mar 41) and will be completed by 0500 hrs DI day.

(b) It is essential that the enemy should not become aware of the assembly and movement will be restricted as follows:—

(i) M–I

> 2 Mahrattas—Movement in rear areas will be reduced to a minimum. Except for small recce parties, movement in the front line is forbidden.

P. T. O.

(ii) DI

No movement in front line by 2 Camerons and 2 Mahrattas between first light and 0700 hours.

(c) Dispersion.

Space is restricted but as wide a dispersion as possible will be maintained at all times.

9. Arty.

(a) See Appendix "C".

(b) Arty Screens will be carried and will be used as directed in 11 Ind Inf Bde No. 13/106/G dated 11 Mar 41. 2 Mahrattas will show screens in the direction of Pt 1572 (3387) when the objective has been captured.

10. R. E.

(a) 4 Fd Coy S & M is placed in support of bns as follows:

> One Sec—2 Camerons
>
> Two Secs— $\begin{cases} 2 \text{ Mahrattas} \\ 1 \text{ Raj Rif} \end{cases}$

(b) Tasks.

> (i) To make tracks forward;
> (ii) To assist in the consolidation by making strong points.

(c) Secs will NOT be employed in any other manner without orders from Bde HQ.

(d) Secs will move to respective Bn areas in rear of the Coy 1 R. F. moving up the track at 0700 hrs DI day. (See App "D".) Other than recce parties, secs will not move further forward until ordered by O. C., 2 Camerons, and Bde HQ in case of the secs in support of 2 Mahrattas and 1 Raj Rif.

(e) HQ 4 Fd Coy S & M will remain in the Indian Dump area.

11. Consolidation.

(a) Immediate steps will be taken on capture of the objective to prevent penetration by counter-attack.

(b) D. F. tasks will be arranged by Bn Comds direct with F. O. O.'s as soon as possible after the objective has been captured.

(c) Forward positions will be sited, whenever possible, in front of the crest line of the objective.

(d) Wire will be erected at first opportunity and at such a distance from forward troops as to put them out of bombing range.

12. A Tk.

(a) Two A Tk rifles per bn may be taken forward to assist, if required, in overcoming enemy strong points.

(b) A Tk Pls remain under comd bns.

13. R. A. F.

See Appendix "E".

P. T. O.____

14. Stores.

(a) Wire Cutters.—Extra cutters are allotted as follows:

    2 Camerons—80

    2 Mahrattas⎫
    1 Raj Rif ⎬—90 each

(b) Sandbags.—At the scale of two per man will be held in dumps for consolidation.

(c) Order of Priority of forward despatch of stores during and after attack.

    Ammunition.
    Water.
    Wire and sandbags.
    Food.

15. Carrying Parties.

(a) Units will arrange for their own carrying parties, under the command of an officer, for the immediate supply of the forward troops during and after the capture of the objective.

Later, it is hoped that mules will be available.

(b) Each bn will provide one carrying party for taking forward wire for F. O. O.'s. C. R. A., 4 Ind Div., is notifying units direct of the time and place these parties will report.

Strength—Six Other Ranks.

(c) All personnel of carrying parties will wear a white armband on the right arm.

16. Secrecy.

(a) No orders, marked maps, etc., will be taken forward of the Starting Line.

(b) Men will be warned particularly NOT to "talk" should they be captured. They may, however, be informed that there is a possibility of Australian troops following them up.

(c) SECRECY is of PARAMOUNT IMPORTANCE.

ADM.

17. Instructions issued separately.

INTERCOMN.

18. Bde HQ will open at HQ present LEFT Bn at 2130 hrs DI–2 day.

19. Location of Bn HQ.

2 Camerons —In area now occupied by RIGHT forward Coy of present LEFT Bn.

1 Raj Rif —CRACK—moving to NEAR FEATURE and later HOGS BACK.

2 Mahrattas—Centre of area now occupied by LEFT Coy of present LEFT Bn. Moving to SLAB ROCK.

P. T. O......

20. Communications.

Sig Offr will arrange for:
(a) L/T and W/T to all bns.
(b) R/T to 2 Mahrattas (to be used ONLY if L/T fails).
(c) L/T, V/T and R/T to HQ 4 Ind Div.

21. L. O.'s (less 4 Raj Rif) will remain with Bns. L. O. 4 Raj Rif will report Bde HQ at 0600 hrs DI day.

22. Synchronisation.

Sig Offr will synchronise with C. R. A., 4 Ind Div., at 0600 hours DI day and pass to units.

23. S. O. S. Signal.

Signals for D. F. after capture of objective are being issued by C. R. A., 4 Ind Div.

24. Password.

From 1800 hours DI–I day to 2359 hours DI day:

KHARTOUM

ACK. (Signed)
Time of signature 1200 hours. Major,
Method of despatch—by D. R. Brigade Major.
DISTRIBUTION: 1 1 R. F.
2 2 Camerons
3 2 Mahrattas
4 1 Raj Rif.
5 4 Raj Rif.
6 A Tk Coy.
7 4 Fd Coy SM.
8 A Coy 17 Fd Amb.
9 Comd.
10 B. M.
11 S. C.
12 Sigs.
13 B. I. O.
14 B. T. O.
15 B. O. O.
16 RIASC Offr.
17 L. O. 1.
18 L. O. 2.
19 L. O. 3.
20 Div L. O.
21 Lt-Col. ——–—.
22 Maj. ——–— (DAQMG).
23 5 Ind Inf Bde.
24 C. R. A., 4 Ind Div.
25 4 Ind Div.
26 5 Ind Div.
27 File.
28}
29} War Diary.

APPENDIX "A"—All copies.
APPENDIX "B"—NOT issued to copy Nos. 6, 14, 15 and 16.
APPENDIX "C"—NOT issued to copy Nos. 6, 7, 8, 11–22, 24–26.
APPENDIX "D"—NOT issued to copy Nos. 6, 8, 14–16.
APPENDIX "E"—NOT issued to copy Nos. 6, 8, 11, 14–20, 22–26.

c. The following outline indicates the general content of the appendixes referred to in the operation order as given in *b,* above:

(1) *Appendix A.*—Reference maps and information on—

(*a*) Enemy.

(*b*) Own troops.

(2) *Appendix B.*—Mimeographed panoramic sketch of terrain occupied by enemy.

(3) *Appendix C.*—Task table of the Royal Artillery, with columns showing the following:

(*a*) Serial number.

(*b*) Time and duration of firing.

1. From.

2. To.

(*c*) Task.

(*d*) Rate.

(*e*) Ammunition.

(*f*) Remarks.

(4) *Appendix D.*—Instructions for brigade reserve.

(5) *Appendix E.*—Air plan.

(*a*) Tasks of supporting aircraft.

(*b*) Air-ground communications.

123. British and U. S. equivalent terms for advance guard and rear guard formations.—See figure 109.

124. British and U. S. equivalent terms for the attack.—See figure 110.

125. Defensive.—*a.* The British *Field Service Regulations,* Volume II (Operations—General), 1935, page 132, makes the following statement on defensive principles:

"The adoption of the defensive does not necessarily imply weakness or inferiority. It may be necessary to gain time for the arrival of reinforcements or for the execution of a decisive maneuvre in some other part of the battlefield or of the theatre of operations. It may also be desirable to induce the enemy to commit himself to a ground favorable to the counter-offensive and to waste his strength in attacks on a well-prepared position; just as some of the most effective falls in wrestling are given by inducing the opponent first to exert his strength in a certain desired direction."

b. The discussion of this doctrine is continued with excerpts from the more recent British War Office publication *Operations,* Military Training Pamphlet No. 23, Part II (Defence), 1939, pages 5–6:

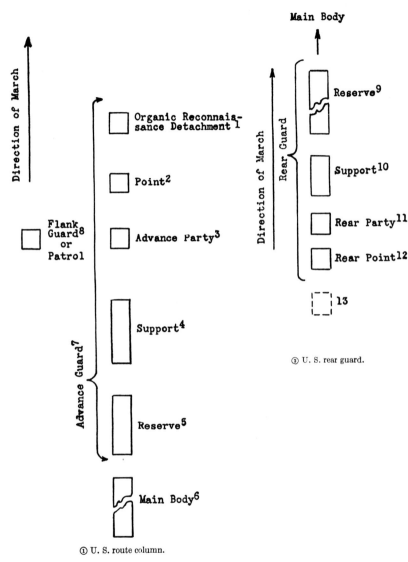

① U. S. route column.

② U. S. rear guard.

British equivalents

Route column:
1. Mobile troops (recce unit).
2, 3, 4. Van guard.
5. Main guard.
6, 7, 8. (Same.)

Rear guard:
9, 10. Main body of rear guard.
11, 12. Rear parties of rear guard.
13. Rear guard mobile troops.

FIGURE 109.—U. S. march dispositions (with equivalent British terminology).

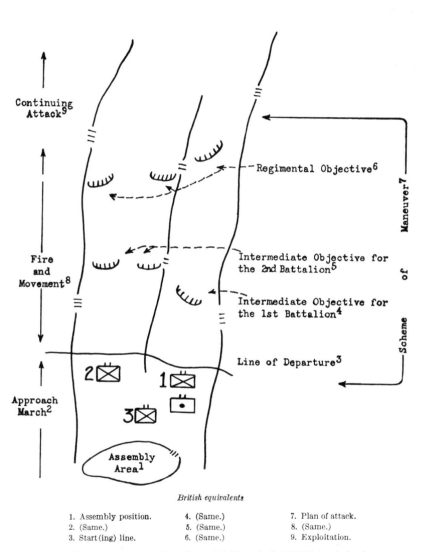

Continuing
Attack[9]

Fire
and
Movement[8]

Approach
March[2]

Regimental Objective[6]

Intermediate Objective for
the 2nd Battalion[5]

Intermediate Objective for
the 1st Battalion[4]

Line of Departure[3]

Assembly
Area[1]

Maneuver[7]

of

Scheme

British equivalents

1. Assembly position.	4. (Same.)	7. Plan of attack.
2. (Same.)	5. (Same.)	8. (Same.)
3. Start(ing) line.	6. (Same.)	9. Exploitation.

FIGURE 110.—U. S. regiment in attack (with equivalent British terminology).

"The advantage which the defence confers upon the defender, where he has freedom of action, is that he has the opportunity to select ground that will allow of the greatest possible development of the fire power of his weapons; and as time allows, the defences can be progressively improved. The chief object of the defender is to reduce and exhaust the enemy's forces with the minimum expenditure of his own. He may then eventually be able, either in the same part of the battlefield or elsewhere, to pass to the offensive and complete the defeat of the enemy; or it may, in certain situations, be sufficient if the enemy is prevented from attaining his object.

"The principal weakness and danger of the defence is that freedom of action and maneuvre is temporarily surrendered and allowed to pass to the enemy, who can choose the time and place of his attack. Active reconnaissance is therefore of great importance. * * *

"Troops allotted to the defence of a locality must defend it to the end without a thought of withdrawal, whatever may happen on their right or left, unless and until their commander receives orders to retire.

"A special feature of the defence imposed by modern weapons is that it must be in depth and designed to withstand attack supported by tanks, heavy artillery fire and aircraft. The power of modern weapons is such that the attacker, by concentrating his effort, can usually make a breach on a limited front and to a limited depth in even an organised and prepared defence."

c. British doctrine in defence is now veering away from the defended line in depth towards heavily armed pockets of resistance in depth or behind an anti-tank obstacle. The enemy is engaged by one after the other of these pockets of resistance, which should be in tank-proof localities. Great stress is now laid on alternate firing positions for all troops in any defensive position, especially infantry and artillery.

126. Organization of defensive position.—*a.* The following excerpt (with slight changes) from British War Office publication *Operations*, Military Training Pamphlet No. 23, Part II (Defence), 1939, pages 10–11, states some British principles for anti-tank defence:

"The occupation and preparation of a defensive position will be protected by covering troops, which will occupy a position to cover the defensive position during this period. The covering position or positions should be sufficiently far from the defensive position to give the covering troops room for delaying action, and should not be so close that the enemy could bring observed artillery fire to bear on the main position. Occasions may arise, however, when, owing to the proximity of the enemy or other causes, the covering troops will be obliged to occupy a closer position which may in extreme cases coincide with that eventually to be occupied by the outposts. The covering troops will usually be provided by complete formations. They may, however, be provided by units thrown out by forward brigades in cases where the covering position is close. They will be withdrawn ultimately into reserve. As they may be required to hold the covering position against enemy attack, they must be strong in anti-tank guns and must be provided with the support of artillery, which will usually be under orders of the commander of the covering troops. Where, however, the position of the covering troops is so close that it is adequately covered by guns of the defensive position, the artillery may more suitably be 'in support' of such covering troops. OP's (observation posts) will always be established on the covering position. The divisional light tank regiment with some medium machine guns will as a rule form part of the covering troops. When a complete formation with its own signal personnel is not provided, an allotment of the necessary signals to the commander of the covering troops must be made.

"The withdrawal of the covering troops will be coordinated along the whole army front. This will usually be effected by higher commanders, who will give the time at which these troops are to be withdrawn. As the units comprising the covering troops, with the exception of the cavalry, will be required to prepare their own positions in the defensive organisation, it will be advantageous if they can be withdrawn in good time. The dominating factor affecting their withdrawal, however, is that they must not be withdrawn until the main position is sufficiently prepared to meet the enemy's attack.

"When the main body of the covering troops is withdrawn, the divisional reconnaissance regiment (battalion), which must be adequately supported by artillery and, when possible, machine guns and anti-tank guns, should remain in observation on or in front of the covering position to gain information and to delay and mystify the enemy as long as possible. These detachments will fall back under pressure, and it is essential that good lateral liaison be maintained to ensure that the movement is properly coordinated.

"A main position will be organised to provide:

"(1) The area of forward defended localities protected by a tank obstacle;

"(2) The brigade (U. S. regiment) reserve area;

"(3) The divisional reserve area protected by a tank obstacle.

"Outposts will be established in front of the line of foremost defended localities (main line of resistance) for local protection. Their role will be:

"(1) To prevent the enemy's reconnoitring troops from obtaining information;

"(2) To obtain information of the enemy's approach;

"(3) To gain such time by resistance as may be necessary to enable the garrison of the main position to prepare for action.

"The distance at which outposts are placed in front of the main position will depend chiefly on the ground. It will be advantageous if they can be placed behind a tank obstacle."

b. British officers have reported that during operations in France in 1940 it often was unavoidably necessary to hold extended frontages. With limited resources this may occur again. Under these conditions it may often be difficult to reconcile the two principles that a position organized for defence against a tank attack must be in the greatest depth possible, and that an obstacle must be kept under small-arms fire throughout its length. However, to keep the whole length of the obstacle under small-arms fire may be possible only at the expense of depth.

c. Under these circumstances depth must be the primary consideration and some gaps in the belt of fire along the anti-tank obstacle must be accepted. If these conditions prevail, however, it is essential to maintain mobile reserves which can counterattack the enemy as soon as the latter has discovered the gaps and commenced infiltration.

Furthermore, these gaps must be constantly observed by day and night either by patrolling or other suitable means in order to get the earliest information of any enemy penetration or other activity.

127. British and U. S. equivalent terms for regiment (British brigade) in defence.—See figure 111.

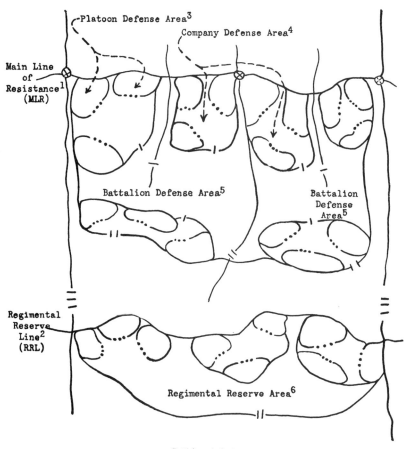

British equivalents

1. (Line of) forward (foremost) defended localities.
2. Brigade reserve position.
3. Platoon sector.
4. Company sector.
5. Battalion sector.
6. Brigade reserve area.

Figure 111.— U. S. regiment in defence (with equivalent British terminology).

128. Tactics of carrier platoon.—*a. Organization.*—The organization of the carrier platoon, an integral part of the rifle battalion (see par. 26*a* and fig. 9), is illustrated in figure 112.

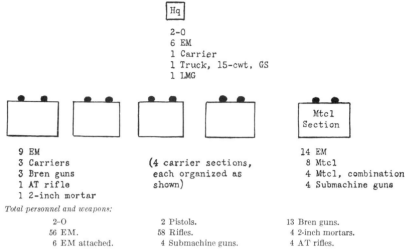

```
                            Hq

                         2-O
                         6 EM
                         1 Carrier
                         1 Truck, 15-cwt, GS
                         1 LMG
```

9 EM
3 Carriers
3 Bren guns
1 AT rifle
1 2-inch mortar

(4 carrier sections,
each organized as
shown)

14 EM
8 Mtcl
4 Mtcl, combination
4 Submachine guns

Total personnel and weapons:

2-O	2 Pistols.	13 Bren guns.
56 EM.	58 Rifles.	4 2-inch mortars.
6 EM attached.	4 Submachine guns.	4 AT rifles.

FIGURE 112.—Organization of the carrier platoon.

b. Characteristics.—(1) The carrier is bulletproof against rifle fire on the same level, but the crew is vulnerable to fire from above, or when the carrier is on a forward slope. It is, therefore, a partially protected vehicle only. (See fig. 113.)

FIGURE 113.—Carriers in close cooperation with infantry.

(2) The carrier can move fast across good country, but will be stopped by trenches, by any obstacle which is a tank obstacle, and by many which are not. There will be occasions, therefore, when it will be unable to follow tanks forward. Continuous scouting will always be necessary.

(3) The light machine-gun detachment, consisting of two men, cannot be expected to do more than keep the gun in action, either in the vehicle or on the ground. Once in action, the detachment has little or no power to protect itself by observation, and is therefore very vulnerable to a quick attack by one or two determined infantrymen. If an isolated position has to be held for any length of time, the three detachments in a section must be sited to provide mutual support. Carriers cannot carry out mopping-up operations.

(4) The period of dismounting from the carrier and getting into action is one of considerable danger to personnel and vehicle. Dismounting must be carried out under cover and very quickly. The carrier, once the LMG is dismounted, is entirely vulnerable, and must either withdraw to the cover of other troops or must be concealed close to the LMG and under cover.

(5) The fire power of the carrier platoon is considerable, and the platoon should for short periods be able to hold a front varying from 500 yards to 1,000 yards according to the depth in which it is disposed. But, as stressed above, gun detachments are very vulnerable unless protected from the flank and rear.

(6) The LMG can give fire as effective from 400 yards as from closer up. There is no need to move close in to a target to gain fire effect.

(7) From these characteristics the tactical employment of the carrier may be deduced. It must be remembered that the carrier is not a light tank; it is an armoured machine designed to convey the LMG from place to place and a machine from which the LMG can be fired if necessary.

c. Carrier platoon in attack.—(1) *Tasks in attack.*—(a) Close cooperation with infantry alone (figs. 113 and 114).

(b) Close cooperation with infantry and infantry tanks.

(c) Flank protection.

(d) Consolidation.

(2) *Close cooperation with infantry alone.*—(a) Throughout the attack, reconnaissance by both the infantry commander and the carrier commander, especially for the purpose of obtaining knowledge of terrain features, must be continuous. Points to be looked for are likely carrier positions, the line of advance, and obstacles to movement.

(*b*) During the advance, the infantry commander may realize that some of his leading troops are held up by fire from enemy defence areas. If the advance is only partially checked, he may decide to move forward his carriers, in the immediate rear of the troops still advancing, to positions from which the carriers can bring fire to bear on the enemy from the flank or rear, and so enable the advance to continue.

(*c*) On other occasions, carriers may be sent wide to a flank to a position from which flanking fire against enemy resistance may be employed.

(3) *Close cooperation with infantry and infantry tanks.*—(*a*) When the infantry attack is supported by a prearranged fire plan, the car-

FIGURE 114.--Carriers in an advance.

riers will usually be best kept in hand as a mobile reserve of fire power. As the attack proceeds, they may be used to infiltrate through gaps and to turn enemy areas which are still holding out, or to guard a flank.

(*b*) The attack against light opposition will often be more in the nature of an advance, and will rely mainly on infiltration and maneuver. In such cases carriers may precede the infantry, reconnoitering for gaps in the defence and flanks of enemy resistance.

(*c*) In an attack in which infantry tanks are cooperating, the role of the carrier platoon, provided that the ground permits of its moving forward, is to advance from fire position to fire position in order to give close support to tanks moving ahead of the infantry. This implies in the first instance close support against anti-tank weapons disclosing themselves within the area of attack and on the flank of the attack, and, subsequently, support against weapons located beyond the objective. In an attack in which the leading echelon of tanks moves directly to the final objective, the carrier platoon will rarely be able to accompany this echelon, but will probably move protected by the tanks of the second echelon. As the infantry with the second echelon of tanks approach the final objective, carriers may go forward to the objective to engage anti-tank weapons located beyond it. But plans will vary in accordance with circumstances, and no stereotyped method can be contemplated.

(4) *Flank protection.*—(a) Flank protection consists not only in stopping enemy counterattacks, but also in the neutralization of enemy fire coming from the flank. Efficient performance of this task depends mainly on good observation.

(b) Carrier platoons and sections employed on this task may be attached to leading rifle companies, or given an independent task directly under battalion control.

(c) The closest cooperation with leading rifle companies should be maintained, and carrier platoon and section commanders should make full use of their carriers for keeping contact.

(5) *Consolidation.*—(a) On reaching an objective there will, as a rule, be some measure of disorganization, and it is then that the attacking troops are most vulnerable to immediate counterattack. The actual objective reached may not be the best ground on which to consolidate. The process of consolidation will therefore include the reconnaissance and organization of the position for defence, the reorganization of troops, the replenishment of ammunition, etc. Carriers will often be most valuable to cover consolidating troops during this very difficult period; and if they are used in this role, they must be relieved as soon as possible.

(b) If the ground is not suitable for the employment of carriers in a fighting role, they may be used to bring forward ammunition of all sorts, mortars, wire, anti-tank mines, and entrenching tools for consolidation.

d. Carrier platoon in defence.—(1) The tasks that may be allotted to carriers in defence are—

(a) To assist the outposts.

(b) To provide a mobile reserve of fire power.

(c) To support counterattack, by dismounted or armoured action.

(d) To give depth to the defensive fire of the battalion.

(2) *Carriers on outpost.*—(*a*) Carriers are suitable for employment with outpost troops, as, by day, they can be established forward of the outpost line and so give early warning of the enemy's approach.

(*b*) If employed in static roles for anything but short periods, they should be supported by infantry. Owing to the limited number of men that crews can provide for observation, carriers are easily stalked and surrounded.

(3) *Carriers as mobile reserve.*—(*a*) A mobile reserve of fire power will enable the battalion commander to support hard-pressed areas, stop gaps, and obtain surprise by fire from unexpected directions. Careful prior reconnaissance by all ranks of the carrier platoon will be necessary in order to insure an intimate knowledge of the battalion area.

(*b*) The battalion commander should, as a rule, hold all carriers under his own command in defence, and not disperse them by allotment to companies.

(4) *Carriers in counterattack.*—(*a*) Carriers can be used quickly and boldly in the immediate counterattack, in either dismounted or armoured action, or they may be used to provide supporting fire from previously reconnoitered positions.

(*b*) Again, all ranks of the carrier platoon should acquire a good knowledge of the terrain by previous reconnaissance.

(5) *Carrier fire power in defence.*—The carrier platoon should rarely be employed in the static role of increasing the depth of the position, unless guns so allotted can also be available as a mobile reserve. At night, or in fog or mist, the LMG's of the carrier platoon can, by means of the tripod, be laid on fixed lines. If the carriers themselves can be concealed close at hand, then it may be possible for the two roles—the provision of depth and a mobile reserve—to be linked, but the retention of a mobile reserve is the first consideration.

e. Carrier platoon in protection.—(1) *Advance and gaining of contact.*— Carriers can be used in the advance and contact phase, when useful short reconnaissances can be made to the front and flanks. The method of movement on roads or across country on all occasions in face of the enemy will be by bounds, and carriers will often be used to take over and hold points gained by reconnaissance troops.

(2) *Flank guards.*—(*a*) Carriers can be used with advantage on flank guards, whether fixed or moving parallel to the column which they are protecting. In both cases their ability to move quickly from point to point can be so used as to give to the enemy the impression that the flank is wider and more strongly held than is actually the case.

(*b*) Carriers can also be used as detached posts on side roads. The distance of these posts will depend on the topography, but, as a rule, they should not be farther than is necessary to safeguard the main column from direct fire or observation.

(c) This duty will usually consist of making temporary barbed-wire concertina road blocks, covered by the anti-tank rifle.

(3) *Rear guards and withdrawal.*—(a) In a withdrawal, the carrier platoon forms a most suitable unit for holding an intermediate position through which groups of the rear guard withdraw, whether the action takes place by day or night.

(b) In this form of action there are unlimited opportunities for initiative. By a skillful maneuvering of the carriers behind ridges, using either dismounted or armoured action, the enemy can be deceived as to the strength of the rear guard. As an alternative rearguard action, on suitable ground, carriers may be left in ambush in concealed and camouflaged positions, holding their fire until the enemy is close enough to be so punished that his advance will be checked.

f. Other uses in war.—(1) Carriers have been found to be of value in—

Reconnaissance.

Intercommunication.

Wood, village, and river fighting.

Raids.

Night operations.

(2) Carriers have also been used frequently to transport—

Small-arms ammunition, grenades, etc.

Tools.

Mortars.

Wire.

Anti-tank mines.

Reinforcing personnel.

Wounded.

(3) *Use of carrier as reconnaissance vehicle.*—The armour and mobility of the carrier permit reconnaissance of all kinds to be carried out with speed and comparative safety. This reconnaissance includes—

(a) Inspection of occupied defence areas by brigade (regimental) and battalion commanders.

(b) Flank reconnaissances to find the location and examine the dispositions of adjacent units.

(c) Short-distance reconnaissances forward of the main line of resistance, in the nature of daylight patrols.

(d) Reconnaissance of successive positions during withdrawals.

(*e*) Close reconnaissance by junior commanders and by intelligence personnel of elements of the defence under fire.

(4) *Intercommunication.*—During battle the carrier has been found to be a good means of intercommunication, and has been used in this capacity by battalion, company, and platoon commanders. Its reliability in getting through messages and information under fire has been proved in action where other methods have failed. It has, in fact, on many occasions replaced the runner in forward areas.

(5) *Wood fighting.*—In spite of the disadvantages of being restricted to roads and trails, and of being liable to casualties from snipers in trees, etc., carriers have been used to advantage in wood fighting. The method has generally been to lie hidden in the undergrowth on the near side of clearings and surprise the enemy as he emerges into the clearings. In such instances it was found necessary to have well-reconnoitered lines of withdrawal.

(6) *River fighting.*—Carriers have been found useful in holding up the enemy at canal and river crossings, especially at some canals where the carriers could move up and down under cover, or even partial cover, of the raised banks, and then, by getting the LMG into position, enfilade a section of the canal. Carriers have also been used to bring up troops with grenades under the banks of canals, the troops throwing their grenades among the enemy on the far side with good effect.

(7) *Raids.*—Carriers have been used with effect to raid and bomb enemy positions held by machine guns, and groups in defence areas. Examples for two such cases follow:

(*a*) On one occasion successful action was carried out when 3-inch mortars shelled some farm buildings, and the carriers, moving around on both flanks, struck the enemy as he withdrew.

(*b*) On another occasion the carriers of one unit penetrated the advanced elements of the hostile infantry, thus slowing up its advance. The raid entailed a cruise along 3 or 4 miles of road within an area occupied by the enemy, and all hostile units which were met either fled or took cover immediately. The appearance of tanks could not have been more effective.

(8) *Transport.*—On numerous occasions carriers have been used to transport munitions and reinforcements across fire-swept terrain, where other means would have proved either impossible or very costly. Carriers have also been frequently used for carrying back wounded.

129. Leaguering[1] **(bivouacs of armoured regiments).**—*a. General.*—Bivouacs of armoured regiments in Libyan desert warfare are called leaguers by the British, and fall into two categories:

(1) Leaguers, both by day and by night, when contact with the enemy is expected.

(2) Leaguers when air attack but not ground attack may be expected. This form of leaguer involves merely dispersion, siting of anti-aircraft positions, digging of slit trenches (see par. 130 *b*), and maintenance of strict light discipline.

b. Principles involved.—Leaguering, when ground attack as well as air attack is expected, involves the following principles:

(1) All-around protection must be secured. Although units may be so sited as to afford mutual protection during the day, this is not possible during the night, because of the danger of firing on other friendly tanks and vehicles in the leaguer.

(2) Every vehicle must halt, facing in the proper direction to move out at a moment's notice if necessary.

(3) Dispersion must be maintained during daylight hours, but visual distance must be maintained after dark.

(4) Perimeter defence must be maintained.

c. Open leaguer.—During the hours of daylight, units are formed into what is known as an open leaguer, which is a form of dispersed bivouac. Vehicles are disposed in generally the same manner as when moving during the day. If air attack is expected, however, intervals and distances may be increased. In this open leaguer an all-around defence is habitually maintained.

d. Close leaguer (fig. 115).—(1) Upon halting for the night, units of the size of a regiment are formed into what is known as a close leaguer. Armoured vehicles, facing outwards, form either a triangle or a square, and the smaller units occupy the leg or side, with 10 to 15 yards between vehicles. Close leaguers are usually formed about dusk; but if the troops believe themselves to have been observed from the air or ground, they often change position after darkness falls. "B" echelon of the supply unit comes forward after dark and moves inside the triangle or square. Unit vehicles then move to the rear of their respective organizations.

---

[1] In British terminology the terms "harbouring" and "leaguering" occur as synonyms of the American word "bivouacking." The British use "harbouring" generally for all temporary camps, and therefore it comes closer to the meaning of "bivouacking" than does "leaguering." The latter term has been applied during the present war particularly to the specific type of "protective formation" employed in Libyan desert operations. The term "leaguering" or "leaguer" was derived by the British from the words "laagering" or "laager," which were used in the days of the South African wagon trains to denote a circular defensive formation, somewhat like that practiced by the American pioneers with their covered wagons.

(2) Night listening posts, as well as day patrols, are kept well out from the leaguer. Armoured vehicles are not used for this purpose. Within the leaguer one tank or other armoured vehicle is detailed to approximately every five vehicles. One man in each vehicle is always on the alert, and these sentries are changed hourly.

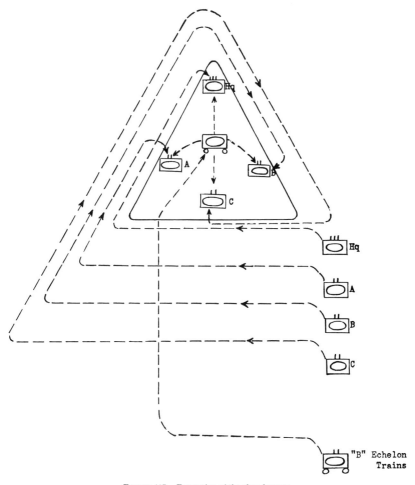

FIGURE 115.—Formation of the close leaguer.

(3) The lights which are necessary for administration, maintenance, and cooking are carefully concealed by tarpaulins. When there is no danger of observation or attack, a leaguer light is shown intermittently in order to assist "B" echelon or other units in finding the leaguer.

(4) Except in cases of emergency, radio silence is observed during the hours of darkness and for at least half an hour before moving into the leaguer area. Just prior to dawn, "B" echelon moves to the rear. When there is no danger of an attack by enemy ground forces, the open leaguer is used for both day and night formations. This is done in order to provide dispersal protection against air attacks.

130. Anti-aircraft defence.—*a. Riflemen and Bren gunners.*— Riflemen and Bren gunners are trained to take anti-aircraft targets while swinging guns through an arc, and to fire with a 12° lead.

b. Slit trenches.—Although passive, the "slit trench" is unquestionably the best means of anti-aircraft defence for the individual. Whenever a unit is halted for any appreciable length of time, men are trained to prepare to dig slit trenches at once. Units which made great use of slit trenches in Greece suffered almost no casualties from air attacks. The slit trench is most effective against dive bombardment aviation. Unit commanders have found that after men realize the protection which is afforded them by the slit trench, they dig slit trenches most enthusiastically and become very nonchalant about air attacks. If there is time, a slit trench should be dug deep enough to allow a man to use a rifle or light machine gun while standing.

c. In bivouac.—In bivouac, anti-aircraft precautions are primarily defensive. Slit trenches are dug; vehicles are dispersed with from 100 to 200 yards between vehicles; and at least one-third of the light machine guns are mounted for anti-aircraft defence. When available, a section of two Bofors guns may be assigned to a bivouac area. Bivouacs are usually by battalion or other small units.

d. On the march.—(1) The Bren guns on Motley mountings are dispersed throughout the column or formation. At least one-third of the light machine guns are tied to cross bows of trucks or are otherwise mounted for anti-aircraft defence. An anti-aircraft sentry is placed on each vehicle. (Openings have been cut out in the tops of all closed-bodied or closed-cab vehicles to make it possible for a sentry to stand on the driver's seat and have his head and shoulders protrude through the top of the vehicle—see par. 113c.)

(2) When the formation is attacked, every effort is made to keep it moving. On the desert when the attack is persistent, vehicles may keep moving and disperse over a very wide area, for they invariably move across country. In Greece, where the roads ran through many defiles and corridors and the air attacks were most persistent, the movements of motor columns were constantly interrupted, and during the evacuation period they had to be made largely during the night.

131. Motor marching.—*a. Definitions.*—(1) *Speed (U. S. equiva-*

lent "rate").—Speed, which is expressed "miles in the hour" (mih), means the average speed over a route, including the time spent on short halts up to 10 minutes in 1 hour, or 20 minutes in 2 hours.

(2) *Cruising speed (U. S. equivalent "speed")*.—The speedometer reading at which a vehicle must travel over open sections of road to maintain a given average of speed (i. e., mih) is known as "cruising speed." It is expressed as "miles per hour" (mph). The relation between speedometer speed and mih depends on road conditions; for example, gradients, defiles, traffic, etc.

(3) *Density (U. S. "density")*.—The general spacing of vehicles on a route is known as "density" and is expressed as "vehicles to the mile" (vtm). Five to ten vtm will probably escape air observation. Ten vtm do not offer a good bombing target. Thirty or forty vtm are suitable densities at night.

(4) *Time past a point (U. S. equivalent "time length")*.—The following formula may be used to obtain the time past a point in minutes:

$$\frac{60 \text{ minutes}}{\text{mih}} \times \frac{\text{Number of vehicles}}{\text{vtm}}$$

Thus the 2,500 vehicles of an embussed (entrucked) division moving at 12½ mih and 10 vtm will take 1,200 minutes, or 20 hours, to pass a point. With allowances for gaps between unit or formation groups of vehicles, this figure becomes approximately 30 hours.

(5) *Group (U. S. equivalent "march unit")*.—A group is a small number of vehicles moving as a formed unit.

(6) *Starting point (SP) (U.S. equivalent "initial point" (IP))*.—The SP is the place at which a column or group is timed onto the route. Columns, groups, etc., pass the SP at the speed and density ordered for the move.

(7) *Traffic control post (TCP) (U. S. equivalent "traffic control point")*.—TCP's are posts along the route through which the move is controlled. Normally, these are not necessary for small moves.

(8) *Dispersal point (U. S. equivalent "release point")*.—The dispersal point is the place where a column or group is timed off the route at the destination area.

b. Responsibility of staff for moves by road.—Decisions concerning movement are made by the commander. The General Staff is then responsible for the logistical aspect: for instance, the order of moves of units and formations. The "G" Staff and the "Q" Staff arrange the move generally. The "A" Staff is responsible for the traffic control arrangements of the move. In an infantry division the sequence will generally be as follows: [2]

---

[2] See paragraph 21*a* and figure 5 for the officers mentioned.

MOVEMENT TABLE.

APPENDIX "A" to 1 Div.0.0.No.5.

```
Route:-         CAMBERLEY - ODHIUM - LONG SUTTON - NEWBURY.
Speed:-         15 m.i.h.
Density:-       10 v.t.m.
Halts:-         At 20 mins to each even clock hour for 20 mins.
S.P.:-          Rd Junc 214632
T.C.P.No.2:-    X rds 284793
Dispersal Point:- X rds 306981
```

Serial No. (a)	Formation or Unit. (b)	To (c)	S.P. Head (d)	S.P. Tail (e)	T.C.P.No.2. Head (f)	T.C.P.No.2. Tail (g)	DISPERSAL Point. Head (h)	DISPERSAL Point. Tail (i)	REMARKS. (j)
1	15 Inf.Bde.	BLEWBURY	0900	1043	1015	1158	1257	1440	
2	40 Fd Regt.	BLEWBURTON	1100	1152	1215	1307	1457	1549	
3	182 Fd Coy.	ASPLEY	1210	1224	1325	1339	1607	1621	
4	18 Lt.A.A.Bty	ROMER	1234	1249	1349	1404	1631	1646	

FIGURE 116.—An actual divisional movement table.

(1) The divisional commander makes the decision regarding a move.

(2) GSO 1 decides on tactical aspects of the move, and consults with AA & QMG regarding the administrative problems of the move and the administrative layout of the division at the end of the move.

(3) GSO 2 writes the general operation order dealing with the move.

(4) GSO 3 (O) with DAQMG arranges the actual move, that is, movement tables, staff tables, graphs, etc.

(5) DAAG (with DAPM) arranges necessary traffic control for the move, obtaining additional traffic control personnel, if required, through GSO 2.

c. Movement (march) table.—See figure 116 for an actual British divisional movement table for a motorized unit.

Traffic Control Post personnel on a movement route; the despatch rider (note T. C. Brassard) is bringing news of a blocked route to the movement control officer.

Chapter 7

MILITARY INTELLIGENCE IN THE FIELD

SECTION I

GENERAL

132. Methods.—The methods followed by the intelligence service of the British Army in the collection, evaluation, and dissemination of military information are similar to those used by the U. S. Army.

SECTION II

ORGANIZATION

133. GHQ.—*a.* The Intelligence Section of GHQ is directed by a General Staff officer known as GSO 1 (I), and is divided into four sub-sections, each under control of a General Staff officer. The general distribution of intelligence duties among the sub-sections is as follows:

Ix—Organization and administration.
Ia—Information.
Ib—Security.
Ic—Censorship, publicity, and propaganda.

b. The organization shown in figure 117 is prepared on the basis of a field force of a strength up to four or five infantry divisions, and may consequently require expansion or alteration to suit any particular campaign.

GSO 1 (I)

Intelligence appreciations. Organization of military intelligence in the field. Liaison with British and allied naval, air, and civilian intelligence services and officials.

IX. ORGANIZATION AND ADMINISTRATION

General organization, coordination, and administration of the military intelligence service in the field. Intelligence appointments. Records, registry, and finance. Editing and printing of intelligence reports, summaries, and publications. Interviews. Liaison with Commandant, Intelligence Corps, on questions dealing with organization, administration, and training of the Intelligence Corps, and with the Field Survey Directorate regarding the issue of maps. General war diary.

Ia. INFORMATION

Coordination of work of subsection and distribution of information. Ia war diary.

Ia. (i) Enemy intentions and operations

Enemy strategy; political intelligence; intentions and plans; enemy tactics and methods of warfare. Situation reports.

Ia. (ii) Enemy order of battle

Order of battle. Identifications of formations and units. Strengths and locations. Discipline and morale. Equipment. Casualties, wastage, replacements, and reserves. Troop movements. Lines of communication and supplies. Interrogation of prisoners of war and study of captured documents.

Ia. (iii) Enemy defences, rear organization, and resources

Enemy defences, artillery, ordnance, munitions, armoured force vehicles, gas. Technical matters relating to rear organizations. Preparation of guide books and route reports.

Ia. (iv) Enemy signals

Enemy signal system, equipment, and traffic. Interception and translation of messages. Corespondence with the enemy.

Ia. (v) Air co-operation

Issue of information to air component. Collection and distribution of air intelligence. Advice to operations section on bombing targets. Photographs.

Ib. SECURITY

Collection of information by special methods. Organization and control of security intelligence. Security of operations and information. Issue of security instructions. Distribution of security intelligence. Ib accounts.

Ib. (i) Collection of information by special methods.

Ib. (ii) Civil security

Counterespionage. Countersabotage. Control of civilians and employment of field security police. Signal security section. Security lists.

Ib. (iii) Military security

Control of the observance of security orders by all military personnel. Elimination of untrustworthy personnel from military establishments. Security of offices. Security of military signal traffic and ciphers. Advice on all forms of military deception, including camouflage. Advice on wireless silence.

Ic. CENSORSHIP, PUBLICITY, AND PROPAGANDA

Coordination and supervision of censorship, publicity, and propaganda in the field, GSO 2 (I) being chief field censor. Liaison with British technical intelligence officers, British and foreign press representatives, attachés, and visitors. Ic war diary and general records.

Ic. (i) Censorship

Postal censorship of private and official correspondence and parcels passing in and out of the theater of war. Telegraph and telephone censorship. Trade and blockade censorship and economic intelligence. Traffic in arms and war material. Special censorship. Communications to and from prisoners of war.

Ic. (ii) Publicity

Press censorship. Press representatives in the field. Study of British, enemy, and neutral press Examination of publicity material for use by Ic (iii) as propaganda and counterpropaganda. Attachés and visitors—control of their movements and censorship of their correspondence. Photographers and artists—control of their movements and censorship of all pictorial matter produced in the field.

Ic. (iii) Propaganda

Propaganda and counterpropaganda for civilians (local and home) and for own and allied forces. Propaganda for enemy forces and civilians. Supervision of propaganda, printing, and distribution.

FIGURE 117.—Organization of the Intelligence Section of the General Staff at GHQ.

c. In addition to the four sub-sections mentioned above, there is a Survey Directorate which is responsible for all questions on surveying and mapping. The organization of this office is as follows:

FIELD SERVICE (FS) DIRECTOR OF SURVEY

ASSISTANT DIRECTOR OF SURVEY

Organizations and administration of the Field Survey Directorate. Field survey personnel, quartering, interior economy, stores, and transport. Field survey war diary and special records.

FS (i) Field Survey	*FS (ii) War Topography*	*FS (iii) Field Survey Maps and Publications*
Acquisition, recording, and indexing of information required for field surveys and maps. Initiation of surveys and coordination of those carried out by other branches. Supply of survey information required by artillery for sound-ranging and flash-spotting, etc.	Topography. Compilation and revision of route and topographical reports (in conjunction with Ix). Topographical interpretation and custody of air photographs, as supplied by air services.	Production, revision, reproduction, custody, and supply of maps and survey publications in the field.

134. GHQ, Home Forces.—The General Staff "I" of the GHQ, Home Forces, is similar in organization to the General Staff "I" of a field GHQ. The major difference is that in the former there is no provision for an Ic section to handle censorship, publicity, and propaganda. The "I" branch of the GHQ, Home Forces, maintains very close liaison with the Directorate of Military Intelligence in the War Office, and with the Admiralty and the Air Ministry.

135. Corps.—*a.* The intelligence duties at corps headquarters are under the direction of the senior General Staff officer and are carried out by a GSO 2, assisted by officers of the Intelligence Corps. Officers for intelligence duties are also allotted to the commander, corps Royal Artillery, and the commander, corps medium artillery. The duties of GSO 2 include—

(1) Coordination of intelligence work within the corps.

(2) Collation of reports from forward areas.

(3) Distribution of any information of value to those who can make best use of it.

(4) Arrangements, in conjunction with the Adjutant-General's branch, for the interrogation of prisoners of war.

(5) Supervision and execution of all security measures prescribed by higher authority.

b. The corps headquarters Deputy Assistant-Director of Survey acts as the advisor on technical subjects.

136. Divisions.—The intelligence duties for divisions are directed by a GSO 1. He has an intelligence staff, whose duties comprise—

a. Coordination and supervision of all intelligence work in the divisional area of operations.

b. Collation of intelligence and its transmission to higher authority.

c. Distribution of information within the division.

d. Arrangements for air reconnaissance and air photography and for the custody, interpretation, and distribution of air photographs supplied to the division.

e. Arrangements for the preliminary examination of prisoners of war.

f. Arrangements for the provision of maps.

137. Infantry brigades.—*a.* The Brigade Intelligence Officer (Bde IO or BIO), acting under the orders of the Brigade Major, co-ordinates all intelligence duties within the brigade and within the limits laid down by higher authority. He is held responsible for the collection, collation, and dissemination of all information obtained within the brigade area of operations.

b. Among the responsibilities of BIO in the field are—

(1) Identification of enemy units.

(2) Watch on enemy dispositions, movements, and field works within the brigade area of operations.

(3) News of, and deductions as to, enemy intentions.

(4) The study of all intelligence reports and summaries.

(5) Topography of adjacent country, particularly as affecting the movement of armoured fighting vehicles.

(6) Distribution (upward and downward) and record of information.

(7) Arrangements for the disposal of prisoners of war and of captured documents.

(8) Supply of maps and air photographs to units.

(9) Security measures to be adopted within the brigade.

(10) Upkeep of the brigade gas map.

c. To assist in the execution of these duties, BIO has at his disposal a small brigade intelligence section.

d. BIO must constantly be prepared to produce for his commander an estimate of the situation from the point of view of the enemy.

e. The responsibilities of BIO in connection with air and ground reconnaissance are as follows:

(1) *Air reconnaissance.*—(*a*) He must be proficient in interpreting air photographs, and should lose no opportunity of studying the air photographs taken.

(b) Information of immediate importance obtained from air photographs must be communicated to units even before the photographs themselves reach them.

(c) He will bring to the notice of the brigade commander all intelligence gleaned from air sources which may affect the operations of his command, and he is responsible, under his orders, for the dissemination of such information to lower units and other troops which may be cooperating with the brigade.

(2) *Ground reconnaissance and observation.*—(a) He should coordinate all patrolling that is being done by subordinate units, in order to prevent wasteful overlapping; he should also coordinate patrol work with flanking brigades and make arrangements to insure that any information so obtained reaches him with a minimum loss of time.

(b) He should coordinate the intelligence work of subordinate units in order to insure that enemy troops which have once been located are kept under continuous observation.

138. Cavalry and tank brigades.—The task of collating information and of keeping the commander informed rests with the Brigade Intelligence Officer.

139. Artillery formations.—The artillery intelligence staff and other personnel of the artillery whose duties involve intelligence work are as follows:

a. *Corps artillery.*—(1) *At Hq, corps artillery.*
   One captain, RA.
   One captain, RA, for liaison with the RAF.

(2) *At Hq, corps medium artillery.*
   One captain, RA   ⎫ (As CBO's (counter-battery officer's) as-
   One lieutenant, RA ⎬ sistants for CB (counter-battery) in-
   One lieutenant, RA ⎭ telligence)

(3) *Duties.*—(a) The captain, RA, appointed to corps artillery Hq for intelligence duties, collects, studies, and collates artillery information from all sources, working in close cooperation with the intelligence section of the General Staff, which he keeps informed of artillery intelligence requirements. He makes a special study of enemy intentions as shown by artillery activities.

(b) The captain, RA, at corps artillery Hq for liaison with the RAF, coordinates within the corps the results of artillery air reconnaissance.

(c) CBO's assistants, in addition to their other duties, are responsible for the intelligence work of the counter-battery office (for example, the location of hostile batteries); the examination and filing of photographs; the keeping of shelling reports, records, and general artillery intelligence from observation posts, the air, flash-spotting posts, and other sources of information. It must be remembered that apart from its value to the artillery, counter-battery intelligence may also furnish a guide to the enemy's intentions and may therefore be of immediate importance to the General Staff. When CB control is decentralized to divisions, CBO's assistants will be attached to divisional artillery Hq, in order to assist in CB work.

(*d*) One of the lieutenants, RA, at corps medium artillery Hq, carries out duties similar to those of the lieutenant, RA, for reconnaissance and intelligence for divisional artillery. He will get much of his information from air observation and air photography and must keep in close touch with the Air Intelligence Liaison Officer (AILO). He must also be in closest liaison with the counter-battery staff.

b. Divisional artillery.—At divisional artillery Hq there is a lieutenant, RA, for reconnaissance and intelligence. His duties are—

(1) To collect information concerning enemy artillery, enemy movements and defences, the position of his own forward troops and artillery, the general situation, and the particular situation on the divisional front.

(2) To collate information and keep an intelligence situation map.

(3) To keep such counter-battery records as are necessary.

(4) To supply information to the General Staff of the division, with whom it is essential that he should work in close cooperation, and to artillery regiments, corps artillery Hq, corps medium artillery Hq, and the artillery Hq of neighboring formations.

140. Intelligence duties in units.—*a.* The personnel for intelligence duties varies with different arms.

b. The duties which the intelligence officer may be called upon to perform include the following:

(1) To organize the system of intelligence within the unit.

(2) To observe and report enemy movements and dispositions.

(3) To study the progress of the battle on the front and flanks of the unit, and to be prepared to give information on the dispositions of his own unit and of friendly troops.

(4) To study the topography of the unit area and of the surrounding country, including lines of approach to and from the enemy's position.

(5) To collect, sift, and collate intelligence reports emanating from within the unit, and to distribute the information so obtained to higher and lower Hq's.

(6) To study the information received from higher authority or

friendly units, and to draw the attention of the unit commander to any items of importance.

(7) To insure that the unit is kept supplied with up-to-date maps and air photographs.

(8) To see that orders are carried out regarding prisoners of war and captured documents and material.

(9) To keep unit intelligence records up to date.

(10) To supervise military security measures within the unit.

Section III

INTELLIGENCE CORPS

	Paragraph
General	141
Commandant	142

141. General.—*a.* The Intelligence Corps is made up of officers and enlisted men with special qualifications and training. This corps is controlled, under the orders of the GSO 1 (I), by the GSO 2 in charge of the organization sub-section of the intelligence staff at GHQ, assisted by the Commandant of the Intelligence Corps.

b. The Commander-in-Chief of each field GHQ is authorized to attach to the intelligence section of the General Staff personnel from the Intelligence Corps. Other sections of the Intelligence Corps are attached to corps and divisional headquarters and to the line of communications (L of C) area.

c. The Intelligence Corps as such does not exist in peacetime.

142. Commandant.—Working in conjunction with the organization sub-section, the principal duties of the Commandant of the Intelligence Corps are as follows:

a. To command the corps and to superintend its organization and administration, and the discipline of its personnel.

b. To carry out any changes in organization rendered necessary by modifications of policy or new developments.

c. To arrange for and to supervise the training of all ranks of the corps.

d. To keep in close touch with the requirements of the General Staff and to provide suitable personnel at short notice for special duties.

AIR COMPONENT INTELLIGENCE

143. General.—The air officer commanding at GHQ and the air force commanders attached to the headquarters of lower formations obtain the following information from army intelligence staffs, air-defence formations, and air-force sources:

a. The order of battle of enemy air forces.

b. Reports of enemy air activity, raids, etc.; this information is generally passed to air headquarters by the air defence organization.

c. Enemy air intentions.

d. Enemy air tactics.

e. Enemy air casualties, losses, wastage, reserves, resources in personnel and air material, repair facilities, details of equipment, development and performance of aircraft.

f. Captured enemy aircraft, equipment, and air-force prisoners.

g. Enemy anti-aircraft defences.

h. Suitable ground objectives for air attack and the effect of raids carried out by their own air forces.

i. General intelligence regarding both air and land operations.

Section V

RECORDS AND MAPS

144. Records of information.—The following records are kept by the brigade intelligence section:

a. "*Enemy Order of Battle Book.*"—Particulars as to the enemy's order of battle fall into the following categories:

(1) Identifications.

(2) Titles, organization, and composition of formations.

(3) Characters of commanders.

(4) Fighting qualities and morale.

(5) Armament and equipment.

b. "*Own Forces Book*"—This information is kept in a book form on the same principle as the "Enemy Order of Battle Book."

c. *Brigade intelligence diary.*—This is a permanent record of information and events and includes all deductions made as a result thereof.

d. Brigade intelligence diary (mobile).—This diary is kept for use when there is an advanced (or rear) brigade headquarters or when the brigade headquarters is on the move and clerical and office facilities are not available.

145. Situation maps.—The maps that should be maintained are—

a. Situation map.—Preferably for a large area (such as that of the division and the flanking divisions).

b. Brigade commander's map.—Portable, covering a suitable area (probably that of the division of which his brigade is a part).

c. Brigade commander's map (duplicate).—This duplication is necessary in order to insure that the brigade commander has an up-to-date map for a sudden move to a reconnaissance, conference, etc., or for use on return from such absence.

d. Situation map (mobile).—Portable, covering a suitable area (from the brigade bivouac area to the forward echelons).

e. Air reports map.—Suitably large area; with tracing cover which can be removed every 24 hours or when detail gets confused; each tracing is numbered, recorded in the brigade intelligence diary, and filed with it; information of both enemy and own troops is recorded as received.

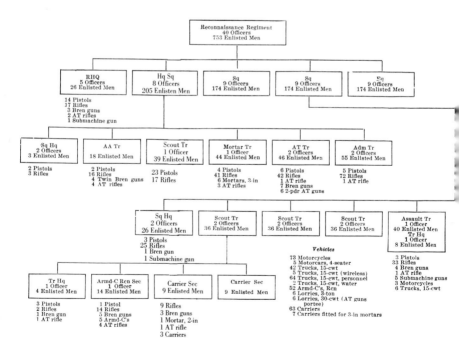

FIGURE 11.—Organization of the reconnaissance regiment (battalion).

224

Chapter 8
ABBREVIATIONS

165. Headquarters, formations, staff, appointments, and services.—These abbreviations are for general use and for addressing messages or correspondence *to*, but many of them are used only by special or technical services or units.[1] Abbreviations for the titles of units are not used when code names are employed. Names and individual designations of officers do not appear in messages unless they are intended for delivery to individuals. Distinguishing letters are to be used with the originator's number on the message form (see par. 51*c*(3) and fig. 34).

a. Headquarters and formations.

Full title	Abbreviation	Distinguishing letter
General Headquarters.	GHQ	------
First (Second, etc.) Army.	First (Second, etc.) Army	------
1st (2nd, etc.) Corps.	1 (2, etc.) Corps	------
1st Armoured Division.	1 Armd Div	------
1st (2nd, etc.) Division.	1 (2, etc.) Div	------
1st Light (Heavy) Armoured Brigade.	1 Lt (Hy) Armd Bde	------
1st (2nd, etc.) Cavalry Brigade.	1 (2, etc.) Cav Bde	------
1st (2nd, etc.) Infantry Brigade.	1 (2, etc.) Inf Bde	------
Royal Regiment of Artillery (RA):		RA[2]
1st (2nd, etc.) Corps Artillery.	RA 1 (2, etc.) Corps	RA
1st (2nd, etc.) Corps Medium Artillery.	MA 1 (2, etc.) Corps	MA
1st (2nd, etc.) Divisional Artillery.	RA 1 (2, etc.) Div	RA
1st (2nd, etc.) Field (Medium, etc.) Regiment.	1 (2, etc.) Fd (Med, etc.) Regt	------
Corps of Royal Engineers (RE):		RE
1st (2nd, etc.) Divisional Engineers.	RE 1 (2, etc.) Div	RE
Royal Corps of Signals (R Sigs):		Sigs
General Headquarters Signals.	Sigs GHQ	Sigs
First (Second, etc.) Army Signals.	Sigs First (Second, etc.) Army	Sigs
1st (2nd, etc.) Corps Signals.	Sigs 1 (2, etc.) Corps	Sigs
1st (2nd, etc.) Divisional Signals.	Sigs 1 (2, etc.) Div	Sigs

---

[1] In addressing a headquarters, the branches of the staff will not be included (e. g., "1 Div" is correct and "Q1 Div" is incorrect), but abbreviations denoting subordinate commanders or services will be included (e. g., "RA 1 Div" and "Medical 2Corps" are correct).

[2] The staff of MGRA, CCRA, CCMA, and CRA (see par. 166) will use the originators' letters "RAO," "RAI," and "RAQ." Units (regiments, battalions, etc.) will use the distinguishing letters "O," "I," and "Q" only.

Full title	Abbreviation	Distinguishing letter
Anti-Aircraft Defence (AAD):		
1st (2nd, etc.) Anti-Aircraft Brigade.	1 (2, etc.) AA Bde	------
Royal Army Service Corps (RASC):		
1st (2nd, etc.) Divisional Royal Army Service Corps.	RASC 1 (2, etc.) Div	ST
Royal Air Force (RAF):		
Royal Air Force Component with the Army in the Field.	Air GHQ	------

b. Staff.

General Staff Branch (G or GS):[3]		
Operations Section.	------	O
Intelligence Section and Intelligence Officers.	------	I
Staff Duties and Training Section.	------	SD
Brigade Majors.	------	O
Signal Officer in Chief, Chief Signal Officers, and their Staffs.	------	X
Adjutant-General's Branch (A):[4]	------	A
Officer in Charge, 2nd Echelon.	O2E	ECH
Staff Captain.	------	A
Quarter-Master-General's Branch (Q):[5]	------	Q
Staff Captain.	------	Q
Movement Control.	------	QM

c. Appointments.

Aide-de-Camp.	ADC	ADC
Camp Commandant.	Camp	CP
Military Secretary.	MS	MS
Personal Assistant.	PA	------

d. Services.[6]

Army Postal (Q).	Postal	P
Canteen (Q).	Canteens	CAN
Chaplains (A).	Chaplains	CH
Engineer Stores (G).	Restores	ES
Graves (A).	Graves	GR
Hirings (A).	Hirings	HGS
Judge Advocate-General (A).	DJAG	JAG
Labour (Q).	Labour	LB

[3] The General Staff is responsible for operations, intelligence, training, and coordination in general. At the War Office and other large headquarters separate branches of the "G" Staff (or "GS") are established. (See notes 4 and 5, below.)

[4] The Adjutant-General's Staff is responsible for personnel administration. It enlists the soldier, pays him, promotes him, looks after his discipline and welfare, supervises his medical arrangements, and eventually discharges or buries him. The "A" Staff also considers the questions of man power and statistics, and in this regard links very closely with the "G" Staff. (See note 5, below.)

[5] The Quarter-Master-General's Staff is responsible for every article that the soldier needs, whether it be clothing, equipment, weapons, ammunition, food, vehicles, petrol (gasoline), or oil. The "Q" Staff is also responsible for movement, except when troops are actively engaged in operations. Operational movement is controlled by the "G" Staff. At every Hq there is an officer who coordinates "A" and "Q" duties.

[6] The letter in parentheses following each service indicates which branch of the staff exercises control.

Full title	Abbreviation	Distinguishing letter
Medical (A).	Medical	M
Dental.	Dental	M
Hygiene.	Hygiene	M
Medical and Surgical.	Medical	M
Nursing.	Nursing	M
Pathology.	Pathology	M
Ordnance (Q).	Ord	OS
Pay (A).	Pay	PAY
Printing and Stationery (A).	Print	PS
Provost (A).	Pro	PRO
Remounts (Q).	Remounts	RM
Supply (Q).	Sup	S
Survey (G).	Survey	CV
Transport (Q).	Tpt	T
Transportation (Q).	Transit	TN
Docks.	Docks	D
Inland Water Transport.	IWT	IW
Light Railways.	Lightrail	LR
Railways.	Rail	RY
Veterinary (Q).	Vet	Vet
Works (Q).	Works	Wks

166. Commanders and staffs.[7]

Title	Abbreviation
Chief of the Imperial General Staff at the War Office	CIGS
Commander-in-Chief	C-in-C
Major-General, Royal Artillery	MGRA
Commander, Corps Royal Artillery	CCRA
Commander, Corps Medium Artillery	CCMA
Commander, Royal Artillery	CRA
Engineer-in-Chief	E-in-C
Chief Engineer	CE
Commander, Royal Engineers	CRE

[7] Staff officers of the rank of colonel and above are ungraded and, in general, exercise a coordinating function over a number of branches. First-grade staff officers, who are graded as lieutenant-colonels, are in charge of branches at the War Office and larger headquarters. Second-grade staff officers are majors; third-grade, captains. Titles according to the branch of the staff are as follows:

	"G" Staff	"A" Staff	"Q" Staff
1st Grade	General Staff Officer, Grade 1 (GSO 1, or G1)	Assistant-Adjutant-General (AAG)	Assistant-Quarter-Master-General (AQMG)
2nd Grade	General Staff Officer, Grade 2 (GSO 2, or G2)	Deputy Assistant-Adjutant-General (DAAG)	Deputy-Assistant-Quarter-Master-General (DAQMG)
3rd Grade	General Staff Officer, Grade 3 (GSO 3, or G3)	Staff Captain (A) (SC(A))	Staff Captain (Q) (SC(Q))

It will be observed that the titles "G1," "G2," and "G3" when used in the British Army relate to gradings, and not to the branch of the staff.

Title	Abbreviation
Signal Officer-in-Chief	Chief Sigs (*formerly* SO-in-C)
Chief Signal Officer	CSO
Commander, Royal Army Service Corps	CRASC
Naval Staff Officer	NSO
Principal Sea Transport Officer	PSTO
Air Officer Commanding	AOC
Chief of the General Staff in the Field	CGS
Deputy Chief of the General Staff	DCGS
Major-General, General Staff	MGGS
Brigadier, General Staff	BGS
General Staff Officer	GSO
Brigade Major	BM
Deputy Adjutant-General	DAG
(Deputy) Assistant-Adjutant-General	(D)AAG
Staff Captain	SC
Deputy Quarter-Master-General	DQMG
(Deputy) Assistant-Quarter-Master-General	(D)AQMG
(Deputy) Assistant-Director of Transportation	(D)AD Tn
(Deputy) Assistant-Adjutant and Quarter-Master-General	(D)AA & QMG (*or* AAQMG *or* AQ)

167. Regiments and corps of Regular Army.[8]—The regiments and corps of the Regular Army are listed in order of precedence, as follows:

a. Household cavalry.[9]

	Abbreviation
The Life Guards [10]	LG
Royal Horse Guards (The Blues) [11]	RHG

b. Mechanized cavalry of the line.—The 20 cavalry regiments of the line have been merged with the Royal Tank Corps to form the Royal Armoured Corps (RAC), which includes the Royal Tank Regiment (R Tanks).[12]

---

[8] Yeomanry (cavalry) and infantry territorial units, many of which are attached to regular cavalry and infantry regiments, respectively, are not included in this list.

[9] Household cavalry and infantry form the King's bodyguard.

[10] Now one regiment; formerly known as The Life Guards, 1st and 2nd, that is, the 1st and 2nd Regiments.

[11] The Royal Horse Artillery (RHA), now mechanized, which is a part of the Royal Regiment of Artillery (see *c*, below), follows the Royal Horse Guards in order of precedence. But when on parade with its guns, it takes the right and marches at the head of the household cavalry. At the present time, two units of The Honourable Artillery Company (HAC) of the City of London, one of the oldest existing military units in Great Britain, are a part of the RHA.

[12] Formerly known as RTR, the Royal Tank Corps then being known as R Tanks.

	Abbreviation
1st King's Dragoon Guards	KDG
The Queen's Bays (2nd Dragoon Guards)	Bays
3rd Carabiniers (Prince of Wales's Dragoon Guards).	3 DG
4th/7th [13] Royal Dragoon Guards	4/7 DG
5th Royal Inniskilling Dragoon Guards	5 Innis DG
1st The Royal Dragoons	Royals
The Royal Scots Greys (2nd Dragoons)	Greys
3rd The King's Own Hussars	3 H
4th Queen's Own Hussars	4 H
7th Queen's Own Hussars	7 H
8th King's Royal Irish Hussars	8 H
9th Queen's Royal Lancers	9 L
10th Royal Hussars (Prince of Wales's Own)	10 H
11th Hussars (Prince Albert's Own)	11 H
12th Royal Lancers (Prince of Wales's)	12 L
13th/18th Hussars	13/18 H
14th/20th Hussars	14/20 H
15th/19th The King's Royal Hussars	15/19 H
16th/5th Lancers	16/5 L
17th/21st Lancers	17/21 L
Royal Tank Regiment	R Tanks

c. Artillery.

Royal Regiment of Artillery [14]	RA

d. Engineers.

Corps of Royal Engineers	RE

e. Signals.

Royal Corps of Signals	R Sigs

f. Household infantry (The Brigade of Guards). [15]

Grenadier Guards (The First or Grenadier Regiment of Foot Guards).	Gren Gds
Coldstream Guards (The Coldstream Regiment of Foot Guards).	Coldm Gds
Scots Guards (The Scots Regiment of Foot Guards).	SG

[13] Two ordinal numbers separated by a diagonal stroke (as 4th/7th) denote two original regiments now merged into one.

[14] The Field Branch takes precedence over the Coast Defence and Anti-Aircraft Branch. (See also note 11, above.)

[15] A "Guards' brigade" is a brigade formed of two or more battalions from these regiments. A "Guards' general" is a general officer promoted to that rank after having served as a field officer in a regiment of Foot Guards.

Irish Guards (The Irish Regiment of Foot   IG
Guards).
Welsh Guards (The Welsh Regiment of Foot   WG
Guards).

g. Infantry of the line.—The 64 Foot Regiments that make up the infantry of the line are numbered from (1) to (91), beginning with The Royal Scots; the last to be formed, The Rifle Brigade, has no number. The numbers are the old numbers by which the regiments were formerly known. Each regiment received a number as it was formed, the number indicating the age and seniority of the regiment (in many cases actually a regiment of one battalion). These numbers no longer have any significance except from a historical and sentimental point of view. The missing numbers refer to disbanded organizations (for example, No. 18 was that of The Royal Irish Regiment, which ceased to exist in 1922) or to junior battalions of existing regiments (for example, No. 52 is the 2nd Battalion of the 43rd Regiment, all battalions of which are known as The Oxfordshire and Buckinghamshire Light Infantry).

The Royal Scots (The Royal Regiment) (1)_ _ _ _   RS
The Queen's Royal Regiment (West Surrey) (2)_   Queen's
The Buffs (Royal East Kent Regiment) (3)_ _ _ _ _   Buffs
The King's Own Royal Regiment (Lancaster) (4)_   King's Own
The Royal Northumberland Fusiliers (5)_ _ _ _ _ _ _   NF
The Royal Warwickshire Regiment (6)_ _ _ _ _ _ _ _ _   Warwick
The Royal Fusiliers (City of London Regiment)   RF
(7).
The King's Regiment (Liverpool) (8)_ _ _ _ _ _ _ _ _ _   King's
The Royal Norfolk Regiment (9)_ _ _ _ _ _ _ _ _ _ _ _ _   Norfolk
The Lincolnshire Regiment (10)_ _ _ _ _ _ _ _ _ _ _ _ _   Lincolns
The Devonshire Regiment (11)_ _ _ _ _ _ _ _ _ _ _ _ _ _   Devon
The Suffolk Regiment (12)_ _ _ _ _ _ _ _ _ _ _ _ _ _ _ _ _   Suffolk
The Somerset Light Infantry (Prince Albert's)   Som LI
(13).
The West Yorkshire Regiment (The Prince of   W Yorks
Wales's Own) (14).
The East Yorkshire Regiment (The Duke of   E Yorks
York's Own) (15)
The Bedfordshire and Hertfordshire Regiment   Bedfs Herts
(16).
The Leicestershire Regiment (17)_ _ _ _ _ _ _ _ _ _ _ _   Leicesters
The Green Howards (Alexandra, Princess of   Green Howards
Wales's Own Yorkshire Regiment) (19).

	Abbreviation
The Lancashire Fusiliers (20)	LF
The Royal Scots Fusiliers (21)	RSF
The Cheshire Regiment (22)	Cheshire
The Royal Welch Fusiliers (23)	RWF
The South Wales Borderers (24)	SWB
The King's Own Scottish Borderers (25)	KOSB
The Cameronians (Scottish Rifles) (26)	Cameronians
The Royal Inniskilling Fusiliers (27)	Innisks
The Gloucestershire Regiment (28)	Glosters
The Worcestershire Regiment (29)	Worc R
The East Lancashire Regiment (30)	E Lan R
The East Surrey Regiment (31)	Surreys
The Duke of Cornwall's Light Infantry (32)	DCLI
The Duke of Wellington's Regiment (West Riding) (33).	DWR
The Border Regiment (34)	Border
The Royal Sussex Regiment (35)	R Sussex
The Hampshire Regiment (37)	Hamps
The South Staffordshire Regiment (38)	S Staffords
The Dorsetshire Regiment (39)	Dorset
The South Lancashire Regiment (The Prince of Wales's Volunteers) (40).	PWV
The Welch Regiment (41)	Welch
The Black Watch (Royal Highland Regiment) (42).	Black Watch
The Oxfordshire and Buckinghamshire Light Infantry (43).	Oxf Bucks
The Essex Regiment (44)	Essex
The Sherwood Foresters (Nottinghamshire and Derbyshire Regiment) (45).	Foresters
The Loyal Regiment (North Lancashire) (47)	Loyals
The Northamptonshire Regiment (48)	Northamptons
The Royal Berkshire Regiment (Princess Charlotte of Wales's) (49).[16]	R Berks
The Queen's Own Royal West Kent Regiment (50).	RWK
The King's Own Yorkshire Light Infantry (51)	KOYLI

[16] The precedence of the Royal Marines is established as follows:

When serving under the Naval Discipline Act (i. e., when landed from HM ships or from naval establishments), they will form part of the naval contingent and take precedence immediately after the Royal Navy. When serving under the Army Act (i. e., when a Royal Marine unit is furnished from a Royal Marine division or from a Royal Marine battalion), they will take precedence after The Royal Berkshire Regiment (Princess Charlotte of Wales's).

Abbreviation

The King's Shropshire Light Infantry (53)_ _ _ _ _ KSLI

The Middlesex Regiment (Duke of Cambridge's Mx
Own) (57).

The King's Royal Rifle Corps (60)_ _ _ _ _ _ _ _ _ _ _ KRRC

The Wiltshire Regiment (Duke of Edinburgh's) Wilts
(62).

The Manchester Regiment (63)_ _ _ _ _ _ _ _ _ _ _ _ _ Manch

The North Staffordshire Regiment (The Prince N Staffs
of Wales's) (64).

The York and Lancaster Regiment (65)_ _ _ _ _ _ _ _ Y & L

The Durham Light Infantry (68)_ _ _ _ _ _ _ _ _ _ _ _ DLI

The Highland Light Infantry (City of Glasgow HLI
Regiment) (71).

The Seaforth Highlanders (Ross-shire Buffs, the Seaforth
Duke of Albany's) (72).

The Gordon Highlanders (75)_ _ _ _ _ _ _ _ _ _ _ _ _ _ Gordons

The Queen's Own Cameron Highlanders (79)_ _ _ Camerons

The Royal Ulster Rifles (83)_ _ _ _ _ _ _ _ _ _ _ _ _ _ RUR

The Royal Irish Fusiliers (Princess Victoria's) R Ir F
(87).

The Argyll and Sutherland Highlanders (Princess A & SH
Louise's) (91).

The Rifle Brigade (Prince Consort's Own) (No RB
number).

h. Other corps.

Reconnaissance Corps_ Recce Corps

Royal Army Chaplains' Department_ _ _ _ _ _ _ _ _ _ RAChD

Royal Army Service Corps_ _ _ _ _ _ _ _ _ _ _ _ _ _ _ _ _ RASC

Royal Army Medical Corps_ _ _ _ _ _ _ _ _ _ _ _ _ _ _ _ RAMC

Royal Army Ordnance Corps_ _ _ _ _ _ _ _ _ _ _ _ _ _ _ RAOC

Royal Electrical and Mechanical Engineers_ _ _ _ _ REME

Royal Army Pay Corps_ _ _ _ _ _ _ _ _ _ _ _ _ _ _ _ _ _ _ RAPC

Royal Army Veterinary Corps_ _ _ _ _ _ _ _ _ _ _ _ _ _ RAVC

Army Educational Corps_ _ _ _ _ _ _ _ _ _ _ _ _ _ _ _ _ _ AEC

The Army Dental Corps_ _ _ _ _ _ _ _ _ _ _ _ _ _ _ _ _ _ AD Corps

Pioneer Corps [17]_ P Corps

Intelligence Corps_ IC

Army Catering Corps_ ACC

---

[17] Formerly the Auxiliary Military Pioneer Corps (AMPC).

	Abbreviation
Army Physical Training Corps_____	APTC
Corps of Military Police_____	CMP
Military Provost Staff Corps_____	MPSC
Queen Alexandra's Imperial Military Nursing Service.	QAIMNS
Auxiliary Territorial Service_____	ATS
Officers' Training Corps_____	OTC

168. Titles of units other than cavalry and infantry.

a. Royal Armoured Corps (RAC). *Abbreviation*

1st Armoured Car Company_____	1 Armd C Coy
3rd Royal Tank Regiment_____	3 R Tanks

b. Royal Regiment of Artillery (RA).

3rd Anti-Aircraft Battery, RA_____	3 AA Bty
1st Anti-Tank Battery, RA_____	1 A Tk Bty
A/E Battery, Royal Horse Artillery_____	A Bty RHA
42nd/53rd Field Battery, RA_____	42 Fd Bty
4th Heavy Battery, RA_____	4 Hy Bty
4th Light Anti-Aircraft Battery, RA_____	4 Lt AA Bty
17th Medium Battery, RA_____	17 Med Bty
2nd Searchlight Battery, RA_____	2 SL Bty
1st Survey Battery, RA_____	1 Svy Bty

c. Corps of Royal Engineers (RE).

100th Army Field Company_____	100 A Fd Coy
103rd (Glasgow) Army Troops Company_	103 A Tps Coy
105th Corps Field Park Company_____	105 Corps Fd Pk Coy
12th (Field) Company, RE_____	12 Fd Coy
6th (Field Park) Company, RE_____	6 Fd Park Coy
19th (Field Survey) Company, RE_____	19 Fd Svy Coy RE
3rd (Fortress) Company, RE_____	3 Frt Coy
109th Workshop and Park Company_____	109 Wkshop and Pk

d. Royal Corps of Signals (R Sigs).

No. 1 Anti-Aircraft Brigade Signals_____	1 AA Bde Sigs
No. 1 (No. 2, etc.) Field Artillery Signal Section.	1 (2, etc.) Fd Arty Sig Sec
No. 1 (No. 2, etc.) Medium Artillery Signal Section.	1 (2, etc.) Med Arty Sig Sec
No. 1 (No. 2, etc.) Squadron, Armoured Divisional Signals.	1 (2, etc.) Sqn Armd Div Sigs

e. Royal Army Service Corps (RASC).

Anti-Aircraft Group Company_____	AA Gp Coy
Ambulance Car Company_____ ____	Amb C Coy

Abbreviation

Armoured Brigade Company	Armd Bde Coy
Armoured Division Ammunition Park	Armd Div Amn Pk
Armoured Division Petrol Park	Armd Div Pet Pk
Armoured Division Reserve Supply Park	Armd Div Res Sup Pk
Armoured Division Troops Company	Armd Div Tps Coy
Bridge Company	Bridge Coy
Corps Ammunition Park	Corps Pk
Corps Petrol Park	Corps Pet Pk
Corps Troops Ammunition Company	CT Amn Coy
Corps Troops Ammunition Sub-Park	CT Amn Sub Pk
Corps Troops Supply Column	CT Sup Col
Divisional Ammunition Sub-Park	Div Amn Sub Pk
Divisional Troops Company	Div Tps Coy
GHQ Troops Company	GHQ Tps Coy
Infantry Brigade Company	Inf Bde Coy
Line of Communication Motor Transport Company.	L of C MT Coy
Motor Ambulance Convoy	MAC
Reserve MT Company	Res MT Coy
Tank Brigade Company	Tank Bde Coy

f. Royal Army Medical Corps (RAMC).

Casualty Clearing Station	1 (2, etc.) CCS
Cavalry Field Ambulance	1 (2, etc.) Cav Fd Amb
Field Ambulance	1 (2, etc.) Fd Amb
Field Hygiene Section	1 (2, etc.) Fd Hyg Sec
General Hospital	1 (2, etc.) Gen Hosp
Light Field Ambulance	1 (2, etc.) Lt Fd Amb
Light Field Hygiene Section	1 (2, etc.) Lt Fd Hyg Sec

g. Royal Army Ordnance Corps (RAOC).

Anti-Aircraft Brigade Workshop	AA Bde Wkshop
Armoured Brigade Ordnance Company	Armd Bde Ord Coy
Army Field Workshop	A Fd Wkshop
GHQ Troops Workshop	GHQ Tps Wkshop
Infantry Brigade Ordnance Company	Inf Bde Ord Coy
Light Aid Detachment	LAD
Ordnance Field Park	Ord Fd Pk
Recovery Section	Rec Sec
Tank Brigade Ordnance Company	Tank Bde Ord Coy

h. Royal Army Veterinary Corps (RAVC).

Mobile Veterinary Section	1 (2, etc.) Mob Vet Sec
Veterinary Evacuating Station	1 (2, etc.) VES